Advance Praise for ***Religious Peacebuilding in the Democratic Republic of Congo***

"This book is a clearly written and empirically grounded study of the role of churches and their followers in the making of conflict and peace in the Great Lakes region of eastern DRC. Alfani carefully places the views of church members in the city of Goma in North Kivu alongside relevant scholarly and theological accounts of the reasons for conflict and concomitant ways of making peace."

David M. Gordan, Professor of History, Bowdoin College

"In this groundbreaking book, Dr. Alfani gives a voice to religious peace activists who are usually voiceless in both the media and academic circles. His many interviewees are part of the silent majority of grassroots religious people and local religious leaders who demonstrate how religious faith and community is central to resilience in the midst of latent war conditions. This remarkable book is the result of courageous ethnographic research that not only sheds new light on the notions of peace and peacebuilding from the perspectives of persons living in a precarious context at many levels: political, economic, and social, but not spiritual! Dr. Alfani's book also provides new contributions in matters of ethnographic theory and methodology when it comes to doing fieldwork in dangerous contexts, sharing his insights with great sensitivity to his informants' need for security."

Patrice Brodeur, Professeur agrégé, Institut d'études religieuses, Université de Montréal

"Roger B. Alfani's work on religion and peace-building makes a significant and welcome contribution to the scholarship on the Eastern Democratic Republic of Congo. Few scholars of the region have done this kind of qualitative research on the subject, particularly in a way that so effectively engages both the leadership and grassroots members of diverse religious communities. Given the significance of religion to the everyday lives of individuals and communities in Eastern Congo, and to their overall understandings and perceptions of peace and conflict, such oversight is, indeed, troubling. Alfani's work makes important steps toward developing a substantive, qualitative, evidence-driven analysis of these issues. But more importantly, he does so with great nuance, paying attention to both the ways in which such communities can contribute to and exacerbate conflict and the ways in which such communities encourage and facilitate peace building."

Nicole Eggers, Assistant Professor of African History, University of Tennessee-Knoxville

Religious Peacebuilding in the Democratic Republic of Congo

Knut Holter
General Editor

Vol. 4

The Religion & Society in Africa series is part of the Peter Lang Humanities list.
Every volume is peer reviewed and meets
the highest quality standards for content and production.

PETER LANG
New York • Bern • Berlin
Brussels • Vienna • Oxford • Warsaw

Roger B. Alfani

Religious Peacebuilding in the Democratic Republic of Congo

PETER LANG
New York • Bern • Berlin
Brussels • Vienna • Oxford • Warsaw

Library of Congress Cataloging-in-Publication Data

Names: Alfani, Roger B., author.
Title: Religious peacebuilding in the Democratic Republic of Congo / Roger B. Alfani.
Description: New York: Peter Lang, 2019.
Series: Religion and society in Africa; v. 4
ISSN 2328-921X (print) | ISSN 2328-9228 (online)
Includes bibliographical references and index.
Identifiers: LCCN 2018058169 | ISBN 978-1-4331-6324-1 (hardback: alk. paper)
ISBN 978-1-4331-6339-5 (ebook pdf) | ISBN 978-1-4331-6340-1 (epub)
ISBN 978-1-4331-6341-8 (mobi)
Subjects: LCSH: Peace-building—Congo (Democratic Republic)—Goma (Nord-Kivu)—Religious aspects. | Peace-building—Congo (Democratic Republic)—Goma (Nord-Kivu)—Case studies. | Goma (Nord-Kivu, Congo)—Religion—21st century.
Classification: LCC BT736.4.A413 2019 | DDC 261.873096751709051—dc23
LC record available at https://lccn.loc.gov/2018058169
DOI 10.3726/b15368

Bibliographic information published by **Die Deutsche Nationalbibliothek**.
Die Deutsche Nationalbibliothek lists this publication in the "Deutsche Nationalbibliografie"; detailed bibliographic data are available on the Internet at http://dnb.d-nb.de/.

The paper in this book meets the guidelines for permanence and durability of the Committee on Production Guidelines for Book Longevity of the Council of Library Resources.

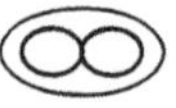

29 Broadway, 18th floor, New York, NY 10006
www.peterlang.com

Printed in Germany

I dedicate this book to my wife, Georgine, and our three children, Esther Henel, Josef-Nissi Salem and David Yadah Alfani

Table of Contents

Abbreviations

ABFMS	American Baptist Foreign Mission Society
ABMU	American Baptist Mission Union
ACCMBK	*Association des Chrétiens Congolais de la Mission Baptistes du Kivu* (Association of Congolese Christians of the Baptist Mission in Kivu)
ACEAC	*Association des Conférences* Épiscopales *de l'Afrique Centrale* (Association of Episcopal Conferences of Central Africa)
AFDL	*Alliance des Forces Démocratiques pour la Libération du Congo-Zaïre* (Alliance of Democratic Forces for the Liberation of Congo-Zaïre)
AIA	*Association internationale africaine* (International African Association)
AIC	*Association internationale du Congo* (International Association of the Congo)
CADC	*Communauté Assemblée de Dieu au Congo* (Community of the Assembly of God in Congo)
CBK	*Communauté Baptiste au Kivu* (Baptist Community in Kivu)
CBCA	*Communauté Baptiste au Centre de l'Afrique* (Baptist Community in the Centre of Africa)

CBFMS	Conservative Baptist Foreign Mission Society
CDJP	*Commission Diocésaine Justice et Paix* (Diocesan Commission for Justice and Peace)
CEF	*Centre Évangélique Francophone* (Francophone Evangelical Centre)
CEHC	*Comité d'études du Haut-Congo* (Upper Congo Study Committee)
CEJP	*Commission Épiscopale Justice et Paix* (Episcopal Commission for Justice and Peace)
CENI	*Commission* Électorale *Nationale Indépendante* (Independent National Electoral Commission)
CEV	*Communauté ecclésiale vivante* (Living Ecclesial Community)
CEVB	Communauté ecclésiale vivante de base (Base Living Ecclesial Community)
CNDP	*Congrès National pour la Défense du Peuple* (National Congress for the Defense of the People)
ECC	*Église du Christ au Congo* (Church of Christ in Congo)
ECZ	*Église du Christ au Zaïre* (Church of Christ in Zaïre)
EIC	*État indépendant du Congo* (Congo Independent/Free State)
EJCSK	*Église de Jésus-Christ sur la Terre par son envoyé spécial Simon Kimbangu* (Church of Jesus Christ on the Earth by His sent one Simon Kimbangu)
ESAM	Evangelization Society Africa Mission
FARDC	*Forces Armées de la République Démocratique du Congo* (Democratic Republic of the Congo Forces)
FIB	Force Intervention Brigade
FTSR	*Faculté de théologie et de sciences des religions* (Faculty of theology and religious studies)
MBK	*Mission Baptiste au Kivu* (Baptist Mission in the Kivu)
MLN	*Mission Libre Norvégienne* (Norwegian Evangelical Mission)
MONUC	*Mission des Nations Unies au Congo* (United Nations Organization Mission in the Democratic Republic of Congo)
MONUSCO	*Mission des Nations Unies pour la Stabilisation du Congo* (United Nations Organization Stabilization Mission in the Democratic Republic of Congo)
M23	*Mouvement du 23 mars* (March 23 Movement)
NBC	Northern Baptist Convention

RCD	*Rassemblement Congolais pour la Démocratie* (Congolese Rally for Democracy)
RDC	*République Démocratique du Congo* (Democratic Republic of the Congo)
SECAM	Symposium of Episcopal Conferences of Africa and Madagascar
SMF	*Svenska Missions förbundet*
UAM	Unevangelized American Mission

Acknowledgments

This book is the product of several years of research including fieldwork in a conflict zone. It was therefore made possible through the instrumentality of a number of people to whom I am sincerely grateful. The contribution of many research participants who placed their trust in me and agreed to share their life's difficult situations, even amidst violent conflicts during the March 23 rebellion. I would like to particularly recognize some of the people who shared their stories, instructed me through personal anecdotes, and provided special advice during my fieldwork in Kinshasa and Goma: my two grandmothers, *Tate* (grandmother) Marthe and *Nya* Doro, who I had the great privilege of seeing last before they pass; former Governor and Mayor Maliaseme; lay Pastoral agent Jacques Maliaseme; and Professor Richard Mugaruka who all passed away before the completion of this book.

I am also grateful to both Professors David Robert and Patrice Brodeur who have helped me throughout my graduate academic years at the University of Montreal. This book grew out of my doctoral thesis under the supervision of the latter. I am also indebted to Professors Nicole Eggers and David Gordon whose critiques and comments of the manuscript were of great value.

Special thanks go to Professor Andrea Bartoli—Dean of the School of Diplomacy at Seton Hall University—who took the time to write the foreword of this book. I substantially benefited from his wisdom, leadership and mentorship while working as researcher on shared projects. In the same vein, I am grateful to the contributions of faculty and administrative staffs of the School of Diplomacy during my Executive MS program. I am equally grateful for the unique academic environment and support of colleagues at Seton Hall University which were conducive for the successful completion of the manuscript. I owe my deepest debt of gratitude to Drs. Nancy Enright and Sister John Bosco Amakwe for their insights and support; Sushant Naidu and Oluwagbemiga Oyeneye, for reading early chapters of the manuscript and their pertinent feedbacks; Sheryl Steadman, Emanuel Hernandez, Patricia Zaini Gracia, and Erick Agbleke, for making my integration at Seton Hall University and in South Orange (New Jersey) much easier.

This book would not have seen the light of the day without the support and encouragement of my family. My parents, Dr. Alfani Shesoko Emile and Lufungula Dorothée, have been instrumental in deciding to embark on a Ph.D. adventure and to write a book. These two decisions represent in some way the results of their immeasurable efforts and sacrifices. They have instilled both in me and all my siblings—to whom I wish to also thank for their support—values of sacrifice, hard work, education, and relationship.

Finally, and most important, I am highly indebted to my lovely wife, Georgine, and our wonderful children, Esther Henel, Josef-Nissi Salem and David Yadah, for their unwavering support, patience and endurance over the years. I dedicate this book to them. I can never thank Georgine enough, for her kind understanding and support throughout my graduate studies and particularly in my absence for fieldwork in a conflict zone.

Foreword

This book is the product of a new synthesis that links the local, cultural, social and political conditions of the Kivus with the peace building, conflict resolution, and conflict transformation contributions. It is good to see the familiarity with Western authors being blended with the originality of authentic testimonies. Peace is not obvious for many trapped by the contradictions of violent experiences produced by inadequate responses to long-term and structural drivers. Yet actively seeking a way out of the spiral of violence, Christians of different churches engage systematically and consistently in peace building. Peace—through the work and commitment of many—becomes the yeast of an emerging community of conscience. While peace might not be completely secured and prevalent, the longing for it is orienting the actions of many. Religion can be divisive and might play a destructive role in human relations. Many scholars have argued the ambivalence of the sacred. Alfani underlines the responsibility of revisiting deep-rooted cultural heritage in the midst of challenges that are at times overwhelming. This responsibility is personal and collective at the same time. It is the duty of those who do not want to be powerless in front of contradictions that seem to overwhelm them. I found touching that the writer references a wide array of authors while describing the need for a new pastoral approach. From a Congolese priest, Jean-Marie Vianney Kitumaini to Johan Galtung, from John Paul Lederach to Edward Azar, up to the American bishops and René Coste. The pathway experienced locally puts prayer and sacramental liturgy at the core of this commitment. Peacebuilding in Goma, through the life of the three churches considered in the study—Roman Catholic, *3ème Communauté Baptiste au Centre de l'Afrique* (CBCA) and *Arche de l'Alliance* (*Arche*)—is made of people believing that their prayer counts, that their education and training of consciences (preaching, homily and catechism of peace) make a difference and that peace can be acted upon in numerous ways. Indeed, the notion of an emerging "community of conscience" is very relevant. Peace is not a moment, it is not a status, it is a dynamic commitment that transforms the lives of communities trying to find alternatives to violence and oppression. The use of Kä Mana's work on the "Christianity of catastrophe" encourages a critical examination of African Christian faith in general and that of the Congo, in particular. The Catholic, *3ème* CBCA and *Arche* Churches of Goma have to be liberated from the burdens of the past, from the heavy load of misunderstanding and hostility. Peacebuilding cannot be but practice informed by the Word, verified in the actual effects that it has on people and measured in the long term consequences of its impact. Goma has a rich history and the churches are deeply rooted in the territory. They weave cultures and populations into the dynamic present, changing themselves in the process. Studying peacebuilding through actual cases is indispensable to advance the knowledge of what is possible and good. Alfani has done a great service by focussing on actors and areas that are in dire need of self-expression, self-determination and self-governance. I am convinced that this is only the beginning of a rich professional career, and I am delighted to learn more in the process.

Andrea Bartoli
Dean, School of Diplomacy and International Relations, Seton Hall University

1 General Introduction

This book is situated primarily within the field of religious studies, while borrowing from other fields because of the topic being studied. Therefore, it is interdisciplinary in nature and includes perspectives from other disciplines such as theology, peace studies, sociology, anthropology, international relations and political science to allow for better understanding of the issue at hand. This introductory chapter is subdivided into five different sections. The first section begins by discussing the problems and goals that motivated this study. In the second section, I focus on the questions inherent to this research that determined the methodology which best suits this study—a qualitative case study method. In addition to the definitions given in the body of the book, I provide, in the third section, flexible and evolving working definitions of important concepts (based notably on the contributions of the research participants) related to this book (e.g., peacebuilding, religion, religious peacebuilding, conflict transformation, and so on). While further definitions emerge in the research findings chapter (Chapter Four), those presented in this third section remain as initial working definitions to better understand the key concepts initially, even if these definitions will be elaborated upon later in the book. The fourth section provides an outline of the chapters that constitute this book. Finally, in the fifth section I discuss about the delimitations (or boundaries) and limitations of this research.

Problems and Goals

The violent conflicts in the Great Lakes region of Africa during the 1990s have remained unsettled and continue to influence socio-political situations throughout the entire region (Lemarchand 2011; Reyntjens and Lemarchand 2011). In its 2000 publication entitled *The Cycle of Conflict: Which Way out in the Kivus?*, African Rights, a London-based organization that conducts studies on human rights abuses, rightly wrote, "The Kivus reflect the wider problems in the Great Lakes, but they can also influence them." Since 1997, three years after the Rwandan genocide that cost more than 800,000 lives in less than 100 days, at least 5.4 million people have died in the Democratic Republic of Congo (DRC), with millions more displaced (Nzongola-Ntalaja 2015). The consequences of these violent conflicts have been mainly felt in the Eastern provinces of the Congo, such as North Kivu and South Kivu where 4.8 million (out of 5.4 million) people have died since 1998 (Coghlan et al., 2008; Roberts 2000). In fact, since the late 1950s, violent conflicts in these latter two provinces have not completely ended as successions of rebellions continue to emerge, with M23 (the March 23 rebellion) being the latest. The people in those areas have endured not only difficult human relationships, but the population in Goma, the provincial capital of North Kivu, has lived with the constant fear of recurring volcanic explosive eruptions.

It is worth indicating here some of the problems and goals this book focuses on in order to facilitate a better understanding of the broader context. *Goals* here include different motives, desires and purposes.

The first goal of this book is to fill a knowledge gap. This gap in the literature chiefly concerns the field of peace studies and its relation to religious actors in the city of Goma. In his book *Qualitative Research Design: An Interactive Approach,* Joseph Maxwell, an American anthropologist who has largely focused his studies on research methods, calls this first category of goals "intellectual" or "scholarly"[1] (Maxwell 2013). Many scholars, particularly in the West and from a variety of disciplines (political science, sociology, ethnography, anthropology and urban studies), have been interested in understanding conflicts in the Kivu provinces (Autesserre 2014; Büscher 2011; Kisangani 2012; Seay 2009; Tull 2005; Vlassenroot and Büscher 2009; Willame 2010; Willame and Verhaegen 1964b). These studies have tended to address those issues at the state level. Only a few studies (e.g., Seay 2013; Prunier 2001) have explored the influence of religion on conflict in North Kivu and Goma in particular (e.g., Mararo 1999, 2005a, 2014a & b). To the best of my knowledge and until now (2019), no one has tackled the issue of conflicts from the bottom-up, including such groups as *Upendo* (love in

Kiswahili) or *Kijiji* (village in Kiswahili) in the *3ème Communauté Baptiste au Centre de l'Afrique* (Baptist Community in the Centre of Africa, *3ème* CBCA) church, or even cell members of Revival churches (e.g., *Arche de l'Alliance*. Unless otherwise specified, *Arche de l'Alliance* refers to the church in Goma, henceforth *Arche*). The inclusion of these churches in understanding conflict from both top-down and bottom-up perspectives is important for several reasons. On the one hand, the demography of these churches consists predominantly of youth and women, who are also recognized as victims of conflicts in general (Trefon 2011; Turner 2013). In the chapter "Congo's War Against Women," of his book *Congo,* Thomas Turner points out that the Democratic Republic of Congo may be the "worst place in the world to be a woman or a child" (2013, 120). In Eastern provinces of the Congo, the rape of women, as well as of men, has primarily been used as a weapon of war (Turner 2013, 128). On the other hand, the reason to include Revival Churches in studying conflicts rests in the structural and numerical growth of this Christian denomination not only in the Congo and Africa, but in Western countries as well.

The second set of goals that drove my research, which may perhaps be considered personal to me and might be of lesser importance to readers than the previous ones, in some ways shed light on my own background for readers of this book. Joseph Maxwell argues that identifying and acknowledging personal goals, instead of hiding or suppressing one's subjectivities in the pursuit of certain objectivities, offer researchers two benefits. First, the researcher is aware of the potential personal (negative) influences on his or her research. Second, the researcher is not deprived of his or her personal creativity as well as questions related to the research that he or she can raise (Maxwell 2013, 24). Since personal goals may seek to better understand certain situations or appropriately address certain questions, as intellectual goals do, they may overlap, and caution is therefore advised.

As a Congolese with family members in this country (DRC), I was particularly concerned about the socio-political situations there. On the one hand, the humanitarian consequences of the 1994 Rwandan genocide and, on the other, of the 1996 *Alliance des Forces Démocratiques pour la Libération du Congo-Zaïre* (Alliance of Democratic Forces for the Liberation of Congo-Zaïre, AFDL) rebellion against the Mobutu-regime and the 1998 *Rassemblement Congolais pour la* Démocratie (Congolese Rally for Democracy, RCD) rebellion against the Kabila-regime, both supported by Rwanda and Uganda, saddened me. My concerns about family members further increased with the January 2002 Nyiragongo volcanic eruption wherein lava flows devastated a large part of the city of Goma. The combination of these difficult situations led me to seek a better understanding of the crises in the North Kivu province and notably its capital, the city of

Goma. In addition, as a Christian, I was particularly interested in the role of churches in such a difficult environment. I therefore elaborated a number of questions to conduct this research.

Methodology

Whether using a quantitative or qualitative approach, the construction of sound research relies chiefly on the quality of its design and methodology. In fact, flaws in either approach may weaken a researcher's findings. The complexity of both the research site and the issues under study (in terms of their sensitive nature) constituted hurdles that needed to be faced and eventually overcome. For instance, conducting research in conflict settings, such as in the Eastern Democratic Republic of Congo (DRC), involves both of these complexities.

Statement of Purpose and Research Questions

The purpose of this book is to understand the role Christian churches play in religious peacebuilding in the city of Goma. Since the late 1950s and early 1960s, the Eastern provinces of Congo have not only continued to experience socio-political instability, but most of the rebel movements have used Goma as their base or rear base. In a context where the remaining authority of the Congolese state is contested, my intent is to explore the contribution of non-state actors, as well as their perception of conflict transformation. In addition to seeking the viewpoints of church leaders on conflicts, I also sought the perspectives of communities at the grassroots level. In other words, social relations, a key component of conflict transformation at the local level, was of particular interest to this study. This research purpose facilitated the formulation of the study questions.

The central question guiding this exploratory research was as follows: How did members of the Roman Catholic, *3ème* CBCA and *Arche* Churches perceive and describe their role in religious peacebuilding in particular, as well as conflict transformation in general, in the DRC and mainly in the city of Goma? From this question emerged the following set of sub-questions. First, how did religious actors—both leaders and followers of the Catholic, *3ème* CBCA and *Arche* Churches in Goma—understand the concepts of peace and conflict? Second, how did they describe conflict in the DRC, and particularly in Goma? In other words, what and who did they consider to be the causes of conflicts in their geographic environment? This question addressed the setting of Goma, in particular. Third, as part of religious organizations, how did they articulate their theology in relation to peace (theology of peace)? This question sought to understand the relationship between their theologies and peace. Fourth, what was the nature of the relationship that religious actors (of the three churches) have (had) within their own organizations and between themselves?

Even though the above four sub-questions may suggest competition or tension between each case and its particular issues, I would rather consider such tensions as supplementary to the purpose of this book.

Qualitative Case Study Approach

Unlike quantitative methodology which focuses primarily on numerical data, and experimental and statistical analyses, a qualitative approach centers on the meaning that participants give to their world—the target groups' experience.[2] In addition, either method, or both (mixed methods), is appropriate for use in case studies (Eisenhardt 1989; Gagnon 2012).

A qualitative methodology was considered appropriate for this study, based on its purpose and research questions. I argue that a quantitative one alone is insufficient. The purpose and research questions provided me with enough materials to opt for a qualitative methodology (Morse and Richards 2002). For Simeon Yates, meaning is at the heart of all qualitative data. That is, it is meant to convey what is being asserted from "what is implied not to be the case" (2004, 148). It takes language and action to define meaning. Qualitative inquiries involve collection and interpretation of gathered information without being solely concerned with quantity and numerical data (Murray 2003). In their book *Designing Qualitative Research,* Catherine Marshall and Gretchen Rossman maintain:

> [H]uman actions cannot be understood unless the meaning that humans assign to them is understood. Because thoughts, feelings, beliefs, values and assumptions are involved, the researcher needs to understand the deeper perspectives that can be captured through face-to-face interaction and observation in the natural setting. (2011, 91)

Furthermore, this book subscribes to a constructivist/interpretive paradigm, which provides ways to tell difficult stories in situations of violent conflict. These issues are usually a challenge to measure by other techniques from the positivist paradigm, such as surveys or experiments (George and Bennett 2005; Gerring 2004; Roy 2006, 168, 170–171; Sullivan 2001; Yin 2009). On the one hand, a case study approach can investigate a contemporary phenomenon in a real-life context with individuals who have experienced or are still facing situations of violent conflict (Yin 2009). On the other hand, a multiple case study approach provides the opportunity to conduct a comparative study, as this study does with respect to three different churches.

Units of Analysis and Cases Selections

The definition of what constitutes a case (or multiple cases) and its selection are key to the case study approach. There is a consensus among authors as to what a case might be. A case, according to Robert Yin (2009), Gary Thomas (2011), Luc Albarello (2011) and others, may include individuals, organizations, institutions, programs and events. The selection of a single or multiple case study approach sets the research boundaries in terms of context and time (Yin 2014; Miles and Huberman 1994). There is no set rule regarding the number of cases to use in case studies. While some suggest that the number of multiple cases should range from three to ten, at the maximum, others such as Perry Chad (1998) refrain from providing numbers, instead he argues that the selection process is at the researcher's discretion. Above all, the primary aim of case selection, as noted by Robert Stake (1995), should be to understand the phenomenon under study.

This research focuses on three religious organizations, that is, three churches (Catholic, Protestant and Revival Churches) and their small Christian communities located in one geographic area (Goma). In other words, this research is a multiple case study of three Christian churches with embedded units of analysis (*Shirika*, *Upendo* and cell groups) located in the city of Goma within the context of conflict, as illustrated in Figure 1.1 on the next page. Christianity occupies a major place in Congolese socio-political life.

Despite the influence of Islam in the Eastern DRC, notably stemming from Arab slave traders in the 19th century from the Zanzibar area, Christianity remains the dominant religion both in Goma and throughout the country.[3] Catholics are in the majority, followed by Protestants and then Revivalists (followers of Revival churches). The Catholic and Baptist Communities in the Center of Africa (*3ème* CBCA) Churches are two of the oldest churches in Kivu province and the city of Goma (founded by missionaries), while the *Arche*/Goma Church is relatively recent (late 1990s). These three cases provide a variety of comparative components, such as their theological and socio-political approaches to peace, as well as their capacity to mobilize resources. A multiple case study offers the potential to broaden the scope of the outcomes (Yin 2009, 58–60).

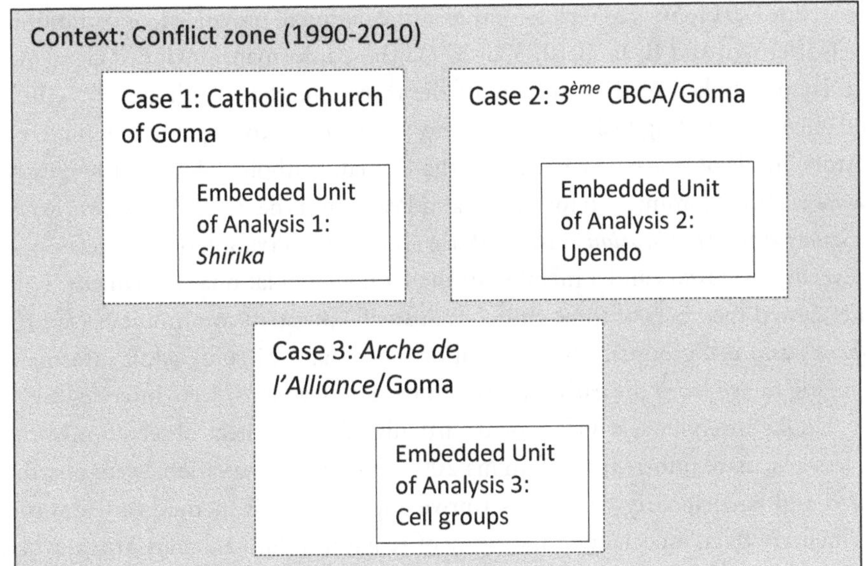

Figure 1.1 Case Studies Design.
Source: Author.

Data Collection Methods

The field research was conducted in Kinshasa and Goma between June and October 2013. The same reasons that justified the choice of qualitative inquiry applied in choosing the data collection methods. In other words, the research questions and triangulation were key factors in determining the data collection methods. A word regarding my sampling method should also be important to mention here.

Since the population to select from was important, though sparse, because of their experiences or their security concerns, I used purposive and quota sampling strategies. While a purposive strategy was chosen because of the resources that were available, a quota sampling strategy enabled me to focus on the population that would contribute in attaining my objectives as well as answering to my research questions. These sampling strategies led my choice of participants to interview, events to attend and who to give my questionnaire. In other words, the selection of people and events were consciously chosen in order to have a representative sample. Three primary sources were used: interviews, direct observations, and a questionnaire.

The first and primary data collection method consisted of interviews with key and specialized informants—or central and peripheral actors, to use Luc

Albarello's (2011, 56–58) terms—either at the national, provincial, or community levels (Bernard and Ryan 2010, 370–371). These informants included clergymen and laymen linked to the structure of the three churches (Catholic, *3ème* CBCA and *Arche*), including bishops, priests, *représentants légaux* (legal representatives), pastors, heads of peace departments—the Roman Catholic Church's *Commission Justice et Paix* (Commission for Justice and Peace) and the *3ème* CBCA's *Justice, Paix et Sauvegarde de la Creation* (Justice, Peace and the Preservation of the Creation)—university professors and a member of the Congolese National Parliament. I also interviewed members of three churches in small Christian communities (*Shirika, Upendo* and cell groups). Thus, a total of more than thirty-six adult informants (ranging in age from the early twenties to the late seventies) were interviewed.

Unlike interviews, which provide articulated data, direct observations bring in less articulate information (Simons 2009, 55). My observations were unstructured and participatory with a descriptive approach. This method provides supplementary data, especially in the study of religion in Sub-Saharan Africa, where importance is given to facial expressions and body language. The two indicators go beyond what is *said and written* about the role of churches in religious peacebuilding, and provide access to *what is actually done*. The direct observations were recorded by taking notes, photographs and audio recordings as I participated in Sunday and mid-week services, meetings and activities held at the grassroots level at the three churches in small Christian communities. For instance, I spent between two to five hours with members of these churches, observing them and taking notes. On one occasion, some attendees forbade me from taking photos and audio recordings; however, they eventually let me do so after I showed them a letter from their leader.

The three churches use different names for their small Christian communities. While the Catholic Church of Goma refers to its own as *Shirika* (from Kiswahili verb *Shirikiana*, meaning to unite), the *3ème* CBCA employs *Kijiji* for its small communities, and Revival churches define the same group as *cell groups*. Thus, my observations in these churches remained qualitative and I used a formal observational instrument as a guide. In addition to interviewing certain members of the small Christian communities in their natural settings, I handed out questionnaires to other members.

Questionnaires were only given to those who were present in the small Christian communities. Their anonymity in responding to the questionnaires was guaranteed. About 140 questionnaires were distributed to members of the small Christian communities. A total of 90 were returned, out of which 70 were considered usable for analysis. Discarded questionnaires were either too difficult to read or had been duplicated by participants. I was conscious of literacy issues, which included reading and/or understanding French. To minimize these issues, I also provided Kiswahili versions, assisted those who were willing to respond immediately, and allowed others to take the questionnaires. I was also aware that people with literacy issues would probably have been assisted in filling it in. The overall objective of using the questionnaire was for triangulation.

Definitions of Key Terms

Religion, Church and Spirituality

Before defining the terms *religion, church* and *spirituality* in the context of this research, I begin by briefly explaining the main components encompassed in the title of this book. The title, "Religious Peacebuilding in the Democratic Republic of Congo," provides various pieces of information. First, the place given to religion and religious actors in peacebuilding is particularly important when it comes to the dynamics found in the Democratic Republic of Congo in general, and in the city of Goma in particular. By peacebuilding, I understand it to mean activities or programs that address injustices and other root causes of conflict with the aim of bringing about peace between peoples.[4] That is, just relationships are at the core of peacebuilding. My understanding of peacebuilding follows that of practitioners and the authors of the book *Working with Conflict: Skills and Strategies for Action* (Fisher, et al. 2000). For them, as well as others, while being conducted in the present, the main aim of peacebuilding is threefold: (1) to understand the causes of conflict; (2) to address past grievances; and (3) to foster long-term stability and justice (Fisher et al., 2000, 14; Lederach and Appleby 2010).

Second, the title of this book also implies my concerns about particular types of actors in conducting peacebuilding activities. Contrary to what peacebuilding is often referred to, my scope in this book does not focus on external actors and their interventions (Barnett, Kim, O'Donnel, and Sitea 2007, 37) nor largely on the degree or kind of state[5] (Barnett and Zürcher 2009, 26–27; Tull 2005). Neither does it refer to the strengthening of the state's capacities (i.e. state-building) as suggested by some, such as Thania Paffenholz who equates peacebuilding with state-building (Paffenholz 2010, 47) or Roland Paris and Timothy D. Sisk (2009, 14) who observe that state-building is not synonymous with peacebuilding but is its sub-component. While external actors, their actions and state-building have their importance, peacebuilding here refers to local actors and their activities aimed at establishing just relationships. Local actors refer to those affected by conflict and violence and who are beneficiaries of transformation activities like churches in the city of Goma.

The importance of religion in this study resided not only in the ubiquity of religious facts in the African context (Ellis and Haar 2004; Idowu 1973; Mbiti 1990) and the Congo in particular, but, as I argue in this research, it also rested in its influence to determine the outcomes of conflicts. Along with the term *religion*, two other closely related terms are associated with it, namely *spirituality* and *church*.

While religion, spirituality and church are three slightly different terms, they are still used interchangeably, both in the literature and in the interviews and observations I conducted during my fieldwork in the Congo (Kinshasa and Goma). The three terms are variously defined and used in the literature and in practice. Whether from scholars or adherents (participants of a religion or a church) themselves, there is no consensus on their definitions nor on criteria to determine them.[4] Although I briefly speak about other religions, including Islam and Kimbanguism, especially in Chapter Three of this book, Christianity is the main religion investigated in this study.

Not only do I regard Christianity as a Western religion introduced by missionaries in the Congo, but also as a religion that is locally owned, and locally (re)interpreted or adapted. In July 1969—after the Second Vatican II and a period when many African states were achieving their political independence—Pope Paul VI recognized, in his homily in Uganda, the necessity of an African Christianity. The latter was to be adapted according to various African contexts and cultures, yet with the "fundamental and indisputable" condition to remain in the "one true [Catholic] Church" (Paul VI 1969; see also Abble 1957). In his book *African Christianity Theology: Adaptation or Incarnation?*, Aylward Shorter follows the same line of thought concerning the definition of, and the criteria for, an African Christianity (1975a). For Shorter, the emergence of an African Christianity can arise through the interpretation of Christianity and the understanding of African realities.

My intention in this book is not to address nor to examine the existence or the absence of African religions or theologies, which other authors, including Africans, have largely documented (Bujo 2008; Bujo and Muya 2002a & b; Idowu 1973; Muzorewa 1985; Parrinder 1974). However, as I suggest in the concluding chapter (General Conclusion), African religious contributions to peace remain an area for future study, especially within the context of dialogue, and within Christianity. However, more specific to this research, the Catholic, *3ème* CBCA and *Arche* Churches are equally regarded as Christian churches despite their doctrinal differences. I do not reserve the exclusive definition of Christian churches to mainline churches, i.e. for the Catholic and Protestant churches, nor do I refer to *Arche* with the pejorative term "sect," as many[5] have described churches that emerge outside the structures of mainline churches (including Kimbanguism). I will subsequently speak about religion in the African context, precisely called *African religions*, in all of their diversity. Before doing that, I will briefly discuss the issue of membership in religious settings, specifically in relation to the three churches in Goma.

Regarding the Catholic, *3ème* CBCA and *Arche* Churches in Goma, I refer to members as *adherents* or *followers*, notwithstanding their positions within their respective religious institutions and organizations. It is not only up to a church member to declare himself or herself one, he or she can also be recognized as such by the church itself. In the case of the three churches included in this study, the former situation is more frequent than the latter. Furthermore, a member is not simply a churchgoer of a single church, indeed some participants have told me of their cross-attendance,[6] but one's membership to a religious organization includes, in the words of Joseph F. McCann (1993), at least four elements of his or her participation in the church. In order of increasing importance, the first element consists of his or her subscription (name), while the second involves monetary (money) participation in the organization. The third requirement of church members is their personal work, time and effort. Finally, members are expected to dedicate their "entire person" to the pursuit of the church's mission.

As for membership in Catholic, *3ème* CBCA and *Arche* Churches in Goma, those I have referred to as *adherents* or *members* expressed little interest in defining the three terms (religion, church and spirituality). While this is partly because they have not been convinced of the relevance of defining them, it does not infer a denial of their realities and their importance in their day-to-day lives. In fact, the French Africanist, ethnologist and anthropologist, Dominique Dimitri Zahan, points out in his book *The Religion, Spirituality and Thought of Traditional Africa* that "spirituality" is the "very soul of African religion" (1979, 1). Elsewhere, the evidence from the fieldwork in Goma echoes what the Nigerian theologian Bolaji Idowu, in his book *African Traditional Religion: A Definition*, stresses as the difference between "religion in practice" and the word "religion" in theory (1973, 4). For example, while some may distinguish between the essence of religion and spirituality by identifying with any one of the three terms (as seen in statements similar to those of a member of the *Arche* church I have called Sambela: "I do not consider myself as a religious person, but rather as a spiritual believer"), the demarcation between religion, spirituality and church is hardly made (sometimes not all). These Western terms seem meaningless in the African context where they do not actually have local language equivalences (Wijsen 2007). However, spirituality is a much more evocative term for Africans.

Contrary to religion and church, which relate more often to either institutions or organizations, and to which members adhere based on specific religious beliefs, teachings, rituals and practices, spirituality is not tied to any boundaries or established rules (Johnston 1994). Spirituality refers here to a transcendent worldview and reality of an individual or group of individuals (community) not necessarily detached from its natural reality, yet intangible, invisible[7] and not bound to any specific time, place or space (Mbiti 1990). In addition, it entails communicating not only with a supreme being, but also, and especially in African contexts, with ancestors.

Talking from an African religion perspective, and even from the Catholic point of view,[8] ancestors are not dead, they have only crossed over to the other side (of death), while continuing to influence and to intervene in the lives of the living, who are still in their special domain (earth) and who may call for their intervention (Mudimbe and Kilonzo 2012; Parrinder 1974; Zahan 1979). Although the role and the area of intervention of these ancestors, divinities[9] or spirits may vary from one African country to another, their presence, reverence, fear, and invocation are broadly recognized in the community. For instance, amidst plagues and drought, they will be called upon and consulted through prayers and sacrifices. Ceremonies like the sacrifice of human lives and animals are performed for them (e.g., in Uganda; in South Africa with the Swazi; and in Ghana with the Ashanti) (Cf. Parrinder 1974, 62–63).

In his book *Prayer in the Religious Traditions of Africa,* the British anthropologist Aylward Shorter emphasizes the importance of prayer to African religion believers who need to express and communicate their faith to ancestral including divinities and other spirits (1975b). Shorter discusses about fifteen different themes (e.g., divine governance, crisis and desperation, conversion and protection from evil, etc.) pertaining to African prayers, which he classifies into four categories (relational, situational, purposive and universal). He includes examples of prayers from different African groups (e.g., the Boran and Kikuyu of Kenya, the Nuer of Sudan, and the Ga of Ghana). One of the themes that might be of immediate interest in this book concerns prayers of, and for, peace as found in Shorter's "universal" category (1975b, 17).

In situations of conflict, including war and violence, African religious believers not only pray for peace, but they also remember, both at individual and group levels, to spend time offering thanks and appreciation for the peace given by divinities (Shorter 1975b, 121–129). These characteristics of peace-related prayers, as illustrated in Shorter's book and others, echo what I subsequently examine in Chapter Four. That is, for African religious believers and Christians in Africa, prayers for peace have external and internal influences such as social order, unity, and harmony (Shorter 1975b, 121).

With regard to the Catholic, *3ème* CBCA and *Arche* Churches in Goma, prayers for peace were constantly said not only in large groups, but also in small groups and in one-on-one settings. While prayers for peace were clear and normal for many Africans in general and Gomatricians in particular, defining or assessing it remained unclear and a subject of debate. For some, prayer was perceived as part of their religion, others described it as their spirituality, and yet others spoke of prayer in terms of a "church-thing."

Defining the terms religion, spirituality and church is further complicated when anthropologists include them in the concept of culture. For them, religion, spirituality and church are cultural elements or, as Stephen Ellis and Gerrie Ter Haar put it, "cultural artefacts" (2007, 389). That is, religion, especially the so-called "new religious movements," falls within the scope of culture rather than being a *sui generis* category. I disagree with this all-encompassing view of religion in culture, in part because of their conceptual dissociation. For this research, I concurred with those who choose not to put them under the same label of culture, such as Frans Wijsen (2007, 21) and Bolaji Idowu (1973). Wijsen's definition of religion suggests it is separate from culture and is included in an invisible world to which African religions can relate (Wijsen 2007, 21, 21n22). Idowu, for his part, strongly critiques the mingling approach to religion and culture, especially in the African context, noting that it has led to errors of identity. He explains:

> It would seem that what happened in the Western world, as it is now happening in Asia and Africa, was that one early religion, more or less aboriginal, formed the cohesive factor of, and gave the foundation complexion to, culture, while another culture was, or other cultures were, superimposed on this. In this way, the fabric of life became a thing made up of strands of various hues and stresses each of which has gone inextricably into the wrap and weft of the complex whole. (Idowu 1973, 5)

Idowu stresses further that "several errors of identity with reference to religion in Africa are results of this confusion between religion and culture: 'heathenism' or 'paganism'" (Idowu 1973). Furthermore, since this book focuses on Christianity, it adopts hybrid and interdisciplinary approaches to the definitions given to religion, spirituality and church. Second, as indicated earlier, it borrows from other disciplines as sociology, anthropology, political science and economics, not to mention other interdisciplinary fields such as peace studies.

The common definition given to *religion* stems from the Latin word *religio* to which is associated either the Latin verb *religare* (to bind together, put together or tie) or *religere/relegere* i.e., to read over. Many scholars, such as the American historian of Religion, Scott Appleby, build their definition of religion based on the term *religare* to support their arguments concerning its binding and communal capacities, and thus its potential to build peaceful relationships (2000). Although I agree with this meaning given to the term "religion," primarily because of the potentialities of peace embedded in this etymological definition, its practicality for precisely studying the three churches in Goma revealed some limitations. For instance, as shown in Chapter Four, the relationships between Catholic and *3ème* CBCA churches are neither openly conflictual nor peaceful, in that they choose not to work in unison.

Scholars, especially sociologists and anthropologists, have alternatively proposed functional and substantive definitions of religion (Willaime 2003/2; Berger 1969). Two functions that may be ascribed to religion include a cognitive function that influences one's behavior, and a function that shapes one's identity. These two functions do not operate exclusively but, rather, they reinforce each other. These functions have clearly been observed for our case studies in Goma. Furthermore, religion provides a vertical connection—with such terms as *divine* or *supernatural*—as well as a horizontal connection. Although this book does not explicitly deal with African religions or spiritualism, the vertical connection includes these African realities which many have already addressed (Bujo 2008; Ellis and Haar 2004, 2007). The horizontal connection of the function of religion, as discussed above, helps to forge closer relationships between people. Likewise, in his book *Sociologie des religions,* the French sociologist Jean-Paul Willaime (1995) observes that religion embodies functional characteristics, in that it fosters solidarity among individuals despite their religious differences.

A tentative and general definition of religion encompasses one's response to what is perceived as sacred, which includes "a creed, a cult, a code of conduct, and a confessional community" (Appleby 2000, 8). I also share an understanding of religion that includes spiritual elements as evoked in the preceding sections. That is, religion in the African context and from a Christian perspective does not necessarily exclude the views of those who believe in ancestors. In addition, this definition of religion is characterized by four components: (1) a *group identity,* through which members identify themselves; (2) *society regulation,* which is based on values that determine one's behaviours; (3) an *ecclesiastic organization,* which is the structure that organizes the group which can also be institutionalized; and (4) a *belief system* that determines the way one thinks (Smith 1970).

Having defined the contours of what I understand the terms religion, spirituality and church to mean, the next definitions I provide (which are associated) are for *religious peacebuilding* and *conflict transformation.* The crucial role and functions given to religious actors in general and church members (leaders and grassroots members) are further discussed.

Religious Peacebuilding and Conflict Transformation

For the scholar and peacebuilder Cynthia Sampson, religion and spirituality are two important components whose vital and dynamic contributions and roles in peacebuilding have not been examined in depth (2007, 273). The focus of this book is, therefore, to fill this knowledge gap and to precisely explore the role of religious institutions (churches) and their corresponding organizations and actors in conflict transformation, from both top-down and bottom-up perspectives.

Religious peacebuilding and conflict transformation are thus the two interrelated conceptual frameworks this research builds upon. Contrary to the latter, the former is rather a relatively more recent field of study (mid-to-late 1990s) originating from the United States (Hertog 2010). Some of the frontrunners in the field of religious peacebuilding—who are predominantly American and from a variety of disciplines (e.g., sociology, theology, history, political science)—include such scholars and practitioners as Douglas M. Johnson Jr. and Cynthia Sampson (authors and editors of the 1994 ground-breaking book, *Religion, the Missing Dimension of Statecraft* (1994), that focused on the contributions of religions to peace); Scott Appleby (author of, for example, the book *Ambivalence of the Sacred: Religion, Violence, and Reconciliation,* 2000); Marc Gopin, author of, for example, *Between Eden and Armageddon: The Future of World Religions, Violence, and Peacemaking* (2000); and John Paul Lederach, author of, among other books, *Building Peace: Sustainable Reconciliation in Divided Societies* (1997). For these authors, as well as others (e.g., Tale 2017; Tesfai 2010), religion carries a twofold role called the "ambivalent of the sacred," or the "paradox" (Hertog 2010; Omer 2015). On the one hand, it can play (as it actually does) a negative role, which they do not deny has the capacity to entice and fuel violence. On the other hand, they side with and capitalize on the positive role of religion as a vehicle to transform conflictual relationships into peaceful and just societies. In *The Ambivalence of the Sacred,* Appleby disagrees with the one-sided view of religion, saying:

> I refute the notion that religion, having so often inspired, legitimated, and exacerbated deadly conflicts, cannot be expected to contribute consistently to their peaceful resolution. I argue to the contrary, that a new form of conflict transformation—"religious peacebuilding"—is taking shape on the ground, in and across local communities plagued by violence. (2000, 7)

The above authors, as well as others, argue that at the core of either one of the two roles of religion reside at least two interrelated elements; that is, change and relationship. During conflicts and violence, relationships between people are not only altered, but grow potentially worse. To put it differently, people no longer perceive each other in the same way. John Paul Lederach associates this particular change in the nature of relationships, which also includes a constructive pathway of conflict, with what he terms a *descriptive transformation* (Lederach 1995, 201). He contrasts this with *prescriptive transformation,* which seeks to transform the structures of conflicts and provide spaces for cooperation, and, as a result, just relationships are provided (Lederach 1995, 201–202). For the anthropologist Carolyn Nordstrom, whose works have largely focused on the Mozambique conflicts (Nordstrom and Robben 1995), understanding the driving cultures (ideas, ideals and interests) of conflicts and power relations is imperative in order to transform them (conflicts) (Nordstrom 1995, 95, 111). Rather than displacing the same paradigms of conflicts, Nordstrom maintains that the nature of conflict, grounded in culture, needs to be changed. Otherwise, she points out, we are faced with the "paradox of consistency embedded in change" (Nordstrom 1995, 106).

In this book, *religious peacebuilding* will refer to the activities that religious actors participate in and put in place for the promotion of peace, as well as peaceful and just relationships. Similar to what Lederach and others have suggested, I understand conflict transformation as a process that does not only seek to end violence (as a short-term objective or a negative peace), but also seeks to comprehend and address the root causes of conflicts with the purpose of establishing healthy, just and right relationships. By *transformation*, I do not only think of personal and social change in general, but I also have in mind economic and structural changes whereby justice serves the cause of peace, both in the short and the long run. Justice is an extremely important concept playing a key role in religious peacebuilding. As such, it cannot be ignored. It is considered one of the preconditions for attaining and sustaining peace.

The questions that arise concerning issues of justice, like the peace with which it sometimes clashes (Allan and Keller 2006; Fixdal 2012), concern not only its definitions, but also its approaches, its actors and its beneficiaries, whether they are victims or bullies. All of these also depend on perspectives as to whose justice is being considered.

Justice, Justpeace and Just Peace

My definition of justice concurs with that of the American political scientist and peace studies scholar Daniel Philpott, as developed in his book *Just and Unjust Peace: An Ethic of Political Reconciliation* (2012). The concern of justice is not limited to rightly addressing past wounds and injustices; it also seeks to restore right relationships. In other words, as Philpott observes, justice borrows from elements of reconciliation (2012, 53). Irrespective of the actors of judicial processes (be they local, national, international, states or non-states), peace must remain at the center of their actions, especially for victims who are, most of the time, ordinary people—the grassroots, less privileged and marginalized people in our society.

Peace studies scholars like Philpott (2012, 11) and Abu-Nimer (2012) argue that religious communities contribute to peace efforts with a justice perspective. They engage in practices of reconciliation which result primarily in the transformation of emotions and attitudes. In fact, justice issues should not only be the concern of states—whose role remains generally unclear and oftentimes challenged especially in conflict zones—but the preoccupation of non-state actors also. The American philosopher John Rawls summarized it as the "first virtue of social institutions" (1999, 3). I thus argue that churches and religious organizations, viewed as social institutions, are well-equipped, because of their beliefs and practices, to offer social justice services. In the context of many religious organizations, social justice is not solely viewed as the addressing of past wounds, but as restoring right relationships through their beliefs and their practices.[10] While peace may be considered as a relatively inclusive objective of all constituents, justice can be problematic in some cases.

Many scholars and practitioners have discussed the link between the concepts of peace and justice. At least two terms have been used to portray the combination of the two concepts (peace and justice), which, as already pointed out, do clash in terms of pre-eminence and significance: (1) *justpeace* (one word); and (2) *just peace* (two separated words). John Paul Lederach has defined *justpeace,* in his 1999 book chapter "Justpeace: The Challenge of the 21st Century," in a threefold manner, as follows:

> 1: An adaptive process-structure of human relationships characterized by high justice and low violence 2: an infrastructure of organization or governance that responds to human

> conflict through nonviolent means as first and last resorts 3: a view of systems as responsive to the permanency and interdependence of relationships and change. (36)

Lederach bases the above definition on three main gaps in peacebuilding initiatives that are all related with the notion of relationships,[11] the: (1) interdependence gap, (2) justice gap and (3) process-structure gap.[12] First, he observes that the interdependence gap broadly points out to two areas where peacebuilders need to focus on. On the one hand, the so-called "horizontal capacity" entails efforts to build constructive relationships amidst conflict between individuals of similar status. This aim has been less troublesome. On the other hand, Lederach believes that the "vertical level" is where the quality of relationships has suffered the most. The flaws at this level originate in the difficulty in establishing mutually respectful and consistent relationships between leaders and grassroots members. Therefore, not only is awareness of the interdependence between both the horizontal and vertical levels important, far more important is the effective coordination of activities and their equal understanding at each level.

The second gap is a justice gap. Influenced by Johan Galtung's views of conflict, Lederach observes that many peacebuilders and practitioners have focused their attention and actions on ending direct violence, while neglecting to address structural violence, and at the same time ignoring the importance of fostering social and economic justice, once war is over (Lederach 1999). He suggests three main ways to address this particular gap. They consist of the integrations of (1) the notion of social justice through education of peacebuilders (state and non-state actors); (2) such fields as conflict transformation and restorative justice, and socio-economic development in peace studies; (3) the capacity to accept and to embrace change even if it demands the reconsideration of established patterns of funding, research, and practice (Lederach 1999, 32).

Third, in the process-structure gap, John Paul Lederach proposes an approach that fosters a change of language when dealing with peace initiatives. For him, conceptualizing peace as either a process or a structure is problematic just as the "resolution" in "conflict resolution" is. While Lederach thinks that the school of conflict resolution falls prey to this process-structure gap and strongly suggests conflict transformation, others (e.g., Ramsbotham, Miall, and Woodhouse et al., 2011) think that they are two similar approaches in peace studies. Lederach critiques conflict resolution, arguing that their focus on "resolution" through a peace agreement undermines the long-term and transformative objectives of peace. He writes: "resolution lends itself to a metaphor that suggests our goal is to end something not desired. Transformation insinuates that something not desired is changing, taking new form" (Lederach 1999, 33).

Lederach's view of peacebuilding in terms of "conflict transformation" can easily be related to the case of the Democratic Republic of Congo where several peace agreements have been ratified without transforming the conflict itself. In sum, the above three gaps developed by Lederach in order to define his *just peace* resonate in this book and aid our better understanding of the combination of peace and justice.

The authors of the book *What is a Just Peace?* explore a concept that, according to them, shies away from the notions of *jus ad bellum* (justice of war) and *jus in bello* (justice during war) in international law, which justify war or violence ("just war"). Rather, they focus on a concept that brings together peace and justice: *just peace*. While most of the authors of *What is a Just Peace?* seem to promote just peace, at least one of them, Yossi Beilin, distances himself from a wrong inference from the term. Beilin (2006), who was an Israeli Justice Minister and a chief negotiator in the Oslo process, argues that the concept of just peace implies the existence and the legitimization of an unjust peace, which diminishes and impedes the value of peace itself. For him, the fact that an "unjust peace" excludes reconciliation, it means that there is no peace at all. Just peace, Beilin further points out, is not only unnecessary and harmful, but it should altogether be avoided (2006, 131). Beilin's own understanding of peace, as well as mine, converges with the meanings of peace as rendered both in Hebrew (*shalom*) and in Arabic (*salaam*), which include justice and integrity (Beilin 2006; see also Steele 2008).

In sum, the Catholic, *3ème* CBCA and *Arche* Churches play a pivotal role in fulfilling a mandate of religious peacebuilding or conflict transformation. At the same time, as religious institutions or organizations and religious actors, they are not immune to the same issues they seek to address. Chapters Four and Five elaborate on the problems and issues the three churches in Goma face, both within and between their institutions and organizations.

Outline of the Book

This book is framed in six chapters including the General Introduction and the General Conclusions. The General Introduction, Chapter One, offers an introduction to this book as it highlights the problem and the motivations of this study. It does not only provide the research methodology, it also defines various concepts used throughout the book. Chapter Two proposes a religious peacebuilding conceptual framework, where key concepts such as conflict, peace, religious peacebuilding, conflict resolution and transformation, and local ownership are examined. Chapter Three focuses on the history of the three Christian churches located in Goma I selected for this study—the Catholic, *3ème* CBCA and *Arche* Churches. Chapter Four of this book presents key research findings. Chapter Five offers a comparative analysis of the above three churches. The last chapter, General Conclusions, concludes the book with a summary of my research findings, theoretical and practical implications, and suggestions for future research.

Delimitations and Limitations

Like any research, using either quantitative, qualitative or mixed methods, this book encountered the same methodological difficulties associated with the unpredictable nature of the field, especially in conflict zones. This does not dispense the researcher from planning and preparation. Unlike the limitations that I present subsequently, I was conscious of a number of delimitations, which included the choice of method, actors, and time range.

First, as I indicated earlier in this introductory chapter, a qualitative method was best suited for this research. This is mainly because of the questions it seeks to answer, which involved, among other things, personal stories. The next delimitation concerns the kind of actors to examine. Religious peacebuilding and conflict transformation in Goma involve not only Christians, but also other traditions and religions, such as Muslims and Kimbanguists, which contribute to peacebuilding enterprises. However, this research was restricted to Catholic, *3ème* CBCA and *Arche* adherents in the city of Goma. In addition, the time scope of this book has been limited to the period between 1992 and 2012.

This study suffered from limitations, which were predominantly associated with both the nature of qualitative study and the risks of conducting research in a war zone-like environment such as Goma. Amidst these uncontrollable limitations, some compromises needed to be made. These included, for instance, ensuring that a sufficient range of views about the subjects of this research (e.g., conflict, peace, ethnicity, leadership, etc.) was obtained. In this section, I present three set of limitations.

The first set of limitations broadly concerned the research site. Not only was it difficult to obtain the approval of the Research Ethics Board, "(similar to the Institutional Review Board in the U.S.)" but at one point, the trip was compromised by the intensification of war in and around the city of Goma. Many contacts, as well as family members, attempted to dissuade me from travelling to Goma. Once in Goma, several scheduled meetings with participants were either delayed or cancelled (e.g., did not show up to meetings, communications with participants were interrupted, etc.). These technical difficulties demonstrate the potential limitations, not only in terms of the choice and availability of people I had to meet, but also the quality of the content (filtered and biased) of our discussions. One of the determining factors was the conflictual nature of the site itself.

The second set of limitations I had to face concerned my own limitations as a researcher. I had to be aware of my perceptions of conflict, potentially influenced by the personal goals I indicated in the opening of this introductory chapter, my religious and ethnic identities, as well as some Western views I may have adopted. During my observations and interviews I was constantly being reminded directly or indirectly of these potential biases. For instance, I was asked: "Who supports your studies?", "Where do you come from?", and "What tribe do you belong to?" Conversely, I had to guard against the influence of certain narratives, which may serve to lobby the cause of one group or another.

The third set of limitations concerned the contribution of followers of religions other than Christianity, such as Islam, to peacebuilding processes in Goma. This study focuses on the role of three Christian churches located in Goma in religious peacebuilding. From a comparative perspective, the inclusion of Islamic groups from Goma would likely have been insightful. In addition, the generalizability of the findings is dependent on the inclusion of other religious and Christian groups.

Endnotes

1. Joseph A. Maxwell distinguishes between three kinds of research goals. These differ from the purposes of a study, which relate to research questions. First, *personal goals* deal with the background and experiences a researcher carries into his or her research. Secondly, he calls *intellectual goals* what one seeks to understand in conducting a given study. Third, *practical goals* refer to research accomplishments. While research questions do not necessarily provide answers to practical goals, the latter inform the former (research questions). Cf. Joseph Alex Maxwell, *Qualitative Research Design: An Interactive Approach*, Thousand Oaks, CA: Sage, 2013.
2. Since the debate between the two traditions (quantitative and qualitative) is ongoing, and although this book does not participate in it (it is not its purpose), I would like to note that both traditions are useful and that each has its own strengths (as well as weaknesses) with regards to research problems

3. Besides estimate of some authors, there are no reliable and updated statistics of religious traditions in Goma. Richard Mugaruka, *Reflexions pastorales: le rôle des églises dans la refondation de l'*État congolais, cinquante ans après son indépendance, Kinshasa: Feu Torrent, 2011; Cyprien Kwibeshya, "L'église et la promotion de la paix dans un monde en conflits: Cas des Pays des grands Lacs," Travail de fin de cycle, Université Libre des Pays de Grands Lacs, 2003.
4. The term *peacebuilding* is often rendered in French either as *construction de la paix* or *consolidation de la paix.* It differs from two other terms related to interventions, namely *peacekeeping* and *peacemaking.* The three terms possess a broad common objective, which is to end conflict. Peacekeeping is generally represented in the United Nations system by the intervention of peacekeepers in order to contain conflict, whereas peacemaking regards the peaceful process that brings conflicting parties together in order to settle conflict and ultimately end war through peace agreement. For further details, see Alfani, Roger Bantea, "Religion et transformation des conflits: le rôle des Églises à Goma en RD Congo (1990–2010)," in Dieng Moda (ed.), *Evolution politique en Afrique: Entre autoritarisme, démocratisation, construction de la paix et défis internes*, Louvain-la-Neuve, Belgique: Academia-L'Harmattan, 2015, p. 90n16; Charles-Philippe David, and Julien Toureille, "La consolidation de la paix: Un concept à consolider," in Yvan Conoir and Gérard Verna (eds.), *Faire la paix: concepts et pratiques de la consolidation de la paix*, Québec: Les Presses de l'Université Laval, 2005, p. 18; O. Ramsbotham, H. Miall, and T. Woodhouse, *Contemporary Conflict Resolution: The Prevention, Management and Transformation of Deadly Conflicts*, Cambridge, UK; Malden, MA: Polity Press, 2011, pp. 23, 146–170, 263–275; Michael W. Doyle and Nicholas Sambanis, *Making War and Building Peace: United Nations Peace Operations*, Princeton, NJ: Princeton University Press, 2006, pp. 10–11; M. D. Toft, *Securing the Peace: The Durable Settlement of Civil Wars*, Princeton, NJ: Princeton University Press, 2010, pp. 150–162; B.F. Walter, *Committing to Peace: Successful Settlements of Civil Wars*, pp. 32–43. I. William Zartman, "Conclusions: The Last Mile," p. 341.
5. While the *degree of state* indicates both its involvement and the tools used for this purpose within a given society, the *kind of state* connotes the interaction between the state and the society.
6. For example, Mark Taylor, an American philosopher of religion, believes that religious scientists should consider at least four prerequisites in examining and defining the concept of religion. First, they need to consider the various functions of religion in its multifaceted complexities. Second, theorists of religion must clarify the way in which different religious networks evolve. The third prerequisite concerns the relationship between religious actors and different characteristics of life (e.g., physical, biological, social, political and economic). Fourthly, since religion is not a firm and static element, Taylor claims that its revision is a plausible consideration. See, Mark C. Taylor, *After God*, Chicago: University of Chicago Press, 2007, p. 4.

7. See for instance, Angang, Dosithée Atal Sa, "L'utilisation de la Bible par et dans les sectes religieuses de Kinshasa." *Cahiers des religions Africaines* 27–28, no. 53–56 (1993–1994) : 431–451 ; Batende, Mwene, "Les sectes : un signe des temps?, Essai d'une lecture sociologique des 'religions nouvelles' issues du christianisme," *Cahiers des religions Africaines* 27–28, no. 53–56 (1993–1994): 25–43; Luboloko, Francois Luyeye, *Les sectes: interpellations et discernement*, Kinshasa: Éditions Le Sénévé, 2013; Moulin, Léon de Saint, and Z. Modio, "La signification sociale des sectes au Zaïre," *Cahiers des religions Africaines* 27–28, no. 53–56 (1993–1994): 247–268; Nkingi, Mweze Chirhulwire Dominique, "Église de réveil: Genèse et modes opératoires," In Kinyamba Sylvain Shomba (ed.), *Les spiritualité du temps présent*, Kinshasa: Éditions M.E.S, 2012.
8. In Chapter Four of this book, I illustrate cross-attendances as well as church-shifting in the Catholic, *3ème* CBCA and *Arche* Churches in Goma. While mobility of this sort is strongly discouraged by church leaders, adherents provide various reasons for doing so. For some, it is materially motivated; others, as shared in Chapter Four, claim that they are not being properly fed (spiritually).
9. The spiritual realm, which is primarily dominated by spirits, according to Mbiti, is not entirely invisible, since it can be revealed to human beings.
10. I still recall at a younger age, in the Catholic Church, being given by Catechist friends some prayers to recite and even going to the tomb of a particular priest to pray for his assistance in our affairs. Protestants, especially Pentecostals, argue that the dead do no longer have any influence among the living. Some will even go further to qualify such practices (communication with ancestors) as witchcraft.
11. Divinities (in plural), since there are generally several of them, are God's creatures and His associates, and whose activities fall in line with His purposes.
12. Several other justice approaches are associated with social justice: (1) transitional justice, (2) distributive justice, (3) compensatory justice, (4) restorative justice, (5) retributive justice, and (6) procedural justice. See Michael D. Palmer and Stanley M. Burgess, "Introduction," in Michael D. Palmer and Stanley M. Burgess (eds.), *The Wiley-Blackwell Companion to Religion and Social Justice*, Chichester, West Sussex; Malden, MA: Wiley-Blackwell, 2012; David Mendeloff, "Trauma and Vengeance: Assessing the Psychological and Emotional Effects of Post-Conflict Justice," *Human Rights Quarterly* 31, no. 3 (2009).
13. While relationships and justice are "dynamic and adaptive," they are not socially limited; rather, they also include political and economic aspects. John Paul Lederach, "Justpeace: The Challenge of the 21st Century," in Paul van Tongeren (ed.), *People Building Peace: 35 Inspiring Stories from Around the World*, Utrecht, Netherlands: European Centre for Conflict Prevention, 1999.
14. These three gaps examined by John Paul Lederach find relevance in the context of this book as it deals specifically with religious institutions and organizations in the city of Goma where conflict and violence have ups and downs.

Bibliography

Abble, A. *Des prêtres noirs s'interrogent.* (2e éd.). Paris: Éditions du Cerf, 1957.

Abu-Nimer, Mohammed. "Building Peace in the Pursuit of Social Justice." In Michael D. Palmer and Stanley M. Burgess (eds.), *The Wiley-Blackwell Companion to Religion and Social Justice.* Chichester, West Sussex; Malden, MA: Wiley-Blackwell, 2012.

African Rights. *The Cycle of Conflict: Which Way Out in the Kivus.* London: African Rights, December 2000.

Albarello, Luc. *Choisir L'étude De cas comme méthode de recherche.* Méthodes en Sciences Humaines. Bruxelles: De Boeck, 2011.

Alfani, Roger Bantea. "Religion et transformation des conflits: le rôle des Églises à Goma en RD Congo (1990–2010)." In Dieng Moda (ed.), *Evolution politique en Afrique: Entre autoritarisme, démocratisation, construction de la paix et défis internes.* Louvain-la-Neuve, Belgique: Academia-L'Harmattan, 2015.

Allan, Pierre, and Alexis Keller. "Introduction: Rethinking Peace and Justice Conceptually." In Pierre Allan and Alexis Keller (eds.), *What is a Just Peace?* Oxford: Oxford University Press, 2006.

Angang, Dosithée Atal Sa. "L'utilisation de la Bible par et dans les sectes religieuses de Kinshasa." *Cahiers des religions Africaines* 27–28, no. 53–56 (1993–1994): 431–451.

Appleby, R. Scott. *The Ambivalence of the Sacred: Religion, Violence, and Reconciliation.* Lanham, MD: Rowman & Littlefield, 2000.

———. "Religion, Conflict Transformation, and Peacebuilding." In Chester A. Crocker, Fen Osler Hampson, and Pamela R. Aall (eds.), *Turbulent Peace: The Challenges of Managing International Conflict.* Washington, D.C.: United States Institute of Peace Press, 2001.

———. "Religious Violence: The Strong, the Weak, and the Pathological." In Atalia Omer, R. Scott Appleby, and David Little (eds.), *The Oxford Handbook of Religion, Conflict, and Peacebuilding.* New York, NY: Oxford University Press, 2015.

Autesserre, Séverine. *Peaceland: Conflict Resolution and the Everyday Politics of International Intervention.* New York, NY: Cambridge University Press, 2014.

Barnett, Michael, Hunjoon Kim, Madalene O'Donnel, and Laura Sitea. "Peacebuilding: What Is in a Name?" *Global Governance* 13, no. 1 (2007): 35–58.

Barnett, Michael, and Christoph Zürcher. "The Peacebuilder's Contract: How External Statebuilding Reinforces Weak Statehood." In Roland Paris and Timothy Sisk (eds.), *The Dilemmas of Statebuilding: Confronting the Contradictions of Postwar Peace Operations.* Abingdon, UK: Routledge, 2009.

Batende, Mwene. "Les sectes: un signe des temps?, Essai d'une lecture sociologique des 'religions nouvelles' issues du christianisme." *Cahiers des religions Africaines* 27–28, no. 53–56 (1993–1994): 25–43.

Beilin, Yossi. "Justice Peace: A Dangerous Objective." In Pierre Allan and Alexis Keller (eds.), *What is a Just Peace?* Oxford: Oxford University Press, 2006.

Berger, Peter L. *The Sacred Canopy: Elements of a Sociological Theory of Religion.* Garden City, NY: Doubleday, 1969.

Bernard, H. Russell, and Gery Wayne Ryan. *Analyzing Qualitative Data: Systematic Approaches.* Thousand Oaks, CA: Sage, 2010.

Büscher, Karen. "Conflict, State Failure and Urban Transformation in Eastern Congolese Periphery: The Case of Goma." Ph.D., University of Ghent, 2011.

Bujo, Bénézet. *Introduction à la théologie africaine.* Fribourg: Academic Press, 2008.

———, and Muya, Juvénal Ilunga. *Théologie africaine au XXIè siècle, Volume II.* Fribourg: Éditions universitaires, 2002a.

———. *Théologie africaine au XXIe siècle, quelques figures Volume I.* Fribourg, Suisse: Éditions universitaires, 2002b.

Chad, Perry. "Processes of a Case Study Methodology for Postgraduate Research in Marketing." *European Journal of Marketing* 32, no. 9–10 (1998): 785–802.

Charmaz, Kathy. *Constructing Grounded Theory: A Practical Guide Through Qualitative Analysis.* London; Thousand Oaks, CA: Sage Publications, 2006.

Chesterman, Simon. "Ownership in Theory and in Practice: Transfer of Authority in UN Statebuilding Operations." *Journal of Intervention and Statebuilding* 1, no. 1 (March 2007): 1–24.

Coghlan, Benjamin, Ngoy, Pascal, Mulumba, Flavien, Hardy, Colleen, Bemo, Valerie Nkamgang, Stewart, Tony, Lewis, Jennifer, and Brennan, Richard. "Mortality in the Democratic Republic of Congo: An Ongoing Crisis." *International Rescue Committee and Burnet Institute, New York and Melbourne,* (2008).

David, Charles-Philippe, and Toureille, Julien. "La consolidation de la paix: un concept à consolider." In Yvan Conoir and Gérard Verna (eds.), *Faire la paix: Concepts et pratiques de la consolidation de la paix.* Québec: Les Presses de l'Université Laval, 2005.

Doyle, Michael W., and Nicholas Sambanis. *Making War and Building Peace: United Nations Peace Operations.* Princeton, NJ: Princeton University Press, 2006.

Ellis, Stephen, and Gerrie ter Haar. "Religion and Politics in Sub-Saharan Africa." *Journal of Modern African Studies* 45, no. 3 (1998): 175–201.

———. "Religion and Politics: Taking African Epistemologies Seriously." *Journal of Modern African Studies* 45, no. 3 (2007): 385–401.

———. *Worlds of Power: Religious Thought and Political Practice in Africa.* New York; Oxford: Oxford University Press, 2004.

Fisher, Simon, Dekha Ibrahim Abdi, Jawed Ludin, Richard Smith, Steve Williams, and Sue Williams. *Working with Conflict: Skills and Strategies for Action.* London; New York: Zed Books, 2000.

Fixdal, Mona. *Just Peace: How Wars Should End.* New York: Palgrave Macmillan, 2012.

George, Alexander L., and Andrew Bennett. *Case Studies and Theory Development in the Social Sciences.* Cambridge, Mass.: MIT Press, 2005.

Gopin, Marc. *Between Eden and Armageddon: The Future of World Religions, Violence, and Peacemaking.* Oxford; New York: Oxford University Press, 2000.

Hertog, Katrien. *The Complex Reality of Religious Peacebuilding: Conceptual Contributions and Critical Analysis.* Lanham, MD: Lexington Books, 2010.

Idowu, E. Bolaji. *African Traditional Religion: A Definition.* London: S.C.M. Press, 1973.

John Paul II. "Centesimus Annus." *Vatican Website.* May 1st, 1991.

———. "Redemptoris Missio." *Vatican Website.* December 7th, 1990.

———. "Slavorum Apostoli." *Vatican Website*. June 2nd, 1985.

Johnston, Douglas. "Introduction: Beyond Power Politics." In Douglas Johnston and Cynthia Sampson (eds.), *Religion, the Missing Dimension of Statecraft*. New York: Oxford University Press, 1994.

Johnston, Douglas, and Cynthia Sampson. *Religion, the Missing Dimension of Statecraft*. New York: Oxford University Press, 1994.

Kisangani, Emizet F. *Civil Wars in the Democratic Republic of Congo, 1960–2010*. Boulder: Lynne Rienner, 2012.

Lederach, John Paul. *Building Peace: Sustainable Reconciliation in Divided Societies*. Washington, D.C.: United States Institute of Peace Press, 1997.

———. "Conflict Transformation in Protracted Internal Conflicts: The Case for a Comprehensive Framework." In Kumar Rupesinghe (ed.), *Conflict Transformation*. Houndmills, Basingstoke, Hampshire: Macmillan, 1995.

———. "Justpeace: The Challenge of the 21st Century." In Paul van Tongeren (ed.), *People Building Peace: 35 Inspiring Stories from Around the World*. Utrecht, Netherlands: European Centre for Conflict Prevention, 1999.

———. *The Little Book of Conflict Transformation*. Philadelphia: Good Books, Intercourse, 2003.

———. "The Long Journey Back to Humanity." In Robert J. Schreiter, R. Scott Appleby, and Gerard F. Powers (eds.), *Peacebuilding: Catholic Theology, Ethics, and Praxis*. Maryknoll, NY: Orbis Books, 2010.

Lederach, John Paul, and R. Scott Appleby. "Strategic Peacebuilding: An Overview." In Daniel Philpott and Gerard F. Powers (eds.), *Strategies of Peace: Transforming Conflict in a Violent World*. Oxford, NY: Oxford University Press, 2010.

Lemarchand, René. "Burundi 1972: Genocide Denied, Revised, and Remembered." In René Lemarchand (eds.), *Forgotten Genocides: Oblivion, Denial, and Memory*. Philadelphia: University of Pennsylvania Press, 2011.

Luboloko, Francois Luyeye. *Les sectes: interpellations et discernement*. Kinshasa: Éditions Le Sénévé, 2013.

Mararo, Stanislas Bucyalimwe. "Kinshasa et le Kivu depuis 1987: une histoire ambigue." In S. Marysse and Filip Reyntjens (eds.), *L'Afrique des grands lacs : annuaire 2004–2005*. Paris: L' Harmattan, 2005a.

———."Kivu and Ituri in the Congo War: The Roots and Nature of a Linkage." In S. Marysse and Filip Reyntjens (eds.), *The Political Economy of the Great Lakes Region in Africa: The Pitfalls of Enforced Democracy and Globalization*. New York: Palgrave Macmillan, 2005b.

———. "La societé civile du Kivu: une dynamique en panne?" In Stefaan Marysse and Filip Reyntjens (eds.), *L'Afrique des grands lacs: Annuaire 1998–1999*. Paris: L'Harmattan, 1999.

———. "Land Conflicts in Masisi, Eastern Zaire: The Impact and aftermath of Belgian Colonial Policy (1920–1989)." Ph.D., Indiana University, 1990.

———. "Land, Power, and Ethnic Conflict in Masisi (Congo-Kinshasa), 1940s–1994." *The International Journal of African Historical Studies* 30, no. 3 (1997): 503–538.

———. *Maneuvering for Ethnic Hegemony: A Thorny Issue in the North Kivu Peace Process (DR Congo), Volume I: The 1959–1997 History of North Kivu*. Bruxelles: Éditions Scribe, 2014a.

———. *Maneuvering for Ethnic Hegemony: A Thorny Issue in the North Kivu Peace Process (DR Congo), Volume II: The 1996–1997 invasion of the "Tutsi without borders" and the remote reconciliation in North Kivu.* Bruxelles: Éditions Scribe, 2014b.

Maxwell, Joseph Alex. *Qualitative Research Design: An Interactive Approach.* (3rd ed.). Thousand Oaks, CA: Sage Publications, 2013.

Mbiti, John S. *African Religions & Philosophy.* (2nd ed.). Oxford: Heinemann, 1990.

McCann, Joseph F. *Church and Organization: A Sociological and Theological Enquiry.* Scranton: University of Scranton Press, 1993.

Mendeloff, David. "Trauma and Vengeance: Assessing the Psychological and Emotional Effects of Post-Conflict Justice." *Human Rights Quarterly* 31, no. 3 (2009): 592–623.

Miles, Matthew B., and Michael A. Huberman. *Qualitative Data Analysis: An Expanded Sourcebook.* 2nd ed. Thousand Oaks: Sage Publications, 1994.

Morse, Janice M., and Lyn Richards. *Readme First for a User's Guide to Qualitative Methods.* Thousand Oaks, CA: Sage, 2002.

Moulin, Léon de Saint, and Z. Modio. "La signification sociale des sectes au Zaïre." *Cahiers des religions Africaines* 27–28, no. 53–56 (1993–1994): 247–268.

Mudimbe, V. Y., and Mbula Susan Kilonzo. "Philosophy of Religion on African Ways of Believing." In Elias Kifon Bongmba (ed.), *The Wiley-Blackwell Companion to African Religions.* Malden, MA: Wiley-Blackwell, 2012.

Murray, R. Thomas. *Blending Qualitative & Quantitative Research Methods in Theses and Dissertations.* Thousand Oaks, Calif.: Corwin Press, 2003.

Muzorewa, Gwinyai H. *The Origins and Development of African Theology.* Maryknoll, NY: Orbis Books, 1985.

Nkingi, Mweze Chirhulwire Dominique. "Eglise de réveil: Génese et modes opératoires." In Kinyamba Sylvain Shomba (ed.), *Les spiritualité du temps présent.* Kinshasa: Éditions M.E.S, 2012.

Nordstrom, Carolyn. "Contested Identities/Essentially Contested Powers." In Kumar Rupesinghe (ed.), *Conflict Transformation.* Houndmills, Basingstoke, Hampshire: Macmillan, 1995.

Nordstrom, Carolyn, and Antonius C. G. M. Robben. *Fieldwork Under Fire: Contemporary Studies of Violence and Survival.* Berkeley: University of California Press, 1995.

Nzongola-Ntalaja, Georges. *Faillite de la gouvernance et crise de la construction nationale au Congo-Kinshasa: une analyse des luttes pour la démocratie et la souveraineté.* Kinshasa; Montréal; Washington, D.C.: ICREDES, 2015.

Omer, Atalia. "Religious Peacebuilding: The Exotic, the Good, and the Theatrical." In Atalia Omer, R. Scott Appleby, and David Little (eds.), *The Oxford Handbook of Religion, Conflict, and Peacebuilding.* New York, NY: Oxford University Press, 2015.

Paffenholz, Thania. "Civil Society and Peacebuilding." In Thania Paffenholz (ed.), *Civil Society & Peacebuilding: A Critical Assessment.* Boulder: Lynne Rienner, 2010.

Palmer, Michael D., and Stanley M. Burgess. "Introduction." In Michael D. Palmer and Stanley M. Burgess (eds.), *The Wiley-Blackwell Companion to Religion and Social Justice.* Chichester, West Sussex; Malden, MA: Wiley-Blackwell, 2012.

Paris, Roland, and Timothy D. Sisk. "Introduction: Understanding the Contradictions of Postwar Statebuilding."In Roland Paris and Timothy D. Sisk (eds.), *The Dilemmas of Statebuilding: Confronting the Contradictions of Postwar Peace Operations.* Abingdon, UK: Routledge, 2009.

Parrinder, Edward Geoffrey. *African Traditional Religion.* (3rd ed.). London: Sheldon Press, 1974.

Paul VI. "Eucharistic Celebration at the Conclusion of the Symposium Organized by the Bishops of Africa: Homily of Paul VI." Kampala, Uganda. July 31st, 1969. https://w2.vatican.va/content/paul-vi/en/homilies/1969/documents/hf_p-vi_hom_19690731.html.

———. "Evangelii Nuntiandi." *Vatican Website.* December 8th, 1975.

———. "Populorum Progressio." *Vatican Website.* March 26, 1967.

Philpott, Daniel. *Just and Unjust Peace: An Ethic of Political Reconciliation.* New York: Oxford University Press, 2012.

Prunier, Gérard. "The Catholic Church and the Kivu Conflict." *Journal of Religion in Africa* 31, no. 2 (2001): 139–162.

Ramsbotham, Oliver, Hugh Miall, and Tom Woodhouse. *Contemporary Conflict Resolution: The Prevention, Management and Transformation of Deadly Conflicts.* (3rd ed.). Cambridge, UK; Malden, MA: Polity Press, 2011.

Rawls, John. *A Theory of Justice.* (Rev. ed.). Cambridge, MA.: Belknap Press of Harvard University Press, 1999.

Reyntjens, Filip, and René Lemarchand. "Mass Murder in Eastern Congo, 1996–1997." In René Lemarchand (eds.), *Forgotten Genocides: Oblivion, Denial, and Memory.* Philadelphia: University of Pennsylvania Press, 2011.

Roberts, Les. *Mortality in Eastern DRC: Results from Five Mortality Surveys.* New York: International Rescue Committee, 2000.

Ross, Marc Howard. *The Culture of Conflict: Interpretations and Interests in Comparative Perspective.* New Haven: Yale University Press, 1993.

Roy, Simon N. "L'étude De Cas." In *Recherche Sociale: de la problématique à la collecte des données,* edited by Benoît Gauthier. Sainte-Foy: Presses de l'Université du Québec, 2006.

Sampson, Cynthia. "Religion and Peacebuilding." In I. William Zartman (ed.), *Peacemaking in International Conflict: Methods & Techniques.* Washington, D.C.: United States Institute of Peace, 2007.

Seay, Laura Elizabeth. "Authority at Twilight: Civil Society, Social Services, and the State in the Eastern Democratic Republic of Congo." Ph.D. Dissertation, The University of Texas at Austin, 2009.

———. "Effective Responses: Protestants, Catholics and the Provision of Health Care in the Post-war Kivus," *Review of African Political Economy* 40, no. 135 (2013): 83–97.

Shorter, Aylward. *African Christian Theology: Adaptation or Incarnation?* London: G. Chapman, 1975a.

———. *Prayer in the Religious Traditions of Africa.* Nairobi: Oxford University Press, 1975b.

Simons, Helen. *Case Study Research in Practice.* Los Angeles: SAGE, 2009.

Smith, Donald Eugene. *Religion and Political Development, an Analytic Study.* Boston: Little, Brown, 1970.

Stake, Robert E. *The Art of Case Study Research.* Thousand Oaks: Sage Publications, 1995.

Steele, David. "An Introductory Overview to Faith-Based Peacebuilding." In Mark Rogers, Tom Bamat, and Julie Ideh (eds.), *Pursuing Just Peace: An Overview and Case Studies for Faith-Based Peacebuilders.* Baltimore, MD: Catholic Relief Services, 2008.

Sullivan, Thomas J. *Methods of Social Research.* Fort Worth, TX; London: Harcourt College Publishers, 2001.

Tale, Steen-Johnsen. *State and Politics in Religious Peacebuilding.* London: Palgrave Macmillan, 2017.

Taylor, Mark C. *After God.* Chicago: University of Chicago Press, 2007.

Tesfai, Yacob. *Holy Warriors, Infidels, and Peacemakers in Africa.* New York; Basingstoke, England: Palgrave Macmillan, 2010.

Thomas, Gary. *How to Do Your Case Study: A Guide for Students and Researchers.* Los Angeles, Calif.: SAGE, 2011.

Toft, Monica Duffy. *Securing the Peace: The Durable Settlement of Civil Wars.* Princeton, NJ: Princeton University Press, 2010.

Trefon, Theodore. *Congo Masquerade: The Political Culture of Aid Inefficiency and Reform Failure.* New York: Zed Books, 2011.

Tull, Denis. *The Reconfiguration of Political Order in Africa: A Case Study of North Kivu (DR Congo).* Hamburg: Institute of African Affairs, 2005.

Turner, Thomas. *Congo.* Cambridge; Malden, MA: Polity Press, 2013.

Vlassenroot, Koen, and Karen Büscher. *"The City as a Frontier: Urban Development and Identity Processes in Goma."* Crisis States Working Paper 61 (Series 2). London: London School of Economics, 2009.

Wijsen, Frans Jozef Servaas. *Seeds of Conflict in a Haven of Peace: From Religious Studies to Interreligious Studies in Africa.* New York, NY: Rodopi, 2007.

Willaime, Jean-Paul. "La religion: un lien social articulé au don," *Revue du MAUSS*, no. 22 (2003/2): 248–269.

———. *Sociologie des religions.* Paris: Presses universitaires de France, 1995.

Willame, Jean-Claude. *La guerre du Kivu: Vues de la salle climatisée et de la véranda.* Bruxelles: Éditions GRIP, 2010.

Willame, Jean-Claude, and Benoit Verhaegen. *Les provinces du Congo: Structure et fonctionnement (Lomami–Kivu Central).* Léopoldville: Université Lovanium, 1964a.

———. *Les provinces du Congo: Structure et fonctionnement (Nord-Kivu–Lac Léopold II).* Léopoldville: Université Lovanium, 1964b.

Yin, Robert K. *Case Study Research: Design and Methods.* 5th ed. Thousand Oaks, CA: Sage, 2014.

———. *Case Study Research: Design and Methods.* Applied Social Research Methods Series. 4th ed. Los Angeles: Sage Publications, 2009.

Zahan, Dominique. *The Religion, Spirituality, and Thought of Traditional Africa.* Chicago: University of Chicago Press, 1979.

Zartman, I. William. "Conclusions: The Last Mile." In I. William Zartman (ed.), *Elusive Peace: Negotiating an End to Civil Wars.* Washington, D.C.: Brookings Institution, 1995.

2 Religious Peacebuilding in Goma

A Conceptual Framework

> Wherever there are human beings, there is conflict. However, in the Congo and particularly in the East, they usually turn into violence. You may leave home in the morning, but you are not sure if you will return in the evening. You sleep and you cannot wait for sunrise out of fear of malicious attacks. (interview of Mastaki, quoted from Alfani 2015, 96)

Introduction

As indicated in the preceding introductory chapter, this book subscribes to the field of religious studies in laying out a conceptual framework of religious peacebuilding and conflict transformation in the city of Goma. While different in their application and the actors involved, these two concepts are often used interchangeably. Two examples may serve as an illustration. The first was already cited in the introductory chapter and comes from Scott Appleby: "religious peacebuilding" is a "new form of conflict transformation" (2000, 7). The second example is from Cynthia Sampson's book chapter "Religion and Peacebuilding," in which she notes that "peacebuilding" and "conflict transformation" are "virtually synonymous" terms (2007, 278).

Like "peacebuilding," "religious peacebuilding" and "conflict transformation" are relatively recent theories. They emerged in the United States, and are spreading, and are being promoted across disciplines such as political science and international relations, as well as sociology, religious studies and theology.

As for any endeavour, having a clear understanding of what one seeks to achieve (in this case, peace) increases the possibility of reaching the given objective. As Oliver Richmond, British Professor of International Relations and Peace and Conflict studies, points out in his book *The Transformation of Peace*, "to know peace provides a clearer understanding of what must be done and what must be avoided, if it is to be achieved" (2005, 207). Seeking this kind of clearer understanding also requires a clearer theoretical understanding of the concept of "peace," which is the aim of this chapter. As this conceptual framework emerges, it will become the pillar upon which the remaining chapters of this book will be built.

This chapter is constructed into five parts besides its introduction and conclusion. I first examine the notions of conflict and peace, which are two of the core concepts of this book. Second, I discuss the concepts of religious peacebuilding and conflict transformation. My attempt in the second section is to compare the two concepts; that is, to describe their similarities as well as their differences. Third, I examine the concept of local ownership. Fourth, I expand on the implementation of both religious peacebuilding and conflict transformation, not only from a top-down approach, but also at the middle and grassroots levels. Fifth, I endeavour to present three theologies of peace based on three Christian perspectives, namely the Catholic, Protestant and Revival ones.

Conflict and Different Kinds of Peace

Despite the difficulty of defining and conceptualizing the term *peace,* many have adopted a series of binary categorizations that include its natures, types, and degrees of achievement. In other words, and even though the aim of this book is not to specifically elaborate on the criteria and indicators of peace, the term *peace* is also suggestive of notions that relate to both qualitative and quantitative dimensions. A binary categorization of peace may, for example, be a perception of peace on an abstract, ascending, and spectrum ranging from negative to positive. Pierre Allan, a political scientist from the University of Geneva, goes even further in his notion of scale to suggest the concept of "global care," which he argues supersedes and is morally superior to positive peace (Allan 2006, 119–120, 129). Whatever the definition given to peace or the adjective that qualifies it, my purpose is not to find the best single definition nor to overemphasize one (*just peace*, *positive peace* or even *global care*) while scorning another (*negative peace*), nor is it to diminish the importance of the various definitions. Rather, my purpose is to find the definitions that best represent the dynamics related to the analysis of the results of this research. In that light, I agree with Oliver Richmond's suggestion that the categorization of peace not only helps in its assessment, but that it also contributes to its planning and, hence, its achievement (2005).

An Understanding of Conflict and Violence

The words of Mastaki, a fictitious name of a peace program coordinator at a church in Goma, quoted at the inception of this chapter, echo what most peace and conflict scholars suggest (Barash 2010; Barash and Webel 2002). For instance, the peace activist and scholar, and former President of the International Fellowship of Reconciliation, Diana Francis, in her book *People, Peace and Power: Conflict Transformation in Action* (2002), presents *conflict* both as a universal reality and as an inevitable situation among humans. Instead of focusing on the cooperative, positive side of conflict, she regrets that many have emphasized its negative counterpart—that which advances competitive relationships. Indeed, some authors (e.g., Azar and Burton 1986; Rabie 1994; Wallensteen 2002) agree that conflict is a universal component that occurs wherever two living entities or more are in direct or indirect interaction. There are also situations where one is in conflict with oneself.

Conflict can also be referred to as incompatible behaviours and actions (Azar and Burton 1986). While conflict may be perceived as inevitable, its escalation to violent acts can nevertheless be prevented. In addition, it is, for some, "a social situation in which a minimum of two actors (parties) strive to acquire at the same moment in time an available set of scarce resources" (Wallensteen 2002, 16). In the same vein, it is also defined as the "actions of two or more parties who contest control over scarce material or symbolic resources" (Ross 1993, 31). Mark Howard Ross posits that both behaviour and perceptions are central in conflict. Others suggest that it is a "normal product of diversity in beliefs and values, differences in attitudes and perceptions, and competing socio-economic and political interests among individuals, social classes, ethnic groups and states" (Rabie 1994, 3). In other words, conflict is understood as a social phenomenon where values, compatibility, differences and interests are at stake. Therefore, for definitional purposes, authors have divided conflict into two categories: (1) interest-related and (2) value-related (Rabie 1994, 3–4; Ross 1993, 16n1). Among many issues associated with the *interest-related* category are state security, regional influence, land and natural resources. The second category, *value-related,* encompasses issues such as political ideologies, religious beliefs, cultural rights, ethnic relations, group identities and the socio-political status of minorities. Value-related conflict is difficult to define, manage and resolve (Rabie 1994, 8, 22–25).

Furthermore, researchers from different fields of study regard conflict in a dichotomous way, which generally includes both internal and external perspectives. The first perspective, internal, focuses on understanding the domestic factors of conflict. Sociologists, anthropologists and psychologists have been at the forefront of such inquiry. The second, external, is dominated by international relations scholars, and focuses on the external factors of conflict (Azar 1990, 5–6). That is, these scholars seek to understand external factors that influence the emergence of conflict. The internal and external perspectives of conflict do not operate in isolation; they overlap and interact with each other.

In addition to the distinction between internal and external perspectives of conflict, authors like the American political sociologist Barrington Moore, Jr. (1978) and the Lebanese political scientist Edward Azar (1990) have included *societal needs* as key factors in conflict. Moore specifies in his book *Injustice: The Social Bases of Obedience and Revolt,* that conflict is embedded in all human beings, irrespective of their origins (1978, 5, 7). Conflict stems from the interaction between individuals and groups, because of the three underlying categories of problems comprising *social coordination* (Moore 1978).

First, the problem of *authority* determines which people are the leaders and followers in all societal activities (e.g., states, organizations, etc.). Second, the problem of the *division of labour* determines which people execute what kinds of work, how and where. The third problem concerns the *distribution of resources,* which includes goods and services collectively. These three kinds of problems are described either as "social needs" or "social imperatives," depending on their degree of strength. Both Moore and Azar maintain that the deprivation of these needs, which the former understands as a "social contract," generates conflict, oftentimes in unison. For the two authors, the provision of these needs is primarily regulated by the state's authority.

Edward E. Azar argues in his book *The Management of Protracted Social Conflict* that unsatisfied basic human needs (security, communal recognition and distributive justice) and development needs (cultural values, images, customs, language, human rights, racial heritage and security) indirectly contribute to the formation of conflict (1990, 2, 9). Prolonged and un-redressed grievances rooted in deprivation and the exclusion of human and development needs are critical factors often exacerbating conflicts, which Azar called "protracted social conflicts" (1990, 2).

In the case of the Great Lakes region of Africa in general, and Goma in particular, one's access to land equates to accessing Azar's superstructure of society. That is, the denial of such a need can only result in grievances and eventually violence, even to the extent of the 1994 Rwandan genocide and several other acts of violence in the Kivu provinces of the DRC. The determining factors of peace and conflict are, first, cooperation and, second, competition. While cooperation may lead to peaceful relationships, competition may result in conflictual ones. One of the research sub-questions that emerges from this question concerns the causes of conflict in Goma.

Negative and Positive Kinds of Peace

Johan Galtung, a Norwegian scholar of peace and conflict studies, is one of the first to have introduced the typology of *negative* and *positive* peace[1] in the mid-1960s (Barash and Webel 2002). In an editorial published in the *Journal of Peace Research* (1964), Galtung identified two extremely opposing views. While we need to shy away from "global complete war" (GCW), we must also move toward "global complete peace" (GCP). Although his perspective of negative peace (as the absence of both violence and war) remains the same, Galtung observed elsewhere, in referring to positive health, that the definition of positive peace constantly changes. For him, positive peace should not only consider the integration of human society, as laid out in his earlier work (Galtung 1964, 2, 3), but it should also further include values such as social justice (Galtung 1969, 189n31).

Galtung equates a negative kind of peace with the absence of war, organized violence and overt rivalries (personal violence). Whereas, in his view, a positive kind of peace not only signifies the absence of structural violence but also includes the "integration of human society" (Galtung 1964, 2). For him, these two dimensions of peace (negative and positive) are self-existing and independent of each other; that is, one does not need the presence of the other to exist. Contrary to what he tried to avoid in his understanding of the word "structural," this book adopts an institutional meaning alluding to religious organizations such as churches (1969, 187n12). In a later article, "Religion, Hard and Soft," Galtung distinguishes vertical from a horizontal form of structural violence, in terms of "economic exploitations and political repression," and "alienation, distance," respectively (Galtung 1997, 441). The elimination of these different manifestations of forms of negative peace does not coincide with the spontaneous existence of positive peace. The structures that shape both personal and structural violence, which are oftentimes invisible with indirect incidences, must be addressed. One way of dealing with such structures is not only to alienate visible forms of violence, but also to foster actions that promote positive peace (e.g., trauma-healing activities, conducting truth commissions and interreligious dialogue). In their article on religion and peacemaking, the English sociologists and peace studies scholars John Brewer, Gareth Higgins and Francis Teeney argue for four strategic spaces that religion occupies in civil society and which foster positive peace: (1) intellectual spaces; (2) institutional spaces; (3) market spaces; and (4) political spaces (Brewer et al., 2010). For them, occupying these spaces enables a double transition which, on the one hand, ushers in a positive peace from a negative one. On the other hand, by occupying strategic spaces, religious actors add political roles to their primary duties (Brewer et al., 2010, 1028).

Furthermore, the word peace embodies religious and spiritual meanings and is generally translated from the Arabic *salaam* and the Hebrew *shalom*. Compared to positive and negative kinds of peace, *shalom* or *salaam* espouses positive peace. *Shalom* and *salaam* mean "wholeness, fulfillment, completion, unity and wellbeing, thereby encompassing both reconciliation and peace" (Steele 2008, 5). This positive dimension of peace further connotes harmony, healing,[2] health and personal fulfillment at personal, social, national and international levels (Coste 1997, 74–80). René Coste, a French Catholic theologian, defines *shalom* both as a "symphony of peace" and a "supreme good and the crown of all divine blessings" (1997, 74–80). Still, to define *shalom*, as a positive peace, many have also included two essential components or values, namely, justice and reconciliation (Coste 1997; Merdjanova and Brodeur 2009; Steele 2008, 6–7). In the same vein, for instance, David Steele (2008) proposes a definition of faith-based peacebuilding primarily focused on justice and reconciliation. For Steele, peace activities initiated by religious groups consist of "effort[s] to assist antagonists to disavow violence of any kind and begin to move toward personal, relational, communal and social wholeness that affirms the need for both fairness/justice and healing/reconciliation" (2008, 8).

In light of the above section, certain research questions arise based on the participants' perceptions of peace and conflict. I formulate them in the following terms: "How do religious actors—both leaders and followers of the Catholic, *3ème* CBCA and *Arche* Churches in Goma—understand the concepts of peace and conflict?," and "How do they describe conflict in the DRC and particularly in Goma?"

Religious Peacebuilding and Conflict Transformation: Religion as a Transformer of Conflicts for a Lasting Peace

Scholars of peace and conflict studies agree that peacebuilding emerged following the wide propagation of the former UN Secretary-General Boutros-Ghali's 1992 *An Agenda for Peace.* The aim of peacebuilding was to institutionalize peace whether by (1) delving into the causal aspects of the given conflict or (2) preventing potential conflicts "without any peace-keeping operation being deployed" (Boutros-Ghali 1992, 19–20). *An Agenda for Peace* focused primarily on post-conflict efforts in the pursuit of peace, where the liberal agenda—political and market liberalization through democratic institutions—prevails. There is a lively debate, in which I will refrain from getting involved, among scholars on the use of the term *post-conflict* in relation to peacebuilding. For instance, in reference to *An Agenda for Peace,* Stephen Ryan rejects in his book *The Transformation of Violent Conflict,* the notion of post-conflict, observing that conflict still exists after peace agreements (2007).

In this book, I will use the concept of peacebuilding in dealing with the city of Goma in particular, not as a "post-conflict" situation, but as an ongoing conflict. I consider a cease-fire situation to be a mere period of quiet that connotes the idea of a *negative peace* (Ryan 2007, 9). Due to its relatively poor results in restoring peace in many conflict regions, especially in Sub-Saharan Africa, some have strongly critiqued liberal peacebuilding (Curtis 2012, 10; Newman 2009; Cousens 2001, 7), whereas others like Roland Paris have advocated for it arguing that those critiques were merely "unfounded scepticism and cynicism" (2010, 338).

Religious peacebuilding connotes the contribution of religion or religious actors to peacemaking. However, this connotation is debated among scholars, primarily because of acts of violence generally attributed to religions and their adherents. This ambivalence between the roles of religions in both peacemaking and violence was developed in the book by Scott Appleby, *The Ambivalence of Religion: Religion, Violence and Reconciliation* (2000). On the one hand, Appleby shares what he defines as the "strong religion" group, which encompasses those who maintain that religion is the cause of and a tool for violence. That is, the so-called "strong religion camp" uses religion to defend or advocate violent acts. On the other hand, his category of "weak religion" comprises those who view religion as a "dependent variable in deadly violence" (Appleby 2015, 34; see also Brewer et al. 2010, 1033). While some argue that religion and religious actors have more often contributed to fuelling conflicts, others claim the opposite, asserting that religious actors can have a positive influence in the same context.

Religious peacebuilding possesses religious elements that believers can consciously use in peacebuilding efforts. On the one hand, it is comprised of beliefs, norms and rituals; and on the other hand, it provides a wide range of religious actors from different backgrounds (individuals, professionals, institutions, etc.), all aiming for peace. The aim of religious actors and organizations' activities consists of (1) transforming conflicts and (2) (re)building both social relations and political institutions characterized by an ethos of tolerance and nonviolence. Their roles also include the fostering of different aspects of justice within society, with cultural and economic inputs. Scholars have also maintained that religious leaders are promoters of both the culture and the value of peace. Both Jean-Marie Kitumaini Vianney and Ignace Ndongala Maduku, two Congolese Catholic priests, stress the place and importance of a peace-related culture in the Congolese socio-political context (Ndongala 2015; Kitumaini 2011).

From Conflict Resolution to Conflict Transformation

Conflict Resolution

The conflict resolution approach focuses on severe and harmful competitive processes and aims to change or reduce their impacts on protagonists. For the political economist Mohamed Rabie, it is meant to restore stability and balance (Rabie 1994, 5–6). Peter Wallensteen proposes in his book *Understanding Conflict Resolution: War, Peace and the Global System* (2002) a twofold definition of this approach (conflict resolution). First, his preliminary definition refers to a "situation where conflicting parties enter into an agreement that solves their central incompatibilities, accept each other's continued existence as parties and cease all violent action against each other" (Wallensteen 2002, 8). Second, he refines it with the addition of such terms as "voluntary" and "armed," as follows: "[conflict resolution] is a social situation where the armed conflicting parties in a (voluntary) agreement resolve to peacefully live with — and/or dissolve — their basic incompatibilities and henceforth cease to use arms against one another." While an *agreement* is basically a formal or informal understanding between conflicting parties, a formal type of agreement is more likely to succeed than an informal one. Furthermore, a "peace agreement" differs from an "agreement of capitulation," in that the outcomes of the first mean that conflicting parties are mutual winners, whereas an agreement of capitulation indicates that one side is victorious over the other (Wallensteen 2002, 8–9). While conflict resolution secures a certain degree of peace, such as a negative kind of peace (e.g., a cease-fire), some maintain that not only are the roles of third parties, who are generally elites, overemphasized and the weaker ones unheard, but the core of conflicts remains unaddressed (Ryan 2007; Francis 2002). Another approach is thus proposed by conflict resolution contenders, who primarily critique conflict resolution on the grounds of its failure to pursue a positive kind of peace, which ensures, for instance, social justice, equality and security. Instead, they put forth the *conflict transformation* approach (Francis 2002).

Religious Peacebuilding as Conflict Transformation

Conflict transformation is the core of peacebuilding. For advocates of conflict transformation (and of the theology of peace, a concept I subsequently examine), mediation and peace agreements are not sufficient to ensure an end to violence and the establishment of sustainable peace (Ryan 2007; Coste 1997, 334). Instead of suggesting new recipes or solutions for violent conflicts – which are largely preconceived without the active participation of the people most directly concerned (primarily victims) — conflict transformation theorists and practitioners argue that fundamental changes are required, especially at the level of relationships (Lederach 2003, 28–30). Conflict changes over time and it carries different forms. Since values and interests are at stake in many violent conflicts, Raimo Väyrynen (1991) and others consider conflict transformation as a key, yet often ignored, approach, to reversing conflict. John Paul Lederach, an advocate of the conflict transformation approach, defines it as a way to "envision and respond to the ebb and flow of social conflict as life-giving opportunities for creating constructive change processes that reduce violence, increase justice in direct interaction and social structures and respond to real-life problems in human relationships" (2003, 14). Lederach's point of departure is that conflicts, as part of human realities, are vectors of change.

Contrary to conflict resolution, which deals with immediate situations, conflict transformation goes further in examining both the pattern of relationships and the context of conflicts. These examinations lead to at least four aspects of transformation on which many conflict transformation observers agree (Alfani 2015; Aquino 2011; Miall 2004; Lederach 2003; Vaeyrynen 1991). The first aspect concerns the vehicles of the transformative approach, i.e. the actors or agents who carry out these transformations. This first consideration is broadly inclusive in nature. That is, the people at the negotiation table include not only armed conflict protagonists but representatives of peace beneficiaries at the grass-roots level. Members of the civil society in general and religious actors in particular are oftentimes invited to play a mediation role. The Catholic Church and the *Église du Christ au Congo* (Church of Christ in Congo, ECC) have been involved in mediating conflicts both at the national and local levels in the Congolese socio-political contexts and at different occasions (Alfani 2015; Nzongola-Ntalaja 2015; Mpisi 2008). Even recently (late 2016), the Congolese Catholic Church (bishops) played a key role in the ongoing political conflict surrounding the expiration of President Joseph Kabila's second and last term which resulted with the signature of the *Accord politique global et inclusif du Centre Interdiocésain de Kinshasa* (Global and inclusive agreement of the Inter-diocesan of Kinshasa) or the so-called *Saint-Sylvestre* (New-year eve) accord on December 31st, 2016.[3]

The second aspect of the transformation approach regards the key issues at stake. Even though this second layer is usually quarrelsome—because of the importance actors give to the matters at stake, and their reservations for reassessing their own agendas (political, economic, etc.)—its success depends primarily on the objectivity accorded to these issues. Third, the idea of transformation provides room to redefine the kinds of relationships which parties involved in conflicts seek to establish and promote. They may include such values as inclusion, respect, reconciliation and justice.

The fourth aspect is a structural transformation. Lederach argues that this last aspect is crucial, because it determines the production and reproduction of conflicts (2003). He believes that conflicts influence the way social structures, organizations and institutions are constructed. This fourth aspect requires a long-term vision which will demand transformation at four levels, a vision that could trigger violence—individual, structural, relational and cultural (Ryan 2007).

Religious Peacebuilding as Local Ownership

Since the mid-1990s, the concept of local ownership has gained considerable attention from scholars in the peacebuilding enterprise. The outcomes of peace processes are more important for *insiders* (local actors and populations), who must abide within the site, than for *outsiders*, who eventually leave conflict zones. Local actors have a relatively better understanding of the root causes of conflicts, as well as their potential transformative components on the grounds of historical, cultural and linguistic resources. However, this concept requires clarification and its related terms, such as participation and collaboration, deserve the same attention. What does *local* mean?

There is no agreement among scholars and practitioners on the limitations of this term. While *local,* from a regional point of view, could refer to a given country, it could also mean a province (from a national perspective) or a city (from a district perspective). For Oliver Richmond and Audra Mitchell, one way in which *local* is understood in the context of peacebuilding is as a "specific socio-geographical space in which peace interventions (and the violence that preceded them) unfold" (2012b, 10–14). The space in question is occupied by individuals and groups that share cultures, traditions, customs and even lifestyles with a wide range of societal statuses. During peacebuilding activities, the given socio-geographical space is shared with external actors (foreign governments, international organizations, multinationals, international NGOs, etc.).

Furthermore, *local* conveys the idea of insiders as opposed to outsiders. Mary Anderson and Lara Olson (2003) define *insiders* in two respects: (1) those who endure the conflict and its consequences and (2) local agencies working for peace purposes. *Outsiders* are people who voluntarily choose to be involved in the conflict zone but have the option of leaving the site at any time.

Ownership is usually linked with local and has a wide range of usage – there cannot be a single, rigid definition of ownership. At the same time, it should not be a pretext for defining a concept according to the context at hand, especially when it leaves room for interpretation with negative consequences. In the context of conflictual situations, ownership portrays at least four meanings: firstly, local actors' perceptions and appreciation of foreign/outsiders' interventions, such as policies and aid; secondly, local actors' participation in decision-making processes (project design and management, budgetary allocations, choice of participants, etc.); thirdly, how and when knowledge/expertise is transferred between insiders and outsiders; and fourthly, the possibility of allowing locals to hold outsiders accountable.

Three Levels of Religious Peacebuilding and Conflict Transformation

Religious peacebuilders intervene on at least three levels, namely at the top-down, middle-range and grassroots levels (Lederach 1997, 38). The top-down approach to religious peacebuilding focuses on key leaders (top-level leaders) in conflicts. For instance, religious leaders, irrespective of their tradition, offer their services as mediators between antagonists. While Newman argues that this approach is a realist exercise that seeks, first and foremost, security and stability, Olive Richmond posits that it focuses primarily on establishing democratic institutions that foster free markets, the rule of law and development (2006a, 379). Autesserre's critiques illustrate the failure of the international community to resolve the conflict in the Congo, despite its deployment of large peacekeeping force (the largest so far, of more than 19,000 people), partly because of its preference for a top-down approach over a grassroots one (2010). The second level of intervention by religious actors is the middle-range or middle-out approach.

The middle-range approach focuses on peace education by way of programs such as problem-solving workshops, training and commissions. This middle-range level is represented by prominent institutional actors—also known as Track II leaders—such as visible and influential religious leaders and heads of NGOs. They are not only influential at the top-down level, but also at the grassroots level, and include both temporal and spiritual aspects in their interventions (Boyle 1992). Because of their authority, credibility and legitimacy, leaders at the middle-range level are also influential and respected at the top-down and grassroots levels, to which they have easy access.

Lastly, the third level of intervention is at the grassroots level. Religious peacebuilding is relatively easy to deploy at the local level by religious organizations located close to local communities, as demonstrated in this book, and particularly in Chapter Three. For instance, the Catholic Church in the diocese of Goma is locally (at the parish level) represented by small communities called *Shirika* in Kiswahili (Living Basic Ecclesial Communities or Basic Ecclesial Communities) which house such programs as the *Commission Justice et Paix* (Commission for Justice and Peace, CJP).[4]

Authors, such as John Paul Lederach (1997, 82), have agreed that conflicts can be addressed at a minimum of three different stages: first, prior to conflict escalation, which is the preventive phase (also known as the phase of conflict management); second, the period of conflict occurrence; and third, the post-conflict stage (structural reform). In order to adequately address contemporary conflicts, it is pertinent to include religious actors in peacebuilding processes at all three stages because of their influence on local populations and their long-term commitment to the latter. Gerard Powers points out that inter-religious collaboration is more effective in complementary peacebuilding efforts than other types of collaboration (2010). The main reason for such a deficiency in bringing about significant results is that participants have not effectively documented their commitments in writing and in terms of their own communities.

Christian Theologies of Peace

A Catholic Perspective on the Theology of Peace

In 1983, tensions between the United States and the Soviet Union, the two superpowers at the time, motivated the bishops of the United States Conference of Bishops to request the development of a so-called theology of peace. While the US-USSR relationship was in relatively good standing during the Second World War, it subsequently deteriorated and reached a low point due to their nuclear arms race which posed a concrete threat to humanity. How did the church in general, and the Catholic tradition in particular, express their viewpoints on war and peace issues amidst such a sensitive situation embedded with political and military aspects? Where was the line drawn between physical and spiritual matters? To put it differently, how does one separate the Church's moral imperative from politics?

The theology of peace emerged in the early 1980s with the publication of the United States Conference of Bishops' pastoral letter entitled *The Challenge of Peace: God's Promise and Our Response* (1983). This letter explicitly indicated the importance of developing a theology of peace. The bishops wrote:

> We are called to be a Church at the service of peace, precisely because peace is one manifestation of God's word and work in our midst. Recognition of the Church's responsibility to join with others in the work of peace is a major force behind the call today to develop a theology of peace. Much of the history of Catholic theology on war and peace has focused on limiting the resort to force in human affairs; this task is still necessary and is reflected later in this pastoral letter, but it is not a sufficient response to Vatican II's challenge "to undertake a completely fresh reappraisal of war." (United States Conference of Catholic Bishops 1983, No. 23)

René Coste—a French Catholic bishop, theologian and former head of France's Pax Christi—took on the challenge proposed by the American bishops to reappraise war and to develop a theology of peace. As a result, he released his book carrying the same term *Théologie de la paix* (Coste 1997). Coste neatly provides in that book tools to theologians and practitioners, particularly Christians, to adequately address contemporary conflicts. His analysis of the concept of theology of peace not only draws from the Catholic writings, it is also enriched by secular fields (e.g., political science, anthropology and sociology), whilst ensuring the practicality of this new approach (Coste 1997). In addition, the concept of theology of peace developed in Coste's book mobilizes also testimonies from believers

(1997, 28).[5] Instead of adopting an ambiguous attitude towards war, the church is now required to assume moral responsibility and to condemn all forms of war, and not while spreading fear and uncertainty, but while inspiring a hopeful, joyful and brighter future in the spirit of the pastoral Constitution *Gaudium et spes* (Vatican Council II, 1965, Nos 4 and 77). A theology of peace involves more than intellectual research. For instance, René Coste states:

> The theology of peace…[is] not only an intellectual pursuit, but an act of faith in the amazing power of inquiry and transformation of history which comes from the biblical message of peace welcomed in the depths of the heart and a practical commitment to ecclesiastic and interpersonal networks which endeavour to promote peace by capillarity, essential to becoming an experience of everyday life. (1997, 39)[6]

Coste considers theology of peace as an act of faith rooted in the Bible with the purpose of transforming relationships through the promotion of peace by capillarity (1997, 39). For him, a theology of peace should not be intellectually limited; rather it should penetrate the heart with the objective of changing one's entire life. In other words, Coste's theology of peace concurs with what is also known as a culture of peace, which inspires human being to have peaceful behaviors not in denying their internal conflicts, but in addressing them as a personal responsibility. As far as the Catholic tradition and, to some degree, the *3ème* CBCA and *Arche* Churches are concerned, a theology of peace is rooted in at least two sources.

First, *revelation* remains a primary source of a theology of peace, despite the terms it may be given (e.g., Word of God, Old or New Testaments) or its theological connotations. For René Coste, the Word of God stands as a fundamental source for a theology of peace to which one is to be exposed. This channel for a theology of peace, according to Coste, cannot be understood through the simple contact with a physical book called the Bible. He argues, however, that its literal interpretation may be misguiding and oftentimes leads to conflict and violence. It is thus important to contextualize and critically interpret the Scriptures. The Holy Spirit bridges the Scripture and the signs of time. Whether seen as the Ruah YHWH, as Roger Alfani uses in his Master of Arts dissertation, or as the Holy Spirit, the presence and attention given to this divine entity contributes to establishing a "region of peace (*shalom*)" (2009, 111). Concerning the theology of peace and the works of the Holy Spirit, René Coste writes:

> The theology of peace shall be built at the hearing of the Holy Spirit [who] addresses us through the Bible and the signs of time and at the deepest of our conscience and that of

> our Christian brothers and sisters…but also in the heart[s] of our human brothers and sisters. (1997, 37)

According to Coste, signs of time are another source of a Catholic theology of peace (1997, 36–37). Signs of time are premonitory elements that nature offers and which many ignore. For instance, René Coste (1997) in *La théologie de la paix* regretfully relates the events that shook the cities of Hiroshima and Nagasaki, while Kä Mana (2000) bitterly describes the 1994 Rwandan genocide in *La nouvelle* évangélisation *en Afrique.*

The Holy Spirit also contributes to the elaboration of a theology of peace, when it regards the interpretation of both signs of time and the Scriptures (Coste 1997, 37). The French theologian Bernard Ugeux shares similar views in his doctoral dissertation (1988, 111). He points out that signs of time encompass the needs of people vested in social, political, economic and cultural garments, which churches are invited to address. This view, in agreement with this theologian, motivated one of the research sub-questions raised in this book: "What are the causes of conflict in Goma?"

I conclude this section with two citations drawn from Kä Mana's *La nouvelle évangélisation,* whose theology will subsequently be elaborated. He writes about the 1994 Rwandan genocide:

> From these people, suddenly emerged a principle of death which imposed itself in my spirit as a missiological nightmare: the macabre manifestation of a Christianity of catastrophe…. (Mana 2000, 77)

He continues few pages later:

> […] This Christianity that was not able to evangelize society in its deep affects, which could not build social dykes against the outbreak of evil and which portrayed everywhere an image of a useless lock posed upon both an African and a universal paganism with no boundaries. (Mana 2000, 84)

Two Means for a Catholic Theology of Peace: Inculturation and Grassroots Approaches

The previous section expanded on the two main sources of a Catholic theology of peace. It is also important to know how this theology can precisely be implemented in conflict situations. For many, notably Catholic authors, one way in which the theology of peace can be transmitted is through the incarnation of the Gospel of Christ (which is also a Gospel of peace) in one's culture (e.g., Coste

1997; Kitumaini 2011; Mana 2000; Mongo 2005; Ugeux 1988). Considered a social approach, it allows for a complete understanding of a human who is "situated within the sphere of culture." (John Paul II, 1991, No. 24).

New Evangelization: Inculturation as a Means for a Catholic Theology of Peace

New evangelization connotes that there was an antecedent form that obviously did not have the intended results, which is the case for the African continent. There is a general consensus that the Church is identified by its propagation of the Gospel of Christ. It is "in fact the grace and vocation proper to the Church, her deepest identity," asserts Pope Paul VI, in his apostolic exhortation *Evangelii Nuntandi,* following the African Synod in 1974 (Paul VI, 1975, No. 14). The cultural aspect cannot be overlooked during this process of evangelization. The apostolic exhortation further explains:

> All this could be expressed in the following words: what matters is to evangelize man's culture and cultures (not in a purely decorative way, as it were, by applying a thin veneer, but in a vital way, in depth and right to their very roots), in the wide and rich sense which these terms have in *Gaudium et spes,* [50] always taking the person as one's starting-point and always coming back to the relationships of people among themselves and with God. (Paul VI, 1975, No. 20)

Inculturation is an encounter initiated by the Gospel with a given man. Even though this is laid out only in Pope Paul VI's 1975 *Evangelii Nuntadii,* scholars have diverged on the precise period this theological concept has been used. For some, inculturation has even been in practice long before its naming. It is understood as a continuous interaction and exchange between the message of Christ and a given culture. As one of the first popes to have used "inculturation," John Paul II, goes in the same direction in defining it as "the incarnation of the Gospel in native cultures and the introduction of these cultures into the life of the Church" (John Paul II, 1985). In another document, Pope John Paul II notes the urgency of inculturation even though he agrees that it is a lengthy, complex and difficult process (John Paul II, 1990, Nos. 52 and 53). There are no denominational boundaries to its usage. Mana, a Congolese Protestant pastor, converges with the Catholic approach, urging for a deep and truthful inculturation that "creates" a society where "human rights are guaranteed, fundamental freedom is ascertained, justice and peace reign, God is announced, Christ is proclaimed, the Spirit of God is spread, and Christianity is presented." How does a theology of peace from a Roman Catholic perspective take root through this process of inculturation? As specified above: through the preaching of the Gospel, a Gospel of peace. That is, to use what has been previously said, an "inculturation" of peace in societies where the culture of peace needs to be reinforced. The pastoral Constitution *Gaudium et spes* is clear about it: "Since, in virtue of her mission received from God, the Church preaches the Gospel to all men and dispenses the treasures of grace, *she contributes to the ensuring of peace everywhere on earth and to the placing of the fraternal exchange between men on solid ground by imparting knowledge of the divine and natural law*" (Vatican Council II, 1965, No. 89, emphasis added).

Coste points out in his book *Théologie de la paix* that promoters of a theology of peace, including missionaries, should not only avoid ecclesial triumphalism and acknowledge their wrongdoings, they should in fact prioritize in their ecclesial mission both the anthropology and ecclesiology of peace (1997, 352–367). These two aspects of a theology of peace that Coste recognizes provide, through its embedded natures of love and solidarity, an opportunity to reach out to fellow Christians and non-Christians.

Having dealt with evangelization and inculturation as two means for a Catholic theology of peace, I will further elaborate and examine its agencies. An ecclesial community can well play the role of an agency of a theology of peace. The following section will examine this kind of pastoral method that focuses on a bottom-up approach.

New Pastoral Approach for Peace: Small Living Christian Communities

Many African countries were embroiled in sociopolitical turmoil in the early 1960s. While many of them obtained their independence, it was accompanied with series of conflicts like protests and rebellions. Administrative roles (clerical and civic) once played by colonists in both Catholic and Protestant churches had to be handed over to local leaders (autochthonous) (Kabongo-Mbaya 1992). During these socio-political challenges, the Congolese Catholic episcopate readjusted both its ecclesiastic approach and its investments, which were already being squandered. In addition, the Congolese Roman Catholic Church was one of the largest religions in the country, followed by Protestant churches, who had a reduced number of ordained priests. As a result of pre-and post-independence violence and instability, suspicions between the Congolese state and the churches, and the imbalanced number of Catholic and "autochthones/indigenous" clergies, it was extremely difficult to respond to their followers' needs and those of the Congolese population in general. Thus, the leaders of the Congolese Roman Catholic Church advocated for a new pastoral approach to be adapted and contextualized to the Congolese reality—a sort of inculturation that fostered human advancement, authentic development and, ultimately, peace in all its dimensions. I will devote upcoming sections to this new pastoral approach, namely Small Living Christian Communities (*Communautés Ecclésiales Vivante de Base*, [CEVBs]).[7]

Authors like Kitumaini and Coste argue that a pastoral approach which fosters peace is likely to be successful when implemented in CEVBs. For Kitumaini, CEVBs reach where parishes and dioceses cannot. Since this new pastoral approach enables laymen to undertake certain responsibilities of priests, as result, they are discharged from other assignments and laymen feel more involved in their communities where the rule of law is relatively non-existent. Kitumaini illustrates the work undertaken by one Congolese Catholic bishop, Alois Mulindwa, who made the development of CEVBs his pastoral priority during his episcopacy:

> In the field of justice and peace, the [Catholic] Church of Bukavu, through the initiative of the diocesan Commission of Justice and Peace, has begun to train paralegals at the parish and CEV levels in order to make the population's rights and duties known and hence provide a basic socio-legal education able to incorporate all mechanisms of taking responsibility over situations of mistakes, of negligence or delays in applying the law. Through this diocesan commission, the Archdiocese of Bukavu challenged the corruption within the state's legal apparatus, because Christians have learned to rely on the Church for conflict resolution. (Kitumaini 2011, 245–267)

The urgent need for a new pastoral approach stressed by the Congolese priest Kitumaini echoes that of the American bishops in their pastoral letter, which Coste calls a "social pastoral letter" (Coste 1997; Kitumaini 2011). The two authors converge on certain aspects of the application of this pastoral letter: (1) prayer for peace and sacramental liturgy; (2) education and training of consciences (preaching, homily and catechism of peace); and (3) deaconry of peace. These three applications will deepen the Gospel of Christ (peace) at the local level and mature believers' knowledge of their rights and responsibilities as various training sessions are carried out. Thus, a community of conscience is certain to emerge (Coste 1997, 381).

Protestant and Revival Churches' Perspectives on Theologies of Peace

Contrary to the Roman Catholic Church, which has a systematic theology of peace, both Protestant and Revival Churches are yet to systematically develop such a theology. However, Kä Mana (also known as Godefroid Mana Kangudie Tshibemba), a Congolese Protestant pastor and one of its prolific African theologians, has suggested, in *La nouvelle évangélisation en Afrique,* a "theology of life," which takes into account some of the Catholics' aspects analyzed above and associates them with Protestant and Evangelical (Revival Churches) theological ingredients.[8] Mana's work analyzes, on the eve of the third millennium, the situation in Africa from a theological perspective. Far from giving a desperate report of the continent's past evangelizations, which have given some relatively positive outcomes, and far from seeking scapegoats, Kä Mana proposes an approach imbued with hopeful possibilities for a new African society: a "theology of life" or a "Christianity of life." Being Christocentric, Mana's theology of life aims to promote life. However, the implementation of such a theology required a theological diagnosis which revealed an issue: the antipode of the theology of life, termed *Christianity of catastrophe*. For him, the Christianity preached so far has not given the anticipated result as proclaimed in the Gospel of Jesus Christ (Mana 2000, 84). Thus, a revision of Christianity is mandatory if the continent of Africa is to experience the redeemed work of Christ: "There is more at stake than changing a society, one needs to change Christianity."[9]

Before looking at this Christianity of catastrophe, what would Kä Mana's definition of theology of peace resemble? Given that Mana is a Protestant pastor, it would be fair enough to ascribe his definition to that tradition. It is also important to mention that all throughout *La nouvelle évangélisation,* he has advocated for an ecumenical approach.

Mana's definition of a theology of peace is closer to that of René Coste's. I will refer to Mana's last chapter, where he outlines four theological perspectives. First, similar to Coste's definition, Mana's type of theology of peace will not only be intellectually based, but it will also include the so-called "evangelical culture." Mana explains:

> Evangelical culture not as intellectual knowledge nor a theoretical mastery of biblical verses to use as arguments…It is not about demonstrating knowledge of the catechism, but it is the result of acts which are not reserved to clergies and God's officials, assumed and ensured by a kind of Christian totally committed to the reconstruction of his country and the promotion of an individual's or community's energy to the development of life. (2000, 210)

Not only does the above citation converge with Coste's definition of a theology of peace, but I also note certain CEVB concepts—of delegating clergies' responsibilities to laymen. Also, in this first perspective, Kä Mana includes a "practical ecumenical" approach for mutual enrichment without confessional boundaries, which corresponds to René Coste's practical engagement. This is similar to his third perspective. Second, along the same lines as the first perspective, Mana proposes that clear and practical programs be established in each denomination (tradition) at visible geographic locations where hope will be deployed and the Gospel will be spread, becoming ferment for a new life. Third, his theology of peace will be what I have defined as one the theological core precepts in Christianity—love—aimed at the hearts of men and women, which is also what Coste suggested for the transformation of history. Mana says, "…If we do not have what he [Apostle Paul] names 'love' and we refer here to the depth of a human being as the manifestation of God, we are missing what is essential" (Mana 2000, 174). Let us turn now to what Kä Mana defines as a "Christianity of catastrophe" and link it at the same time to his theology of life.

To address the deadly conflicts which have had multiple effects on Sub-Saharan Africa in general, and the Great Lakes of Africa in particular, Kä Mana proposes a total rupture with the so-called "Christianity of catastrophe." For him, the latter encompasses the fertile devices missionaries sowed during the colonial period in Africa, which are still producing such issues as subordination and the dependence of African societies on Western religious organizations. In *La nouvelle évangélisation,* Mana observes that some Christian denominations have, sadly, reproduced the same kind of Christianity that does not promote the dignity of humanity, nor its full transformation or freedom. He uses a sevenfold characteristic to define the full spectrum of this gangrene (Mana 2000, 83–98). The first characteristic of his Christianity of catastrophe, *Christianity of power*, is built upon the foundation of power. Many have observed that the relationship between Western missionaries and African populations suffered from coercion (Kabasele 1993; Mana 2000; Mudimbe 1982, 1994). For instance, colonists and missionaries embarked on the same boats to African lands with different and oftentimes complementary purposes. In addition, as is generally put, while the Gospel was offered with the right hand, the left hand simultaneously served to administer both force and violence to the evangelized population. The Gospel of the powerful was then forced upon the poor and weak. Kä Mana believes that the Christianity of power displayed a type of pyramidal hierarchy which systematically enforced itself. In sum, Mana's Christianity of power is a "colonial Christianity inspired by violence" (Mana 2000, 86).

Second, Mana identified the *Christianity of the monopoly of truth,* which refers to the belief held by those in power. That is, because I am in power, I should be right, if not all the time, then most of the time. This kind of Christianity is not only presented as the truth, but as the only way to address the truth. The only point of view that matters is that of the person in power. Deprived of his or her freedom of creativity and action, a convert is bound by mental chains to his or her leader. In other words, until the leader approves it, there is no conviction of being right in the eyes and heart of subordinates and ordinary people.

Third, Mana's *Christianity of mask and duplicity* means that one can put on a mask or a garment while portraying opposing objectives contrary to what is set forth, i.e. the rhetoric and action do not match. Speaking of the Kivu's conflictual context, for instance, the article by Mararo Bucyalimwe (1999), *"La société civile au Kivu: une dynamique en panne?"* expressed similar concerns about the duplicity of civil society in general, and Christian leaders in particular. These attitudes have consequently led to ambivalence about the Christian faith. He believed that three ambiguities have stemmed from this kind of Christianity: (1) sharing the Gospel and occupation motives; (2) the bearer of the message and his or her culture and inborn ways of doing things; and (3) the infeudation of the African approach to the *Gospel of the Other*; i.e. subordinating the African interpretation of the Gospel to those that come from abroad (Mana 2000, 89–90).

Fourth, the importance given to money (or mammon) and its centrality to the evangelization is what Mana calls the *Christianity of capital*. This Christianity, dominated by the power and influence of "mammon," has infected the Christian Church globally with economic capital. Those who have the means of monetary production are the targets of the clergies (priests and pastors) who, in return, impose their agenda (e.g., favours, elections, etc.). This Christianity of capital occurs when the Church is being led by the market economy.

Fifth, the *Christianity of spectacle and folklore* is mainly based on numbers and quantity, rather than the quality of change. In this kind of Christianity of catastrophe, Kä Mana notes that the qualitative aspects of believers are ignored at the expense of their numbers (Mana 2000, 94). He reflects on the process by which new Christian members are quantitatively transformed in their day-to-day faith life. For him, some Christian traditions, especially Protestant traditions, have rather overemphasized the quantitative aspects (physical and material) of their belief. It is more often, observes Mana, about the numbers of saved and baptized followers, buildings, priests, crusades, and so on. Many Africans can hardly tell the difference between their faith and their personal responsibility to positively transform their continent.

Sixth is the *Christianity of individual (personal) salvation,* which supports the centrality of the Gospel only at the personal level rather than also aiming to transform of the community. The anchor that once tied communities with common socio-political objectives has been replaced with individualism. The colonial missionaries were more interested, according to Kä Mana, in ushering individuals to Heaven/Paradise rather than positively transforming their communities (2000, 96). Mana recommends a rupture with this kind of Christianity, which focuses only on the individual while despising the community of origin.

Seventh, Kä Mana deplores a Christianity built on theological divisiveness and reflects on the proliferation of Christian denominations especially Protestant groups. For him, this kind of Christianity, called *Christianity of division,* weakens the message they intend to share and jeopardizes ecumenical attempts. As one considers the number of denominations that exist, one is immediately aware of the divisions that characterize this kind of Christianity. It is limited to demonization in its various forms between Catholics, Protestants, Revival Churches, etc. Mana expresses some of his concerns as he raises strong doubts about the possibility of achieving an African ecumenism in the following terms:

> When one considers how ecumenism is demonized among evangelical Christians; when one sees the disdain the princes of Catholicism display towards leaders of Independent churches, they often assimilate as charlatans seeking both fame and dubious social visibility; when one analyses the visceral anti-Catholicism of some fundamentalist Protestants; when one considers important diverse missionary strategies in modern-day Africa, we cannot but see that an African Christian world united by its faith is a long way off. (2000, 97)

This Christianity of division discredits the Christian faith and its message to its recipients (Mana 2000, 210–211). This last aspect of the "Christianity of catastrophe" sheds light on the nature of relationships that Christian traditions, such as the Catholic, *3ème* CBCA and *Arche* Churches in Goma, can have. It thus raises another research sub-question of this book: "What is the nature of the relationship that religious actors (from the three churches) have both within their own organizations and between themselves?"

The seven components of the "Christianity of catastrophe" illustrate in several ways the state of the African Christian faith in general and that of the Congo in particular. For the church in general, and the Catholic, *3ème* CBCA and *Arche* Churches of Goma in particular, to be relevant in society and to contribute to religious peacebuilding, they need to assess themselves as Kä Mana suggests. This analysis of Mana's Christianity of catastrophe can be used as a model for a theology of peace for the above three churches.

I will now consider Mana's theology of life, which is similar to the Roman Catholic theology of peace described above. Kä Mana's theology of life is developed based on seven layers of convictions that seek the transformation of "Christianity" (2000, 212). In other words, this Protestant theologian formulates certain pastoral recommendations that foster the promotion of life.

The seven convictions developed in *La nouvelle évangélisation* are a response to the seven characteristics of a Christianity of catastrophe. The first conviction is to have a Christianity based on equality, where the power embedded in the *agape* by the Spirit of God takes precedence over the divisiveness between the powerful and the weak, the rich and the less privileged, etc. (Mana 2000, 174–175). The new evangelization will not be anchored in the structures of exploitation or domination. Human life will be advanced in its entirety.

The second conviction relates to the rupture of the monopoly of truth that some believe they have. This type of Christianity gives way to a humble spirit that one understands to be a servant, and a vessel to be used by the truth—he who sacrifices himself for humanity.[10] Truth does not belong to one denomination, but it is a quest for everyone that no one can claim to have attained. In other words, Kä Mana disagrees with the belief purporting that the *vérité* about God is an exclusive possession of the church. He categorically disavows these thoughts:

> All pyramidal, monolithic and totalitarian presentation of the truth about God from men or human institutions which claim to be the unique owners of the genuine truth is inacceptable. It is only through plural, multiple, diverse and honest quests that men acquire their humanity as they share the word and mutually hear what God addresses to peoples and individuals in the world. (Mana 2000, 175)

While the second conviction of Kä Mana stands as an antidote to the *Christianity of the monopoly of truth* (from his repertoire of the Christianity of catastrophe), the third conviction builds on the so-called pact of transparency (Mana 2000, 176). The objectives of this new evangelization are to foster the promotion of life in total openness. The fourth conviction of Mana proposes, in the same vein as the previous one, is to qualitatively transform individuals to become agents of transformation for their communities and societies. The fifth conviction is a warning, as observed by Jesus Christ, that one cannot serve God and mammon. Although material goods contribute to one's wellbeing, these should not be the primary focus under a Christianity of life. The sixth conviction is related to the community, although the individual initiates it. That is, the salvation of an individual should not be limited to himself or herself alone; it must be expanded to the community. In addition, personal salvation is seen as the salvation of one's family, community and nation. Lastly, the seventh conviction promotes a fertile ecumenism where doctrinal division does not end up dividing families and communities.

In order to effectively deal with a theology of peace from the perspective of Revival Churches, one can consider the seven components of a Christianity of catastrophe and observe whether they are applicable. As specified earlier, Revival Churches do not emphasize the theological issues as do the Roman Catholic and Protestant Churches.

Revival Churches have not established a theology of peace as the Roman Catholic Churches have done, or as the ECC churches (*Église du Christ of Congo*, Church of Christ in Congo; referred to as "communities") advocate. Revival Churches, as mentioned earlier, place an emphasis on immediate needs. This is relatively easy, due to the proximity of priests or pastors to their members. This is what the Roman Catholic Churches, as Bernard Ugeux warned not to, have tried to do by establishing CEVBs (*Communautés Ecclésiales Vivantes de Base,* Small Living Ecclesial Communities). The admonishments of Mana, as well as other authors (e.g., Matangila 2006; Mbanzulu 2009; Mugaruka 2011; Nkingi 2012; Sekanga 2009), concern the promotion of unrealistic hope and illusions, which obviously echo in the preaching of pastors of Revival Churches.

Conclusion

The purpose of this chapter was to lay the groundwork for the subsequent chapters. From the conceptual framework presented in this chapter, a number of research questions were raised, leading to the choice of the methodology I used, i.e., qualitative.

To further our understanding of religious peacebuilding as it applies to Goma, I first presented the concepts of conflict and peace with emphasis on two kinds of peace: negative and positive. I then dealt with the concepts of religious peacebuilding and conflict transformation, which I considered as transformers of conflict into lasting peace. Afterwards, I analyzed the contributions of local populations to the development of a religious peacebuilding framework. While those at the grassroots need to be included in the quest for lasting peace, leaders at the top-down and middle-range levels must also not be ignored. In the final part of this chapter, I concluded with a theology of peace that integrates the perspectives of the three Christian traditions, i.e., Catholic, Protestant and Revival Churches.

Endnotes

1. While many have considered Johan Galtung as the inventor of the negative-positive peace typology, others have argued that it was Martin Luther King Jr. For instance, Jason A. Springs insists that the typology came from King's understanding of Jesus's words in the Gospel according to Matthew 10:34–39. See Jason A. Springs, "Structural and Cultural Violence in Religion and Peacebuilding," in Atalia Omer, R. Scott Appleby, and David Little (eds.), *The Oxford Handbook of Religion, Conflict, and Peacebuilding*, 2015.
2. The notion of healing not only refers to an individual recovery, it may also be applied to a community. While healing often involves physical recovery from disease or illness, it also includes psychological recovery, with the ultimate aim of restoring and rebuilding good relationships between communities, survivors and perpetrators. In fact, survivors and perpetrators may still be experiencing sufferings, especially in situations where they (survivors and perpetrators) may have to share common geographic space. For further discussion, see Geneviève Parent, "Peacebuilding, Healing, Reconciliation: An Analysis of Unseen Connections for Peace," *International Peacekeeping* 18, no. 4 (2011): 379–395; Nicole C. D'Errico, Christopher M. Wake, and Rachel M. Wake, "Healing Africa? Reflections on the Peace-building Role of a health-based Non-Governmental Organization Operating in Eastern Democratic Republic of Congo," *Medicine, Conflict and Survival* 26, no. 2 (2010): 145–159; Dominique Le Touze, Derrick Silove, and Anthony Zwi, "Can There Be Healing without Justice? Lessons from the Commission for Reception, Truth and Reconciliation in East Timor," *Intervention: International Journal of Mental Health, Psychosocial Work & Counselling in Areas of Armed Conflict* 3, no. 3 (2005): 192–202; Johan Galtung, *Peace by Peaceful Means: Peace and Conflict, Development and Civilization*, Oslo: International Peace Research Institute, 1996.

   I cannot complete this section without indicating the notion of healing from an African perspective. Broadly, healing in many African countries is associated to the causes of sicknesses, which are generally attributed to witchcraft (*Kindonki* in Lingala or *Bulozi* in Kiswahili), ancestors and divinities in general. In other words, sicknesses are generally interpreted as consequences of bad relations with ancestors. For studies that specifically examine the issue of healing in the African context, see Nicole Eggers, "Kitawala in the Congo: Religion, Politics, and Healing in 20th–21st Century Central African History," Ph.D. Dissertation, University of Wisconsin-Madison 2013; David Westerlund, *African Indigenous Religions and Disease Causation: From Spiritual Beings to Living Humans*. Leiden; Boston: Brill, 2006.
3. My objective is not to access the effectiveness of the mediating roles of religious actors, which may be interesting and enlightening researches. Recent interviews of

Goma residents shared in the online newspapers Peace News are revealing. While one interviewee expresses his excitement over the signature of *Saint-Sylvestre* agreement that has prevented an open conflict, another one is more doubtful in the sincerity of this umpteenth agreement since the independence. Many may interpret the role of both the Catholic Church and ECC as of the state's (Zaïre and DRC) rescuers. See Georges Nzongola-Ntalaja, *Faillite de la gouvernance et crise de la construction nationale au Congo-Kinshasa: une analyse des luttes pour la démocratie et la souveraineté*, Kinshasa; Montréal; Washington: ICREDES, 2015, pp. 260–262; John Oryang, "Can Peace Succeed in the Democratic Republic of Congo," *Peace News*, May 4, 2017 (https://www.peacenews.com/single-post/2017/05/04/Can-Peace-Succeed-in-the-Democratic-Republic-of-the-Congo).

4. The main objective of the Catholic Commission for Justice and Peace in Goma (and elsewhere in the Congo) consists of mediating and amicably settling local conflicts at the local level to avoid costly and time-consuming legal proceedings. If disputes are not resolved at the *Shirika* level, those cases are transferred to the next higher level called the *quartier*, then to its parish level (*Commission paroissiale Justice et Paix*, CPJP) before ending up at an upper level, the *Coordination diocésaine Justice et Paix* (Diocesan Coordination for Justice and Peace, CDJP). Unlike Revival Churches such as the *Centre Évangélique Francophone Arche de l'Alliance/Goma,* where similar local programs are absent, the parishes of the Protestant church *3ème Centre Baptiste au Centre de l'Afrique* (*3ème* CBCA) of both Goma-ville and Birere have their own commission for justice and peace, called the *Commission Justice de la Paix et Sauvegarde de la Création* (Commission for Justice and Peace and the Preservation of the Creation, JPSC) exclusively at the parish level (not in *Kijiji*). However, *3ème* CBCA's JPSCs are not as functional as the Catholics' CDJPs, and they have only been implemented as pilot projects in some parishes.
5. The pastoral letter from the American episcopacy specifies that the biblical vision of the Kingdom of God will be central to the contribution of social and political science.
6. This is the my own translation from the original text in French.
7. In this book, I will be using the acronym "CEVB" when referring to "small living Christian communities," "communautés écclesiales vivantes de base" and "communauté de base." Besides their linguistic and time period differences, these three terms have the same meaning. CEVB is the latest term, and some like Kitumaini choose to remove "base" from "communauté ecclesiale vivante." See Jean-Marie Vianney Kitumaini, *Nouveaux enjeux de l'agir socio-politique de l'Église face aux défis de la société en Afrique: application à l'Archidiocèse de Bukavu (RDC) à travers ses magistères successifs: en marge du premier centenaire de l'évangélisation de l'Archidiocèse de Bukavu, 1906–2006*, Paris: Harmattan, 2011, pp. 257–258.
8. For further details on Kä Mana's Congolese political views and his profile see Stanislas Bucyalimwe Mararo, *Maneuvering for Ethnic Hegemony: A Thorny Issue in the*

North Kivu Peace Process (DR Congo), Volume II: The 1996–1997 invasion of the "Tutsi without borders" and the remote reconciliation in North Kivu., Bruxelles: Éditions Scribe, 2014b. Freddy Mulongo, "Dix questions à Kä Mana," *Reveil Net*, 8 avril 2009 (http://reveil-fm.com/index.php/reveil-fm.com2009/04/08/336-10-questions-a-ka-mana).

9. René Coste, *Théologie de la paix*, Paris: Éditions du Cerf, 1997, p. 381.
10. In this context, Kä Mana seems to compare truth with the Word of God and Jesus Christ.

Bibliography

Alfani, Roger Bantea. "Religion et transformation des conflits: le rôle des Églises à Goma en RD Congo (1990–2010)." In Dieng Moda (ed.), *Evolution politique en Afrique: Entre autoritarisme, démocratisation, construction de la paix et défis internes.* Louvain-la-Neuve, Belgique: Academia-L'Harmattan, 2015.

———. "The Role of the Ruah YHWH in Creative Transformation: A Process Theology Perspective Applied to Judges 14." M.A., Université de Montréal, 2009.

Allan, Pierre. "Measuring International Ethics: A Moral Scale of War, Peace, Justice, and Global Care." In Pierre Allan and Alexis Keller (eds.), *What is a Just Peace?* Oxford: Oxford University Press, 2006.

Anderson, B. Mary, and Lara Olson. *Confronting War: Critical Lessons for Peace Practitioners.* Cambridge, MA: Reflecting on Peace Practice Project, Collaborative Development Action, 2003.

Appleby, R. Scott. *The Ambivalence of the Sacred: Religion, Violence, and Reconciliation.* Lanham, MD: Rowman & Littlefield, 2000.

———. "Religion, Conflict Transformation, and Peacebuilding." In Chester A. Crocker, Fen Osler Hampson, and Pamela R. Aall (eds.), *Turbulent Peace: The Challenges of Managing International Conflict.* Washington, D.C.: United States Institute of Peace Press, 2001.

———. "Religious Violence: The Strong, the Weak, and the Pathological." In Atalia Omer, R. Scott Appleby, and David Little (eds.), *The Oxford Handbook of Religion, Conflict, and Peacebuilding.* New York, NY: Oxford University Press, 2015.

Autesserre, Séverine. *The Trouble with the Congo: Local Violence and the Failure of International Peacebuilding.* Cambridge; New York: Cambridge University Press, 2010.

Azar, Edward E. *The Management of Protracted Social Conflict: Theory and Cases.* Aldershot: Dartmouth, 1990.

———, and Burton, John W. *International Conflict Resolution: Theory and Practice.* Boulder, CO: Lynne Rienner, 1986.

Barash, David P. *Approaches to Peace: A Reader in Peace Studies.* (2nd ed.). Oxford, NY: Oxford University Press, 2010.

———, and Charles Webel. *Peace and Conflict Studies.* Thousand Oaks, CA: Sage Publications, 2002.

Boutros-Ghali, Boutros. *An Agenda for Peace: Preventive Diplomacy, Peacemaking and Peace-keeping.* New York: United Nations, 1992.

Boyle, Patrick M. "Beyond Self-Protection to Prophecy: The Catholic Church and Political Change in Zaire." *Africa Today* 39, no. 3 (1992): 49–66.

Brewer, John D., Gareth I. Higgins, and Francis Teeney. "Religion and Peacemaking: A Conceptualization." *Sociology* 44, no. 6 (2010): 1019–1037.

Coste, René. *Théologie de la paix.* Paris: Éditions du Cerf, 1997.

Cousens, Elizabeth M. "Introduction." In Elizabeth M. Cousens, Chetan Kumar, and Karin Wermester (eds.), *Peacebuilding as Politics: Cultivating Peace in Fragile Societies.* Boulder, CO: Lynne Rienner, 2001.

Curtis, Devon. "Introduction: The Contested Politics of Peacebuilding." In Devon Curtis and Gwinyayi Albert Dzinesa (eds.), *Peacebuilding, Power, and Politics in Africa.* Athens: Ohio University Press, 2012.

David, Charles-Philippe. "Does Peacebuilding Build Peace." In Ho-Won Jeong (ed.), *Approaches to Peacebuilding.* New York: Palgrave Macmillan, 2002.

———, and Toureille, Julien. "La consolidation de la paix: un concept à consolider." In Yvan Conoir and Gérard Verna (eds.), *Faire la paix: concepts et pratiques de la consolidation de la paix.* Québec: Les Presses de l'Université Laval, 2005.

D'Errico, Nicole C., Christopher M. Wake, and Rachel M. Wake. "Healing Africa? Reflections on the Peace-building Role of a Health-based Non Governmental Organization Operating in Eastern Democratic Republic of Congo." *Medicine, Conflict and Survival* 26, no. 2 (2010): 145–159.

Eggers, Nicole. "Kitawala in the Congo: Religion, Politics, and Healing in 20th–21st Century Central African History." Ph.D. Dissertation, University of Wisconsin-Madison 2013.

Francis, Diana. *People, Peace and Power: Conflict Transformation in Action.* London: Pluto Press, 2002.

Galtung, Johan. "An Editorial." *Journal of Peace Research* 1, no. 1 (1964): 1–4.

———. "Violence, Peace, and Peace Research." *Journal of Peace Research* 6, no. 3 (1969): 167–191.

———. *Peace by Peaceful Means: Peace and Conflict, Development and Civilization.* Oslo: International Peace Research Institute, 1996.

———. "Religions, Hard and Soft." *Cross Currents* 47, no. 4 (1997): 437–450.

Jeong, Ho-Won. "Peacebuilding Design: A Synergetic Approach." In Ho-Won Jeong (ed.), *Approaches to Peacebuilding.* New York: Palgrave Macmillan, 2002.

John Paul II. "Centesimus Annus." *Vatican Website.* May 1st, 1991.

———. "Redemptoris Missio." *Vatican Website.* December 7th, 1990.

———. "Slavorum Apostoli." *Vatican Website.* June 2nd, 1985. Johnston, Douglas. "Faith Based Organizations: The Religious Dimensions of Peacebuilding." In Paul van Tongeren, Malin Brenk, Marte Hellema, and Juliette Verhoeven (eds.), *People Building Peace II: Successful Stories of Civil Society.* Boulder, CO: Lynne Rienner, 2005.

———. "Introduction: Beyond Power Politics." In Douglas Johnston and Cynthia Sampson (eds.), *Religion, the Missing Dimension of Statecraft.* New York: Oxford University Press, 1994.

Kabasele Lumbala, François. *Le christianisme et l'Afrique une chance réciproque.* Paris: Karthala, 1993.

Kabongo-Mbaya, Philippe B. *L'Eglise du Christ au Zaïre: formation et adaptation d'un protestantisme en situation de dictature*. Paris: Karthala, 1992.

Kitumaini, Jean-Marie Vianney. *Nouveaux enjeux de l'agir socio-politique de l'Église face aux défis de la société en Afrique: application à l'Archidiocèse de Bukavu (RDC) à travers ses magistères successifs: en marge du premier centenaire de l'évangélisation de l'Archidiocèse de Bukavu, 1906–2006*. Paris: Harmattan, 2011.

Lederach, John Paul. *Building Peace: Sustainable Reconciliation in Divided Societies*. Washington, D.C.: United States Institute of Peace Press, 1997.

———. "Conflict Transformation in Protracted Internal Conflicts: The Case for a Comprehensive Framework." In Kumar Rupesinghe (ed.), *Conflict Transformation*. Houndmills, Basingstoke, Hampshire: Macmillan, 1995.

———. "Justpeace: The Challenge of the 21st Century." In Paul van Tongeren (ed.), *People Building Peace: 35 Inspiring Stories from Around the World*. Utrecht, Netherlands: European Centre for Conflict Prevention, 1999.

———. *The Little Book of Conflict Transformation*. Philadelphia: Good Books, Intercourse, 2003.

———. "The Long Journey Back to Humanity." In Robert J. Schreiter, R. Scott Appleby, and Gerard F. Powers (eds.), *Peacebuilding: Catholic Theology, Ethics, and Praxis*. Maryknoll, NY: Orbis Books, 2010.

Lederach, John Paul, and R. Scott Appleby. "Strategic Peacebuilding: An Overview." In Daniel Philpott and Gerard F. Powers (eds.), *Strategies of Peace: Transforming Conflict in a Violent World*. Oxford, NY: Oxford University Press, 2010.

Lemarchand, René. "Burundi 1972: Genocide Denied, Revised, and Remembered." In René Lemarchand and Filip Reyntjens (eds.), *Forgotten Genocides: Oblivion, Denial, and Memory*. Philadelphia: University of Pennsylvania Press, 2011.

———. *The Dynamics of Violence in Central Africa*. Philadelphia: University of Pennsylvania Press, 2009.

Lemarchand, René, and Filip Reyntjens. "Mass Murder in Eastern Congo, 1996–1997." In René Lemarchand and Filip Reyntjens (eds.), *Forgotten Genocides: Oblivion, Denial, and Memory*. Philadelphia: University of Pennsylvania Press, 2011.

Little, David. "Religion, Violent Conflict, and Peacemaking." In David Little (ed.), *Peacemakers in Action: Profiles of Religion in Conflict Resolution*. Cambridge; New York: Cambridge University Press, 2007.

Little, David, and R. Scott Appleby. "A Moment of Opportunity?: The Promise of Religious Peacebuilding in an Era of Religious and Ethnic Conflict." In Harold G. Coward and Gordon S. Smith (eds.), *Religion and Peacebuilding*. Albany: State University of New York Press, 2004.

Mana, Kä. *La nouvelle évangélisation en Afrique*. Paris; Yaoundé: Karthala; Clé, 2000.

Mararo, Stanislas Bucyalimwe. "Kinshasa et le Kivu depuis 1987: une histoire ambigue." In Stefaan Marysse and Filip Reyntjens (eds.), *L'Afrique des grands lacs: annuaire 2004–2005*. Paris: L' Harmattan, 2005a.

———. "Kivu and Ituri in the Congo War: The Roots and Nature of a Linkage." In Stefaan Marysse and Filip Reyntjens (eds.), *The Political Economy of the Great Lakes Region in Africa: The Pitfalls of Enforced Democracy and Globalization*. New York: Palgrave Macmillan, 2005b.

———. "La societé civile du Kivu: une dynamique en panne?" In Stefaan Marysse and Filip Reyntjens (eds.), *L'Afrique des grands lacs: Annuaire 1998–1999*. Paris: L'Harmattan, 1999.

———. "Land Conflicts in Masisi, Eastern Zaire: The Impact and aftermath of Belgian Colonial Policy (1920–1989)." Ph.D., Indiana University, 1990.

———. "Land, Power, and Ethnic Conflict in Masisi (Congo-Kinshasa), 1940s–1994." *The International Journal of African Historical Studies* 30, no. 3 (1997): 503–538.

———. *Maneuvering for Ethnic Hegemony: A Thorny Issue in the North Kivu Peace Process (DR Congo), Volume I: The 1959–1997 History of North Kivu*. Bruxelles: Éditions Scribe, 2014a.

———. *Maneuvering for Ethnic Hegemony: A Thorny Issue in the North Kivu Peace Process (DR Congo), Volume II: The 1996–1997 invasion of the "Tutsi without borders" and the remote reconciliation in North Kivu*. Bruxelles: Éditions Scribe, 2014b.

Matangila, Alexis. "Pour une analyse du discours des Eglises de réveil à Kinshasa: Méthode et contexte." *Civilisations* 54, no. 1–2 (2006): 77–84.f

Mbanzulu, Kinkasa Salomon. "Problematique de succession dans les églises de reveil: crise de la mission." Mémoire (Licence), Université Protestante au Congo, 2009.

Merdjanova, Ina, and Patrice Brodeur. *Religion as a Conversation Starter: Interreligious Dialogue for Peacebuilding in the Balkans*. New York: Continuum International Publishing Group, 2009.

Miall, Hugh. "Conflict Transformation: A Multi-Dimensional Task." *Berghof Research Center for Constructive Conflict Management* (2004).

Mongo, Nomanyath Manyath Mwan-Awan-A, David. "Les églises de réveil dans l'histoire des réligions en République démocratique du Congo: questions de dialogue œcuménique et interreligieux." Doctorat, Université Lille III—Charles de Gaulle, 2005.

Moore, Barrington. *Injustice: The Social Bases of Obedience and Revolt*. White Plains, NY: M.E. Sharpe, 1978.

Mpisi, Jean. *Kivu, RDC: La paix à tout prix!: La Conférence de Goma (6–23 janvier 2008)*. Paris: L'Harmattan, 2008.

Mudimbe, V. Y. *The Idea of Africa*. Bloomington: Indiana University Press, 1994.

———. *The invention of Africa: Gnosis, Philosophy, and the Order of Knowledge*. Bloomington: Indiana University Press, 1988.

———. *L'odeur du père: essai sur des limites de la science et de la vie en Afrique noire*. Paris: Présence africaine, 1982.

Mudimbe, V. Y., and Mbula Susan Kilonzo. "Philosophy of Religion on African Ways of Believing." In Elias Kifon Bongmba (ed.), *The Wiley-Blackwell Companion to African Religions*. Malden, MA: Wiley-Blackwell, 2012.

Mugaruka, Richard. *Reflexions pastorales: le rôle des églises dans la refondation de l'État congolais, cinquante ans après son indépendance*. Kinshasa: Feu Torrent, 2011.

Mulongo, Freddy. "Dix questions à Kä Mana." *Reveil Net*, 8 avril 2009 (http://reveil-fm.com/index.php/reveil-fm.com2009/04/08/336-10-questions-a-ka-mana).

Ndongala, Maduku Ignace. "Autoritarisme étatiques et régulation religieuse du politique en République Démocratique du Congo: Analyse discursive de la parole de épiscopale catholique sur les élections (1990–2015)." Ph.D. Dissertation, Université de Montréal, 2015.

———. “Le ministère des prêtres en Afrique.” In E. Babissangana and Nsapo Kalamba (eds.), *Qu'as-tu fais de ton frère? Mélanges en l'honneur de Mgr Jan Dumon*. Kinshasa: Publications Universitaires Africaines, 2012.

Newman, Edward. “Liberal Peacebuilding Debates.” In Edward Newman, Roland Paris, and Oliver P. Richmond (eds.), *New Perspectives on Liberal Peacebuilding*. New York: United Nations University Press, 2009.

Nkingi, Mweze Chirhulwire Dominique. “Eglise de réveil: Génese et modes opératoires.” In Kinyamba Sylvain Shomba (ed.), *Les spiritualité du temps présent*. Kinshasa: Éditions M.E.S., 2012.

Nzongola-Ntalaja, Georges. *Faillite de la gouvernance et crise de la construction nationale au Congo-Kinshasa: une analyse des luttes pour la démocratie et la souveraineté*. Kinshasa; Montréal; Washington, D.C.: ICREDES, 2015.

Omer, Atalia. “Religious Peacebuilding: The Exotic, the Good, and the Theatrical.” In Atalia Omer, R. Scott Appleby, and David Little (eds.), *The Oxford Handbook of Religion, Conflict, and Peacebuilding*. New York, NY: Oxford University Press, 2015.

Oryang, John. “Can Peace Succeed in the Democratic Republic of Congo.” *Peace News*. May 4, 2017. (https://www.peacenews.com/single-post/2017/05/04/Can-Peace-Succeed-in-the-Democratic-Republic-of-the-Congo).

Parent, Geneviève. “Peacebuilding, Healing, Reconciliation: An Analysis of Unseen Connections for Peace.” *International Peacekeeping* 18, no. 4 (2011): 379–395.

Paris, Roland. “Saving Liberal Peacebuilding.” *Review of International Studies* 36, no. 2 (2010): 337–365.

Paris, Roland, and Timothy D. Sisk. “Introduction: Understanding the Contradictions of Postwar Statebuilding.” In Roland Paris and Timothy D. Sisk (eds.), *The Dilemmas of Statebuilding: Confronting the Contradictions of Postwar Peace Operations*. Abingdon, UK: Routledge, 2009.

Paul VI. “Eucharistic Celebration at the Conclusion of the Symposium Organized by the Bishops of Africa: Homily of Paul VI.” Kampala, Uganda. July 31st, 1969.

———. “Populorum Progressio.” *Vatican Website*. March 26, 1967.

Powers, Gerard F. “Religion and Peacebuilding.” In Daniel Philpott and Gerard F. Powers (eds.), *Strategies of Peace: Transforming Conflict in a Violent World*. New York: Oxford University Press, 2010.

Rabie, Moḥamed. *Conflict Resolution and Ethnicity*. Westport, CT: Praeger, 1994.

Ramsbotham, Oliver, Hugh Miall, and Tom Woodhouse. *Contemporary Conflict Resolution: The Prevention, Management and Transformation of Deadly Conflicts*. (3rd ed.). Cambridge, UK; Malden, MA: Polity Press, 2011.

Richmond, Oliver P. “Patterns of Peace.” *Global Society* 20, no. 4 (2006a): 367–394.

———. “The Problem of Peace: Understanding the ‘liberal peace.’” *Conflict, Security & Development* 6, no. 3 (2006b): 291–314.

———. *The Transformation of Peace*. New York: Palgrave Macmillan, 2005.

Richmond, Oliver P., and Audra Mitchell. *Hybrid Forms of Peace: From Everyday Agency to Post-liberalism*. Houndmills, Basingstoke, Hampshire; New York, NY: Palgrave Macmillan, 2012a.

Richmond, Oliver P., and Audra Mitchell. “Towards a Post-Liberal Peace: Exploring Hybridity via Everyday Forms of Resistance, Agency and Autonomy.” In Oliver P. Richmond and Audra

Mitchell (eds.), *Hybrid Forms of Peace: From Everyday Agency to Post-liberalism*. Houndmills, Basingstoke, Hampshire; New York, NY: Palgrave Macmillan, 2012b.

Ross, Marc Howard. *The Culture of Conflict: Interpretations and Interests in Comparative Perspective*. New Haven: Yale University Press, 1993.

Ryan, Stephen. *The Transformation of Violent Intercommunal Conflict*. Aldershot, England: Ashgate, 2007.

Sampson, Cynthia. "Religion and Peacebuilding." In I. William Zartman (ed.), *Peacemaking in International Conflict: Methods & Techniques*. Washington, D.C.: United States Institute of Peace, 2007.

Sekanga, Freddy Bomay. "Les rôles d'un prophete: regard sur les prophetisme des églises de reveil de Kinshasa." Mémoire (Licence), Université Protestante au Congo, 2009.

Springs, Jason A. "Structural and Cultural Violence in Religion and Peacebuilding." In Atalia Omer, R. Scott Appleby, and David Little (eds.), *The Oxford Handbook of Religion, Conflict, and Peacebuilding*. New York, NY: Oxford University Press, 2015.

Steele, David. "An Introductory Overview to Faith-Based Peacebuilding." In Rogers Mark, Tom Bamat, and Ideh Julie (eds.), *Pursuing Just Peace: An Overview and Case Studies for Faith-Based Peacebuilders*. Baltimore, MD: Catholic Relief Services, 2008.

Touze, Dominique Le, Derrick Silove, and Anthony Zwi. "Can There Be Healing without Justice? Lessons from the Commission for Reception, Truth and Reconciliation in East Timor." *Intervention: International Journal of Mental Health, Psychosocial Work & Counselling in Areas of Armed Conflict* 3, no. 3 (2005): 192–202.

Ugeux, Bernard. "La pastorale des petites communautés chrétiennes dans quelques diocèses du Zaïre." Ph.D. Thesis, Institut Catholique de Paris, 1987.

———. *Les petites communautés chrétiennes, une alternative aux paroisses?: l'expérience du Zaïre*. Paris: Éditions du Cerf, 1988.

United States Conference of Catholic Bishops, "The Challenge of Peace: God's Promise and Our Response A Pastoral Letter on War and Peace," 1983.

Vatican Council II. "Gaudium et Spes." December 7th, 1965. http://www.vatican.va/archive/hist_councils/ii_vatican_council/documents/vat-ii_const_19651207_gaudium-et-spes_en.html

Väyrynen, Raimo. *New Directions in Conflict Theory: Conflict Resolution and Conflict Transformation*. London: International Social Science Council; Sage Publications, 1991

———. "To Settle or to Transform? Perspectives on the Resolution of National and International Conflicts." In Raimo Väyrynen (ed.), *New Directions in Conflict Theory: Conflict Resolution and Conflict Transformation*. London: International Social Science Council; Sage Publications, 1991.

Vlassenroot, Koen, and Karen Büscher . "The City as a Frontier: Urban Development and Identity Processes in Goma." *Crisis States Working Paper 61 (Series 2)*. London: London School of Economics, 2009.

———. "Humanitarian Presence and Urban Development: New Opportunities and Contrasts in Goma, DRC." *Disasters* 34, no. 2 (2010): 256–273.

Wallensteen, Peter. *Quality Peace: Strategic Peacebuilding and World Order*. New York: Oxford University Press, 2015.

———. *Understanding Conflict Resolution: War, Peace, and the Global System*. London; Thousand Oaks,CA: Sage Publications, 2002.

Westerlund, David. *African Indigenous Religions and Disease Causation: from Spiritual Beings to Living Humans*. Leiden; Boston: Brill, 2006.

3

From Missionary Works to Local Churches in Goma

Introduction

Religious institutions such as the Catholic Church and Protestant *3ème Communauté Baptiste au Centre de l'Afrique* (Baptist Community at the Centre of Africa, *3ème* CBCA) of Goma exhibit complexity in their roles and functions, particularly in an environment where the state's capacity to provide goods and services is limited and ethnic identity issues are very sensitive topics. For instance, the Catholic Church is considered to be an institutional and hierarchical organization that stands out as an important non-state organization in Goma in at least three ways. First, it is one of the oldest non-state organizations in North Kivu that still provides many goods and services across the province, namely education and health services, and is consequently an incontestable major employer. Second, the Catholic Church structures, overall organization and networks extend to places where the Congolese administration is non-existent, which furthermore allows it (the church) to assume functions that are either complementary or substitutive in regard to the Congolese State (Hermet 1973). Third, the Catholic Church is notable for its capacity to mobilize resources, particularly from its international networks.

Although this book does not follow an entirely historical path in its methodology, it does attempt to chronologically identify important events related to the establishment of Christianity in the Congo in subsequent sections. I begin this chapter with a brief presentation of the emergence of the city of Goma in its socio-political context. Next, I discuss the penetration of the Christian faith during the so-called First and Second Evangelizations of the Congo. I then address the relationship between the Leopoldian state during the colonial period and missionaries (specifically Catholics and Protestants). Following that is a discussion regarding the emergence of the Protestant *3ème Communauté Baptiste au Centre de l'Afrique* Church and early prophetic movements initiated by Congolese Kimpa Vita Béatrice, Simon Kimbangu and Kitawala. In the last two sections, I first grapple with the creation of the Goma's Church *Arche* and then, I outline three kinds of local pastoral approaches, namely, the Catholic, *3ème* CBCA and *Arche* Churches, which have been adopted at the grassroots level.

From Ngoma to Goma: A General Overview

> It is difficult for me to tell you precisely why Goma brings together so many people from different places. These include, for instance, internally displaced populations (*wakimbizi*), refugees, innumerable international NGOs and international celebrities. Many come, pass through Goma on their way to Masisi or Walikale, while others stay and do what they have to do and eventually leave. We can only observe and keep quiet. So, as embedded in its name in Kiswahili, Ngoma means "drum": it calls, it gathers, and it warns those who can discern its [Ngoma] sound. That is the mystery of Goma… Don't forget also that this city used to be called the Switzerland of Africa and I think it still is. (interview with Tuungane, pseudonym of a participant)

> Cities attract friends and enemies…[They] inevitably carry baggage from their individual and collective pasts that have to be understood. (Freund 2007, vii–viii)

The Kivu[1] province consists of two different entities, the North and the South with their respective provincial capitals, Goma and Bukavu. Although the focus of this book is on the former, it is imperative to understand the overall history of the Kivu region due to its ongoing socio-political transformations.

Disputes over the Kivu territories began after the German Count Gustav Adolphe von Götzen's discovered Lake Kivu in approximately 1894. Leaving the area and heading west in June of that same year, Götzen believed that the "country presented conditions to establish a future colonization headed by the Germans" (Willaert 1973, 57). Goma was among the first border posts in the Eastern *État*

Indépendant du Congo (EIC) that Belgian authorities erected in the early 1900s amidst intense contestations with both the Germans and, to a lesser extent, the British, over territories in the Great Lakes region. This move was a relatively new focus of the European colonists, who were initially interested in the occupation and control of the western Congolese territories. The erections of these posts—Belgians in the Congo (Goma) and Germans in Rwanda (Gisenyi)—were strategically chosen; not only to mark their (Belgians' and Germans') presence in the area, but to further counteract potential opponents.

In July 1960, one month after the independence of Congo, the country experienced a series of socio-political instabilities, starting with the army's revolt. Two years later, in August 1962, the transformation of the district of North Kivu to a province (including other pre-existing 4 provinces from the colonial period), 1 of the 22 provinces (including the capital ex-Léopolville) fuelled existing intense conflicts between ethnic communities, notably between supporters and challengers of Kivu's new frontiers (Willame and Verhaegen 1964a, 1964b).[2] This redrawing process of the Congolese boundaries, also called the *Provincettes* era, included the attachment of two contested territories, Goma and Rutshuru, to the North Kivu province. However, due to strong divergences between territorial protagonists, these contested territories were placed under the Kasavubu government's jurisdiction, whilst awaiting the result of a referendum. In view of the upcoming referendum, the Banyarwanda legislators, in favour of attaching Goma and Rutshuru to the new Kivu Central province, began distributing "Congolese identification cards to Tutsi refugees" in both territories (Willame 1997, 50). The continuous influx of Rwandan refugees into North Kivu as well as rumours about the Banyarwanda's conquest of the Rutshuru, Goma, Walikale and Kalehe's territories created a Hutuland that further complicated interethnic relations (Kisangani 2012, 175; Willame 1997, 50).

Beside the fact that the Banyarwanda community was mostly represented in Goma and Rutshuru, there were at least two rationales for their resistance to the dismantling of Kivu. On the one hand, the province of Kivu served as their stronghold in both the provincial and the state administrations where they were already established, thus creating what Jean-Claude Willame called a Rwandan "diaspora" (1997, 48). On the other hand, economic competition between the Banyarwanda and Nande communities over the province motivated their objection to dismember what they perceived as their territory (Willame 1997, 48). In other words, the controversial and conflictual erection of the North Kivu province with the inclusion of both Goma and Rutshuru, coupled with ethnic identification issues, were the core components of contention lying behind the race for political and economic hegemony throughout the region. The emergence of the province of North Kivu on 14 August 1962 exacerbated existing ethnic conflicts, notably between the Banyarwanda (Hutu and Tutsi) and other ethnic groups (Hunde, Nyanga and Nande) (Willame and Verhaegen 1964b, 69–70).[3] For the Banyarwanda, the dismantling of the Kivu province meant taking away their control of a large territory (Willame 1997, 48). As demonstrated later in this chapter, Chapter Four and Chapter Five, religious organizations have not been left behind in this race of territorial control.

In addition, these tensions coincided with the Congolese constitution, which some have considered discriminatory toward the Banyarwanda population. The latter, being largely represented in both the Goma and Rutshuru regions, perceived its dismemberment from Kivu province as a threat to their power. Nonetheless, a referendum in the two territories led to the scission of the initial province into a total of three provinces, namely Central Kivu, Maniema and North Kivu. However, the new North Kivu province lasted only four years (until 1966) before its reintegration into the Kivu province, and North Kivu (as well as the South Kivu and Maniema) remained the district of the Kivu province for another twenty-two years (i.e. in 1988).

The city of Goma, the so-called "Switzerland" of Central Africa, is the current capital of the North Kivu province with an estimated population of over 1 million inhabitants in 2017, and a surface area of approximately 76 km^2.[4] The city surrounds the Mont Goma volcano to which it owes its name, according to some, and which was also taken from *Ngoma* in Kiswahili meaning drum (Mpisi 2008). For others, *Ngoma* referred to the sound of volcanic eruptions and others pointed to the sound of splashing of waters into the caves, which one can still hear today around Hotel Karibu or the governorate (former Mobutu's house in the *quartier* Himbi). Goma is located approximately 2,000 km from the country's capital, Kinshasa, or approximately two (2) hours by plane. In the north, it is bordered by a volcano, in the south by Kivu Lake, while in the east by the Rwandan border (Gisenyi) and the west by new districts extending toward the city of Sake. Two *communes* (counties), Goma and Karisimbi, divide the city and form the existing eighteen *quartiers* (districts). Many agree that the first inhabitants of Goma were of the Kumu ethnic group; however, the current multiethnic composition does not reflect a predominant presence of the Kumu ethnic group (Alfani 2015).

The city of Goma and its surrounding areas continue to pay the costly consequences of the humanitarian crisis following the Rwandan genocide in 1994 and the rebellions that the country experienced in the 1990s and mid-2000s. In addition, the Rwandan genocide caused an inflow of close to one million Rwandans into the Democratic Republic of Congo (DRC) through Goma, where refugee camps were installed. The first war that targeted the Mobutu regime began in Goma. A few months after the overthrow of the Mobutu regime by the *Alliance des Forces Démocratiques pour la Libération* (AFDL), which was led by Laurent Désiré Kabila, a second war began in the city of Goma. This was instigated by former allies of the new regime in Kinshasa, which was further supported by Rwanda. A third war consisted of another rebellion, the March 23 Movement (M23), which started in the province of North Kivu in May 2012. While they were defeated by the Congolese army in 2013, with the help of the (United Nations Organizations Stabilization Mission in the Democratic Republic of Congo (MONUSCO) and its FIB (Intervention Brigade Force), many M23 rebels took refuge in Rwanda and Uganda. From there, many leaders and armed forces tried to influence the situation in the Congo and, as a result, are considered threats to the peace and stability of Kivu provinces in particular and DRC in general.

Missionaries in the Congo (1482–1959): First and Second Evangelizations

Historians have agreed that the Congo[5] was evangelized on two different occasions. The first evangelization period occurred between 1482 and 1835 in two sequential phases over two hundred years. While the first phase dates back to the late fifteenth century, the second phase is positioned in the mid-seventeenth century (Randles 1968). The first evangelization is described as the earliest contact between inhabitants of the Kingdom of Kongo and Europeans. The second period of evangelization took place between early 1880s and late 1950s.

It was on January 8, 1455 that the first papal bull, *Romanus Pontifex,* was issued by Pope Nicolas V that offered King Affonso V of Portugal full sovereignty over Portugal's overseas current and future possessions (Comby 1992; Neill 1966). By this "crusade and demarcation's bull," as well as others of the fifteenth century, Portugal was not only given the right to disown "pagans'" properties and lands, it was also entrusted with the responsibility of evangelizing and establishing Christian premises under their control such as schools and monasteries (Comby 1992, 97). Contrary to the first bulls that favoured Portugal as the sole nation authorized to explore and evangelize, Spain expressed interests analogous to the Spanish-born Pope Alexander VI (Borgia). In 1493, the latter granted the requests of King Ferdinand and Queen Elisabeth/Isabella (Spanish sovereigns) by issuing three bulls (two *Inter Cætera* followed by *Eximiae devotions sinceritas*). For instance, Spain was given authority over discoveries of explorers (e.g., Christopher Columbus). Furthermore, the first and second *Inter Cætera* bulls gave legal exploration rights to the king of Spain over lands in America, in addition to the king of Portugal over lands in Africa in the name of Christian doctrine (M'Bokolo 1977). These bulls were also meant to prevent conflicts between the two countries as far as the quest for new lands was concerned. The pontiff put in place two patronage systems—*patronato* (Spain) and *padroado* (Portugal)—which granted the two European states several privileges over territories including ecclesiastical and administrative oversights (Comby 1992).

A year before the publication of the above three bulls, Diogo Cão, a Portuguese explorer, made a historical discovery in 1492 while searching for a route between the Atlantic and Indian Oceans: the mouth of the Kongo River. This discovery eventually led him to the Kingdom of Kongo, where he and his companions erected a *padrão* ("pillar") that sealed their discovery. Thus, the first contact between *mindele* (a plural form of *mundele,* meaning "white people" in the Kikongo language) and black people in Kongo occurred (Neill 1966, 38, 284). The early contacts between these two groups went beyond physical aspects in including cultural exchanges.

While Europeans offered their religion (Christianity) with the conversion of Africans from "paganism," they seemed either to have less to offer or their guests (Europeans) demonstrated more willingness to offer than to receive (from Africans). In other words, exchanges between the two groups were tainted with several forms of inequality. It is worth mentioning at this point the provocative book by the Nigerian novelist Chinua Achebe *Hope and Impediments,* which not only underscores the importance of a Euro-African partnership but also points out its impediments (1990). For Achebe, one cannot talk of true partnership between people of different continents while undermining the notion of equality. Stated differently, being partners means respecting each other's values and beliefs. The first encounters between Europeans and Africans proved the opposite. For example, seeking to transform their hosts, Europeans ensured that Africans changed their names to Western Christian names. For them, real conversion or "westernization" passed through this process. Two kings of the Congo, Mbemba Nzinga Nkuwu and Nzimga Mbemba became John I and Affonso I, respectively. Another form of conversion included the adaptation of Western rules and regulations (customs).

The evangelization of the Kongo did not occur as anticipated by the Portuguese, who left few years later for Angola. Portuguese missionaries were confronted with several obstacles. First, they received little support from local communities at the grassroot level compared to local elites, who were mostly Christian, and certain priests ordained in Portugal. The second obstacle that Portuguese missionaries encountered in the Kongo was financial. Missionaries had to dissociate themselves from the slave trade, as their livelihoods depended on the selling of slaves to America, whereas Portugal reduced its financial support for its missionaries because Africa was no longer among its top priorities.

In summary, the first evangelization period concluded on a relatively negative note early in the nineteenth century in terms of its objectives. Over the course of approximately two centuries, greater than 434 Europeans missionaries ventured into the Kongo. However, only few of them returned to their home countries.

There is general consensus that the second evangelization of the African continent commenced during the mid-1800s. As far as the Congolese territory was concerned, this period was marked by the penetration of new European missionaries both in the west, occupied by the Portuguese, and in the east, under Arabic occupation. While the second evangelization was similarly indicative of the arrival of Protestant missionaries from Europe and America, it also showed the implication of Arabs[6] in Eastern Congo.

Motivated primarily by the conquest of new territories, scientific research and the international economic crisis (Long Depression) that came later, Europeans were among the first to arrive in the Great Lakes region of Africa in 1857 when Richard Burton and John Speke were sent by England's Royal Geographical Society to explore the sources of the Nile River (Roberts 2013). In 1894, three Belgian officers (Lange, Long and Chargeois) failed to penetrate the Kivu region in part because of the local population's resistance to foreigners. A few years later, their fellow Belgian, Commandant Francis Baron Dhanis, as head of the colonial forces, was able to advance towards the North Kivu area as he engaged in fighting against Arabs (Nelson 1992; Smythe 1900). Similar to the Europeans, the Arabs endeavoured to increase their influence along the shores of the Tanganyika, in Eastern Congo, as far as the Nyangwe region. The eastern Congolese territories were completely under their control, which they held with the assistance of the Congolese who were under their allegiance. In fact, any European attempt (e.g., Livingstone and Cameron) to join Nyangwe remained unsuccessful because of the resistance from both the local population and the Arabs. Hamed Bin Mohammed el-Murjebi (or Tippu-Tib or Tippu-Tip), a renowned Zanzibari slave trader who became governor for the *État Indépendant du Congo* (Independent/Free State of Congo: hereafter, EIC) in the Nyangwe region, facilitated Europeans' activities in the area. For instance, his relationship with Henry Morton Stanley went as far as exchanging goods and services. He and his troops actually accompanied

Stanley further into the interior of the Congo. As a result of Stanley's expedition and discovery, many other Western powers, such as Belgium, began to show an interest in Central Africa.

The desire of the Belgian King, Leopold II, to acquire more territories and to enlarge his territorial influence beyond his European kingdom led him to convene an International Geographical Conference. The Belgian capuchin historian Auguste Roeykens observed that King Leopold II was not considered an internationalist; however, he used every opportunity at the international level, including hosting a geographical conference, for his own personal, national and local benefits (1955). The conference was given a much greater philanthropic benevolent connotation compared to its later outcomes, which he and other close collaborates already knew. Prior to the conference that was held in Brussels between 12 and 14 of September 1876, Leopold II needed to convince his European neighbours of its importance. For instance, in addition to insisting on the importance of exporting European civilization to the "savages," they further stressed the urgency of saving them from the Arabs' barbaric slavery. The opening remarks made by the Belgian King to the Geographical Conference's audience were carefully crafted as they emphasized both scientific and humanitarian ends, while explicitly cautioning any expansionist intentions:

> To open to civilization the only part of our globe where it has yet to penetrate, to pierce the darkness which envelops whole populations, it is, I dare to say, a crusade worthy of this century of progress… Needless to say, in bringing you to Brussels I was in no way motivated by selfish designs. No, gentlemen, if Belgium is small, she is happy and satisfied with her lot. My only ambition is to serve her. (Pakenham 1991, 21)

Even though representatives from other Western countries occupied important positions during that conference, King Leopold II was in charge of its entire agenda along with Pyotr Semenov, a Russian geographer, who presided over the conference. One of the results of the meeting was the creation of an organization, the *Association Internationale Africaine* (AIA), with King Leopold II elected as first chairman of the established executive committee, named the International Committee, a position he unexpectedly occupied the following year (Hochschild 1998, 42–46; Roeykens 1955). In addition, National Committees were established in each of the participants' countries to support the International Committee. The latter included, besides its chairman, King Leopold II, three other executive members, namely the British Bartle Frere[7], the French Jean Louis Armand de Quatrefages and the German Gustav Nachtigal. Hesitant to have the Belgian flag fly over a territory he considered his own personal conquest, King Leopold II created a new one; specifically, a gold star with a blue background, which respectively referred to the enlightening civilization brought to the darkened and wandering Congolese people.

In November, two months after the creation of the AIA, Baron Greindl and Antoine Galezot assumed the new positions of General Secretary and Treasurer, respectively. Although the majority of the conference participants agreed on the need to civilize African nations through evangelization, they also noted how important it was for the AIA to remain neutral in dealing with other religions and denominations. AIA's activities in Africa included fundraising, most notably in Europe, and setting stations (also known as posts) in Africa. Despite the creation of the AIA, its materialization, which required significant human and financial resources, remained uncertain.

Nonetheless, King Leopold II employed his many contacts (e.g. renowned international geographers, explorers, religious leaders, businessmen and diplomats) to influence Western powers to support his plan to control the Congo basin. Georges Nzongola-Ntalaja explained it well in his book *The Congo from Leopold to Kabila: A People's History*: "King Leopold II had used all the public relations facilities that money could buy, including lobbyists, celebrities and ghost writers, to depict his business venture in Africa as a humanitarian endeavour against slavery, disease and ignorance" (2002, 38). General Henry Shelton Sanford is a good example of someone King Leopold II used to lobby for him both in his home country, the United States, and in Europe where he worked as an ambassador. Besides being a successful businessman in Florida, Sanford similarly worked as a diplomat, generally in Europe and particularly in Belgium. He is not only recognized as the man who helped Leopold recruit Stanley, but also as someone who played an important role in persuading the Republican president and his acquaintance, Chester Alan Arthur, as well as his administration, to support Leopold II's objectives in the Kongo.

On behalf of King Leopold II and the executive committee, Sanford and Baron Greindl attempted to contact Henry Morton Stanley, who successfully completed his second African expedition, to recruit him for the *Association Internationale Africaine* (AIA)'s plans to work in the Congo. Stanley's disinterest in the AIA advance was doubly motivated. He wanted to share and reveal his findings in England, and yet he was chiefly concerned about finishing his book on his successful previous African adventure. After several weeks of negotiations between Stanley, the AIA executive committee and its stakeholders, a preliminary contract was signed between Stanley and Leopold II on 30 October 1878. Upon invitation from the Belgian King at the Royal Palace, on 25 November 1878, a stakeholders' meeting entrusted Stanley with organizing AIA's first expedition under a new organization named the *Comité d'études du Haut-Congo* (Upper Congo Study Committee, CEHC). Members of the CEHC included Leon Lambert, a Belgian banker, and William Mackinnon, founder of the Imperial British East Africa Company (Nzongola-Ntalaja 2002, 15–16). Two weeks later, Stanley was officially hired by the CEHC for a three-year contract. Only one year after the existence of the CEHC, the King of Belgium initiated a third organization called the *Association Internationale du Congo* (AIC). On 17 November 1879, the CEHC was dissolved, which gave rise to the AIC. This dissolution, as argued by the Congolese historian Isidore Ndaywel è Nziem (1998, 275), consolidated not only Leopold II's hegemony over the Congo, but it also meant hampering the ambitions of the Franco-Italian officer Savorgnan de Brazza, who Leopold II considered an opponent in the race over the Central African territories, particularly after Brazza's refusal to join the AIA.

Whether comparing the King's benevolent activities in the Congo with those of the Americans in Liberia or the agreements between King Leopold II and Congolese local chiefs with those of the Americans and Indians, Sanford ensured that King Leopold's letters to President Arthur properly pleaded his case. In fact, he even rewrote some letters on the King's behalf so that they would be well received in Washington (Bontinck 1966; Ndaywel è Nziem 1998, 275). On 22 April 1884, the United States publicly endorsed Leopold II's plan to rule over the Congo Basin through his two associations, namely the AIA and the AIC. The purpose of these "twin" associations remained—for reasons many believed to be deliberate—unclear and vague. Allen Roberts, in his book *A Dance of Assassins,* illustrates this attitude with a quote from the Belgian king: "Care must be taken not to let it be obvious that the Association of the Congo and African Association are two different things" (2013; see also Bontinck 1966; Nzongola-Ntalaja 2002).

The endorsement read by the then Secretary of State, Frederick Theodore Frelinghuysen, is as follows:

> The Government of the United States announces its sympathy with and approval of the humane and benevolent purposes of the International Association of the Congo, administering, as it does, the interests of the Free States there established and will order the officers of the United States, both on land and sea, to recognize the flag of the International African Association as the flag of a friendly Government. (cited in Hochschild 1998, 81)

Although support from the United States in regard to Leopold II's plans in the Congo was obvious and sounded humanly appealing (civilization and the abolition of the slave trade), Europe was not as enthusiastic. In fact, some countries demonstrated their reluctance, mainly because of their similar interests in African territories. As in the United States, Leopold II used the same strategies with his European neighbours—whether in France, Germany or England—to advocate his plans. Initiated by the German Chancellor, Otto von Bismarck, European powers gathered in Berlin on 15 November 1884 to resolve issues related to their activities in a vast and "unoccupied" Africa, most notably in its central area (Herbst 2000, 74–76). As a result of this gathering, which ended on 26 February 1885, several decisions were made that meant to ensure the control of each power over its piece of African territory. Therefore, the powers represented at the Berlin Conference shared the African territories between themselves like a "cake," as it is often described. In fact, Leopold II signified such desire in "obtain[ing] a part of his magnificent African cake" in a letter written to his Ambassador in England (Pakenham 1991, 22). North Americans also took part in the conference, meaning that participants were not only Europeans.

The United States sent delegates that included a strong supporter of Leopold II, Henry Shelton Sanford, while the United States government had already expressed their consent to the Belgian king's claims over the Congolese territory without passing the Berlin Act. The Belgian king received Congo as his share, granted that the participants of the Berlin Conference recognized the statehood of his AIA in February 1885. A few months later, King Leopold II declared the *État Indépendant du Congo* (EIC) over which he could now "officially" rule as a sole sovereign with Boma as the capital. King Leopold II strategically chose this Congolese port town as the new state capital for two main reasons: (1) to dissuade the Portuguese's ambitions over the city, and (2) to easily access the interior of the country as well as its exit routes back toward Europe. While the king's representative in the Congo, Administrator-General Sir Francis Walter de Winton—who replaced Henry Morton Stanley—made the announcement at Banana on 1 August 1885, he also informed the Western powers of the establishment of the EIC (Keith 1919, 63–65; Slade 1959, 73–77).

In May 1888, the papal decree *Ut in amplissimo congo independetis territorio* announced the creation of the Apostolic Vicariate of the Independent Congo, led by the Congregation of the Immaculate Heart of Mary of Scheutveld (Scheut). Two years earlier, the Propaganda had approved King Leopold II's request to establish an educational institution to primarily train priests for his AIC.[8] Two men from the Belgian Catholic Church made a tremendous contribution to the realization of this project: one is the Archbishop of Malines, Goossens, and the other is the court chaplain to the Belgian king, Bishop Van Weddingen. Besides being under the direct jurisdiction of the first (Cardinal Goossens), the overall project was also placed under the Belgian king's umbrella. Whether in person or through emissaries, the Archbishop of Malines ensured that Rome received adequate documentation and took all means to accelerate the delivery of the project. Both his June 1884 trip to Rome and that of the canon bishop Gauthier served these purposes. In April 1885, the latter brought documentation to the Propaganda that summarized several intentions of the Louvain-based African seminary, namely the preliminary status of the institution and the structure of the seminary that gave first and sole preference to Belgians. Quoting from one such document, Marcel Benedictus Storme wrote:

> The Congo Directorate requires that Belgian chaplains and their posting territories "rely on the immediate authority of the S.C. Propaganda, without the intermediary of any foreign religious authority. The International Association of Congo being a sovereign and independent State, the Directorate would not be pleased seeing foreigners gain considerable influence through religious actions." (1975, 278)

Cardinal Giovanni Simeoni[9], prefect for the Congregation for the Propaganda of Faith, adopted the project presented by Bishop Gauthier. The Catholic University of Louvain, in Belgium, was supportive of the project and agreed to headquarter the seminary on land that had already been allotted by Jean de Hemptinne (Storme 1975, 277). In October 1886, the African seminary opened with Abbot Jacques Forget as director. The Belgian king's main purpose for this project was to ensure his hegemonic presence in the Congo, even in the missionary field. He had a hard time seeing the French being the only Catholic missionaries in Congo, hence his intense activism in Rome to ensure their replacement by the Belgians (Slade 1959, 141).

As a result of the continuous pressure exerted by Leopold II on both the Belgian missionaries and the Propaganda, coupled with the influences of the Scheut Fathers' interest in the Congo and the Sacred Congregation of Faith, other Belgian congregations began flooding into this new missionary field. As mentioned earlier, others, such as Ngomo Okitembo (1998), have also indicated that Cardinal Lavigerie's European anti-slavery awareness and mobilization campaign contributed to the convergence of Belgian congregations in the Congo.

Missionary Roles: Interdependence of Missions in the Colonial State

The rise of the État *Indépendant du Congo* (Independent State of Congo, EIC) in August 1885 revealed other aspects of the relationship between King Leopold II and missionaries concerning what was at stake as well as their respective interests in Central Africa in general. Prior to 1885, the Congo-owning Belgian king was friendly with actors from origins other than his own; however, he later became more of an intransigent ally. His preference for his fellow countrymen over others was now the open rule of his associations or the so-called Congolese's property. This criterion also applied to religious actors operating or planning to do so in Congo and with whom he had previously worked. While the King Leopold II's attitude towards foreigners applied to many other actors as well, this book focuses specifically on religious ones. As previously noted, all avenues and means interested him, under the condition that they contributed to his main objective: to establish a sole sovereignty in what he considered his private domain, Congo. He attained this objective through the internationally wide recognition of his two associations that resulted in the creation of the EIC: *Association Internationale Africaine* (AIA) and *Association Internationale du Congo* (AIC). Contrary to Western Congo, the Arabs not only impeded the establishment of the new state in Eastern Congo, but they furthermore encumbered missionary activities.

Threatened by Arabs in the eastern regions of the Congo, missionaries (Catholics and Protestants) relied on the EIC's army (*Force Publique*) for their security. What seemed to be largely security concerns were also featured in religious conflicts between Christianity (supported mainly by missionaries) and Islam. In Maniema, for instance, where the Arabs had economic and political control, Islam served as a local form of resistance against colonialism. Apart from security issues, administrative burdens for missionaries were added, who needed a state authorization to operate in the Congolese territory, particularly in its eastern areas (Maurel 1992, 216). Missionaries, particularly Catholics and their hierarchies, worked jointly with the EIC in the Congo.

Under the leadership of Pope Pius IX, the Vatican followed the Belgian king's projects and activities in Africa and chiefly in the Congo with great interest. The Congolese philosopher Vumbi-Yoka or Valentin-Yves Mudimbe (1994, 106) observes in his book *The Idea of Africa* that the pope saw in the works of Leopold II in Central Africa an opportunity for the Catholic Church to compensate for the loss of the Papal states (temporal power of the pope) in the late 1870s. Therefore, the Catholic Church was working in such a way as to please Leopold II. On at least three occasions, the Supreme Pontiff expressed his approval of the Belgian king's works in Central Africa and encouraged other Catholic members to support his activities. In 1876, for example, Marcel Storme noted in *Rapport du Père Planque, de Mgr Lavigerie et de Mgr Comboni sur l'association internationale Africaine*, that Pope Pius IX was "well disposed to support the King's project" and "recommended particularly, the apostolic vicariate, Bishop Comboni, contacting Leopold II" (1957, 23).

Understanding the importance of this religious institution in his African projects, the King ensured he included it (the Catholic Church) in his triumvirate, of which the other two components involved the Belgian State and Belgian economic interests. The interests of the EIC and missionaries intertwined in several ways. They were both convinced of their superiority over local populations, who they sought to civilize. Although the methods were slightly different, the civilizing missions of the colony and the missionaries were not only self-assigned, but they were mutually shared and commonly approved. On the one hand, Missionaries recognized their role in the transformation of both the spiritual and moral status of the colonized to "meet" that of Westerners. Until "indigenous" became Christians, they were in fact not civilized. Although the general consensus of that century indicated the superiority of Christian civilization over non-Christians, Friedrich Stenger (2001, 53), a member of the White Fathers, disagreed that all missionaries equated civilization with westernisation. Alternatively, colonial states and notably the EIC served to solidify the physical existence of their colonies. Ultimately, the aims of both the EIC and missions in the Congo concerning indigenous peoples coincided and were furthermore mutually supportive in their activities.

However, the more missionaries from various denominations and different nationalities became interested and involved in the evangelization of the Central African region, the more Leopold II became anxious about increasing competition over the control of those territories. For instance, Belgian Catholic congregations were not initially attracted to missionary work in the Congo. On the contrary, Leopold II's intense pressure on such missionaries as the Belgian Jesuits and Scheuts influenced their decision to accept his offer.[10] Instead, the Sacred Congregation of the Faith responded favourably to his desire, expressed in written form, to have Belgian missionaries from the Louvain seminary replace those of the French. In the same vein, the king was granted jurisdiction over the Congolese ecclesiastic territory. As a result, Catholic missionaries from other countries, such as France, lost their rights in the Congo. For instance, in 1891 the Propaganda summoned the congregation of the Holy Ghost Fathers to leave the Independent State of Congo. Ultimately, Leopold II's strategies consisted of undercutting those missionaries through the Holy See. For example, he requested the intervention of Pope Leon XIII to persuade the reluctant Belgian Scheut missionaries to join the Congolese mission, a request they finally accepted in 1888.

The Belgian king was more concerned with not leaving the Central African field freely open to other missionaries, whom he was convinced were extensions of their respective countries. Another illustration of this was the favour he demonstrated towards Catholic missionaries. Unlike Belgian Protestants' missions, the Belgian kingdom exclusively subsidized missions described as "national," namely Catholic ones. Several missionaries attempted, with difficulty, to dissociate themselves from the Leopoldian works. Although missionaries of diverse nationalities, proclaimed their African humanitarian objectives, their close ties with colonial powers, which did not always run in the interests of local African population, still lingered. The French historian Claude Prudhomme and others have pointed to similarities in degrading approaches (both physical and psychological), engaged by both missionaries and colonialists to local populations (Mudimbe 1982, 1988; Prudhomme 1995, 10). Another missionary who had a vision equal to that of the Belgian king of Central Africa and whose approaches have also been criticized is the French Bishop Charles Martial Allemand Lavigerie. This founder of the *Societé de Notre-Dame d'Afrique* (White Fathers) and head of the Central African missionaries claimed that the intervention of Europeans, particularly missionaries was a way to set the "poor sons of Shem" free from both slavery and ignorance (Kitumaini 2011, 20n25; Storme 1957).

The interests of Bishop (later Cardinal) Lavigerie for the African continent were similar to those of King Leopold II.[11] While the two were initially attracted to North Africa, the latter had a head start in exploring Central Africa. The Belgian king saw in the Archbishop of Algiers' Central African projects an opportunity to secure his own challenged authority and presence in Eastern Congo. To this end, he was ready to offer his financial assistance to the activities of the White Fathers under two exclusive conditions reserved at his discretion, namely (1) the choice of priests, who had to be only, or primarily, Belgian and (2) their posting locations. In 1879, Lavigerie accepted Leopold II's offer of assistance, which initially materialized with 20 scholarships to young Belgian missionaries. However, their personal ambitions intersected with their national and religious identities. That is, the Belgian king was more concerned about his own national identification, while the Cardinal, a Frenchman, was primarily preoccupied with his missionary denomination and that of advancing the interest of his own congregation. While Leopold II engaged at the state level, as well as at the ecclesiastical level, the Cardinal maintained a strong network of contacts in the Vatican. Working at the Holy See as an auditor,[12] Charles Lavigerie, a young abbot at the time, not only had the opportunity to grow this network, but also to fine-tune skills that later proved to be helpful both in his life and career. As an auditor, he was called to deal both in religious matters and situations that required extreme discretion and diplomacy. Jean-Claude Ceillier, a French member of the White Fathers' congregation, observed in his book *Histoire des missionaires d'Afrique*:

> This position not only had religious and legal aspects, but also included diplomatic dimensions, which gave the beholder [Lavigerie] numerous occasions to meet, at the highest level, both leaders of religious and diplomatic matters; this is the context in which Lavigerie was often received by the Holy Father, with whom it appears he had a close relationship. (2008, 17)[13]

Ceillier not only insists on the memorable time the Cardinal had at the Holy See, he likewise shows the importance of the position he occupied, which in some way facilitated his (Lavigerie's) future ecclesiastical projects. In fact, for two years (1861—1863) after his Rome assignment, Pope Pius IX rejected his (Lavigerie's) initial request for a transfer to another posting. Nonetheless, it was granted a few months later. On 22 March 1863, the young abbot was consecrated bishop at the Italian church Saint-Louis des Français and he was additionally provided with a position in Nancy, France, where he exercised his episcopacy for four years (1863–1867) (Ceillier 2008). His African adventure began in the Algerian capital, Algiers, in May 1867, where he also founded his congregation, *Société des Missionnaires de Notre Dame d'Alger* (Society of Missionaries of Notre Dame of Algiers) in October 1868.[14] The society's change of name, to *Société de Missionnaires d'Afrique* (Society of Missionaries of Africa), implied or at least revealed his apostolic ambitions for other African regions, particularly its equatorial regions. Among other steps that confirmed his aspirations included an important letter, commonly known as the *Mémoire secrète* (Secret Memoir), addressed to the Sacred Congregation of the Propaganda.[15] The content of the letter revealed not only the underlying social, political and religious stakes at hand, but also the dynamics between different actors, both active and passive.

At the Propaganda's demand, through its prefect Cardinal Alessandro Franchi, many heads of Catholic missionaries working in Africa sent their reports regarding the advancement of the Catholic faith throughout the continent. The context of this demand coincided with the AIA's initiatives in Central Africa and whose main aims included not only the exploration of Equatorial Africa, but more importantly its unexplored interior. While the initial demand of Cardinal Franchi was to obtain their views on the AIA, they (the missionary heads) used the opportunity to share their concerns and to promote their own works, oftentimes at the expense of other fellow Catholic missionaries. While the first reports coming from leaders such as Father Ignace Schwindenhammer of the Holy Ghost congregation and Father Auguste Planque of the Society of African Missionary supported the AIA's project in Africa, the report Cardinal Lavigerie issued, known as the *Mémoire secrète*,[16] strongly critiqued both his fellow missionaries and the AIA (Storme, 1975: 263). As a result of this report, the Propaganda opted for Lavigerie, who, according to the Propaganda, presented a stronger case.

Once he received the backing of Rome in response to his letter that stressed the importance of Christianizing ("Catholicizing") Central Africa, an initial group of White Fathers' missionaries headed from Marseilles to the Great Lakes region (Slade 1959, 130, 139). In February 1878, the new pope, Leon XIII, continued much in the same vein as his predecessor (Pius IX), which consisted of encouraging initiatives that reinforced the Catholic presence in equatorial Africa, i.e. the evangelization of the Great Lakes region through the creation of Catholic missionary posts. The Archbishop of Algiers was allowed by Pope Leon XIII to create the missions of Nyanza and Tanganyika (which later became Provicariates). During the same month of September, two missionary centres, northern and southern Congo, were established. After sub-delegating his authority in the Equatorial Africa, Lavigerie conferred on himself the new title of "Apostolic Delegate of Sahara and Sudan" (Ceillier 2008, 32).

King Leopold II and Charles Lavigerie shared several characteristics and ambitions, which were demonstrated in the African fields. For instance, the two spearheaded the anti-slavery campaign with fairly similar objectives. Not only were Arabs regarded as common enemies of both Leopold II and Lavigerie, they (Arabs) likewise strengthened their argument among the European public regarding the anti-slavery project. Ruth Slade accurately identified one of their joint actions in the late 1800s, which aimed to reinforce their common goals:

> With remarkable success Cardinal Lavigerie was able to marshal and present the facts about the slave trade in Central Africa so that he both excited the pity of humanitarian Europe and encouraged the active intervention of European governments, intent on their own imperialist plans. His crusade was of the greatest value to Leopold II. At the anti-slavery Conference held in Brussels in 1889–90, the King used humanitarian sentiment to secure larger revenue for the Congo State. (1959, 36–37)

Put another way, Slade attempted to show how the anti-slavery campaigns of both Lavigerie and King Leopold II served their own purposes. The Belgian king and the EIC's position against the Arabs were consolidated with the benediction of the European powers. The two men also shared suspicions concerning Protestant congregations. They both demonstrated extreme anxiety toward Protestants, whom they considered their competitors. They were not only perceived as religious competitors, but they were further regarded as potential political opponents. According to King Leopold II, the French congregations active in the Congo, the Holy Ghost Fathers[17] (also known as Spiritans) and the White Fathers, worked in the interest of their own country, France.

Protestant Missionaries: Early Activities in Kivu

Having concentrated on the Catholic involvement in the Congo in the preceding sections, this section examines the activities of Protestant missionaries in the Congo with particular emphasis on its eastern regions. I do not intend to focus on all missionary groups, as this might divert from the purpose of this book. However, it is my aim to provide an overview of the presence of Protestant missionaries in Eastern Congo, primarily in today's North Kivu and the development of those that contributed or influenced the creation of the contemporary *3ème* CBCA. As subsequent elaborations will display, the premise of Protestant missionaries not only included, like the Catholics, the desire to evangelize and/or civilize the Congolese people, but it additionally fostered inland penetrations. The other two purposes of this section are to understand the motivations and *modus operandi* of Protestant missionaries. Reaching interior territories not only preoccupied states and missionaries, private sectors and several other stakeholders were equally interested in the adventures.

Protestant missionaries settled and expanded throughout the Congo during at least three main periods. In the early 1850s, David Livingstone (1813–1873), a Scottish Protestant and medical doctor, initiated the period with his first African adventure in South Africa. He then headed north towards East Africa and ultimately ended up in Eastern Congo. His exploration motivated many other missionaries, who responded positively to his appeal to evangelize the area in the late 1890s and early 1900s. After the pioneering work of missionaries in the late 1880s, most of the Protestant missionaries were established in the early 1900s, known as the second expansion period, which continued until the 1920s. The focus of many explorers and missionaries consisted of inland penetrations both from the western and eastern Congolese borders. The third period of Protestant expansion covered the period after the First World War until the late 1950s and witnessed a wave of evangelical and non-denominational missionaries. In addition, two main issues marked this third period of the mission's expansion, namely (1) financial difficulties caused primarily by the two World Wars that caused the withdrawal of many missions (Catholics included), and (2) increasingly embittered relations between missionaries and local populations driven by the emancipation movements seeking autonomy.

In the mid-1800s, a British Protestant and industrialist, Robert Arthington, who believed in the soon Second Coming of Jesus Christ, decided to invest in missionary activities in Central Africa by preaching and promoting the Gospel. As a result of this decision and under a sense of urgency, Arthington proposed financially supporting two missionary societies already established in Central Africa under the sole condition that they would progress inland.

First, the pioneering works of the Baptist Missionary Society (BMS) in Africa—a continent that had always been sought after by the society—began its expansion towards Congo and Angola after establishing itself in Cameroon. Seven months after their difficult initial trip[18] to Congo, in July 1878 Baptist missionaries George Grenfell and Thomas J. Comber carried out their new assignment into the then capital of the Kingdom of Kongo, Sao Salvador (now Mbanza Kongo). Three others (William Holman Bentley, H.E. Crudgington and John S. Hartland) joined later on the first two missionaries with whom they sailed toward the Pool area in January 1881.

Second, in 1877 Pastor Alfred Tilly of Cardiff, J. and R. Cory, James Irvy, Henry Gratten and his spouse Fanny Guinness founded the Livingstone Inland Mission (LIM). This society, argued David Lagergren (1970) and contrary to Slade in 1959, was initiated by Pastor Tilly. The LIM was patterned after the British Protestant James Hudson Taylor's China Inland Mission, which he (Taylor) created in 1865 with the main objective of reaching the centre of China with the Gospel (Braekman 1960, 59–60). In addition to the BMS and LIM, other Protestant groups from other nationalities including Nordic countries joined the Congo field for missionary work with a particular interest in eastern regions, such as the Kivu province.

In 1884, upon their departure from the Congo, the LIM transferred their missionary assets to both the American Baptist Missionary Union (ABMU) and the non-Baptist Swedish mission *Svenska Missions förbundet*, which had to start its own station because of denominational differences with the American Baptist Foreign Mission Society (ABFMS).[19] A few years later, in 1921, another Swedish mission, *Mission Libre Suédoise* (Free Swedish Mission, MLB), arrived in Congo and spread across the Kivu areas (e.g., Walikale [1931], Ntoto [1932], Pinga [1935], Bukavu [1948] and Ndofia [1955]). During that same year, Gunnerius Tollefsen of the *Mission Libre Norvegienne* (Norwegian Evangelical Mission), a Pentecostal missionary organization based in Norway, erected stations in Nya-Kaziba (1922) and Moganga (1928). The Evangelization Society Africa

Mission chose to establish its station in Shabunda in November 1922. Another American Protestant mission on which I will focus is the Unevangelized African Mission (UAM) (Braekman 1961).

From Baptist Missionaries to Congolese Churches: Emergence of the *Communauté Baptiste au Centre de l'Afrique*

Charles Hurlburt, an American pastor who knew President Theodore Roosevelt, embarked on missionary work in Eastern Africa, particularly Kenya, where he aimed to establish the ground work for the African Inland Mission (AIM) with the perspective of expanding eastward into the Belgian Congo. His acquaintance with the retired American President Roosevelt who visited the region in 1909–1910 facilitated his entrance into the African field, particularly in the Congo (Stauffacher 1977, 73). In fact, President Roosevelt ensured the materialization of the Belgian king's support of AIM and its missionaries in the Congo (Stauffacher 1977, 82).

While his time in Africa, accompanied by his family, was relatively limited, his son Paul Hurlburt spent several years in the Kivu areas. His early years in Kenya initiated the young Hurlburt into missionary work and acquainted him with African culture. In addition to the Kiswahili language he learned in Kenya—one of the languages spoken in Eastern Congo—Paul Hurlburt also learned Kinande, a language spoken by the Nande people, who make up the majority of members of the current *3ème* CBCA Church. These two assets distinguished him from other missionary groups, providing him with a greater proximity to local people and facilitating his access to the Congolese community (Nelson 1992, 29–47).

Writing about Paul Hurlburt's linguistic advantage of speaking local languages, Jack Nelson, son of American missionaries in Eastern Congo, noted in his book *Christian Missionizing and Social Transformation* that it was one of his Hurlburt's "hallmarks, endearing him to the Banande people" (1992, 31). Hurlburt and other AIM missionaries began their journey in Lubero, a territory situated near the Ugandan border and north of Goma, before moving to a northern neighbouring city, Katwa (previously known as Misebere). The first station was erected in this city of Katwa. They continued setting up other stations in present day North Kivu, totalling five (5) by 1940: Katwa and Kitsombiro in 1928, Ruanguba in 1932, Mushweshwe in 1938 and Kikundu in 1940. In 1946, six years after the creation of the last station, the Conservative Baptist Foreign Mission

Society (CBFMS)—later called *Mission Baptiste du Kivu* (Baptist Mission in Kivu, MBK)—took over the UAM's work, which included the five stations (Braekman 1961, 217).

Following similar doctrinal guidelines of the UAM's pioneers in the Congo, the MBK missionaries encountered swelling contestations with their local leaders and members for three reasons. First, both UAM and MBK missionaries did not remunerate their local workers whose labours Belgian authorities judged to be voluntary when the matter was brought to their attention. The plaintiffs were unable to provide proof—such as a written contract—against those they called employers.

The second reason aggravating conflicts between MBK missionaries and both local members and leaders in particular included the ministerial recognition of the latter (local church leaders). Although trained and experienced, MBK missionaries still denied Congolese "pastors," and evangelists-teachers official ordinations, which, as Jack Nelson has pointed out, would have negatively impacted them if granted. Nelson wrote:

> [T]he most revealing of the deviations that CBFMS missionaries made from the indigenous policy was their reluctance to ordain African pastors. Though church leaders, especially those who graduated from the Bible Institute at Rwanguba, were referred to as pastors (wapastor; wachungaji)...formal ordination was not extended to them. To many missionaries, ordination was equated with a certain educational level not available to Africans; further, it was felt that as previously only missionaries had held ordained status, African pastors would be inclined to become conceited if ordination was extended to them. (1992, 61)

The restraint of native ordinations was not singular to the MBK and Baptist missionaries only; the so-called "indigenous policy" was also common within the Protestant societies in the Congo. As a result of independence movements in the country, Congolese pastors began to be officially ordained (Nelson 1992, 62).

Third, UAM's refusal of the state's educational subsidies was regarded as the "straw that broke the camel's back" as far as the relationship between Baptist missionaries and the natives were concerned. Two factions emerged out of this conflict involving educational subsidies, forming on the one side their supporters (educational subsidies) and on the other side their contenders. The former, predominately represented by natives, insisted that MBK missionaries accept the subsidies, while the latter stood by their decision not to accept under any circumstances state financial assistance for educational purposes.[20]

Although Baptist missionaries supported their own schools, they were limited by the extent to which they could meet their converts' demands and expectations. A primary certificate was the highest level of education offered, including at MBK schools, as well as others in the country. However, diplomas issued by any non-Catholic schools were neither acknowledged in higher education when this was possible, nor in the workplace, wherein most jobs were mainly provided by the state.[21] These two interrelated impediments exacerbated the prevailing tensions between the Baptist missionaries and their adherents, who among other things could not understand the refusal of educational subsidies while accepting medical subsidies at the same time. One of the ways they expressed their grievances was to raise the issue on a yearly basis during the MBK annual meetings, beginning in the mid-1950s. The three-day conference that was held, from 18–21 August 1959, in Burungu triggered the end of the cohabitation period between supporters and opponents of educational subsidies.

While the two groups agreed to participate at the conference with the issue of subsidies on the agenda, all of the MBK missionaries backed out to "boycott" the conference (Nelson 1992, 79). At the end of the conference, the Congolese participants interpreted the obvious absence of missionaries as a betrayal and rejection, thus leading to the creation of their own ecclesial structure, the *Association des Chrétiens Congolais de la Mission Baptistes du Kivu* (Association of Congolese Christians of the Baptist Mission in Kivu, ACCMBK) with Lawy Bakulu Birikoliko as the president. Nonetheless, only eight (8) days following the creation of the ACCMBK, on 29 August 1959 the missionaries' response was twofold with the expectation of abating the conflict: they declined the subsidies, yet they signed the *Convention Scolaire.*

Two other consecutive meetings were required to calm down the heated tensions between missionaries and Congolese people of the Baptist denomination. The first meeting, held from 16 to 19 September 1959, during which the missionaries presented their peace plan, did not resolve the issue of education subsidies. The second meeting (that was held from 29 September to 3 October in the same year), which this time brought together both missionaries and government agents, influenced the former to accept education subsidies. As Nelson pointed out, at least three reasons led the missionaries to endorse the subsidies:

> In view of the increasing political unrest, the demand of the African Christian constituency, the intervention of the Government and having sought the mind of the Lord; seeing no other alternative, we accept government subsidies for our schools. (1992, 82)

As schools opened on 20 October 1959, three mission stations (Katwa, Kitsombiro and Rwanguba) began to receive education subsidies following the MBK missionaries' signing. Yet, the long contention in the MBK was far from over, particularly amid markedly deteriorating socio-political conditions at the dawn of several African countries' independence, which, in the Congolese case in particular, led to a series of rebellions (e.g., Kashamura in Kivu). MBK missionaries contested to the colonial authority the legality of Congolese dissidents for using the name *Association des Chrétiens Congolais de la Mission Baptistes du Kivu*, which was later changed to *Synode des Églises Protestantes Baptistes du Kivu* (Synod of Protestant Baptist Churches in Kivu).[22]

As previously mentioned, Protestant churches are embodied in the organization structure named the *Église du Christ of Congo* ([Church of Christ in the Congo, ECC]; previously the *Église du Christ au Zaïre* [Church of Christ in Zaïre, ECZ]). The arrival of Jean Bokeleale, the first African Secretary General of the *Conseil Protestant au Congo*,[23] as head of the ECZ facilitated the implementation of a single Protestant Church in Zaïre, depicting a broad spectrum of Protestantism in the country. Although independent in their activities, adherents of the ECC, officially called *communautés* (communities), functioned under this organization's umbrella.[24] Congolese local churches that joined the ECC were numerically identified. The emergence of the *Communauté Baptiste du Kivu* (Baptist Community of Kivu, CBK) clearly illustrates this point.

Seeking to resolve ongoing internal conflicts in the Baptist church in Kivu (MBK), the leader of the ECC, Jean Bokeleale, suggested the creation of a Baptist community, which later became the *3ème Communauté Baptiste du Kivu* (3rd Baptist Community in Kivu, *3ème* CBK) (interview with Mwenge, pseudonym of a participant). However, one faction of the MBK rejected Bokeleale's suggestion and instead formed the *Communauté des* Églises *Baptistes du Kivu* (Community of the Baptist churches of Kivu) also identified under the ECC platform as the *55ème Communauté des* Églises *Baptistes du Congo-Est* (55th Community of Baptist Communities of East-Congo, 55ème CEBCE). The CBK was later renamed *3ème Communauté Baptiste au Centre de l'Afrique* (Baptist Community in the Center of Africa, *3ème* CBCA) keeping its third identification within the ECC, thus *3ème* CBCA.[25]

It is worth noting here that besides subsidy issues, ethnic factors strongly contributed to the split of the MBK. While supporters of government subsidies were mostly Nande, Hunde and Shi, as well as members of the CBK groups, anti-subsidy supporters sided with missionaries and were mostly adherents of the CEBCE, in addition to members from the Kinyarwanda-speaking community.

The Emergence of New Religious Movements in Colonial and Post-Colonial Congo

Three decades after the independence of the Congo, the Congolese religious sphere started witnessing an ongoing proliferation of new religious movements. These were considered new, primarily because of their religious distinction from mainline churches from which their leaders usually (but not always) emerged. In other words, the majority of these leaders came from local (also referred to as indigenous) constituents of mainline churches (previously known as missionaries), namely Catholic and Protestant churches and have therefore been critically labelled as sects. Some of these groups have rejected this terminology, while others like researcher David Mongo (2005), categorized them as *soft* as opposed to *hard* (groups deriving from religions other than Christianity) religious movements. However, their emergence can be traced back to the late 1880s and early 1900s during the colonial period, while the Congolese postcolonial era showed a sustained growth of these movements. In addition, *new religious movement* not only included the notion of religious change, as Beckford and others (Beckford 1986) alluded to, but it also coincided with important socio-political and cultural transformations (Nelson 1989).

In *Charismatic Renewal and the Churches,* the American Catholic theologian and monk Kilian McDonnell (1976, 20–21) distinguished at least three theories that scholars (particularly sociologists and cultural anthropologists) have used to explain the emergence and expansion of new religious movements. First, social disorganization results from difficult (sometimes violent) encounters between different cultures, which include religious persons, from either rural or urban backgrounds. These situations are conducive to the emergence of social groupings based on common attributes and bonds. This theory likens to my research findings and particularly with members of *Arche*/Goma. The example of Mamie (a fictitious name) is illustrative of this theory. For this member of *Arche* who recently moved to the city of Goma, her new place of worship is another family where she has met brothers and sisters. When I asked why she chose *Arche de l'Alliance*/ Goma, unlike her parents who attend a Catholic parish, she observed:

> For me, it is first and foremost an integration issue. When we arrived in this city, I attended the Catholic Church along with my parents. Ever since a brother invited me to *Arche*, I have stayed. My mother is Catholic, but all of us children go there [*Arche*]. I don't know how to explain it to you—I felt welcome from the very first time. It was as if I knew everyone there. You don't feel lost. I have been working with the children at Sunday school for several years now.[26]

The second theory explaining the emergence and rapid growth of new religious movements rests on three forms of deprivation. While economic and social deprivations embody the difficulties of acquiring material things to cope with one's social life, ethical deprivation mainly consists of people perceiving their lives as unfulfilled in terms of their value systems. New religious movements, observed Kilian McDonnell (1976), offer alternatives to these people in that they gain a sense of accomplishment and satisfaction.

The other theory is what McDonnell calls psychological maladjustment. This theory suggests that some individuals are mentally predisposed to be much more attracted to given activities, especially those that are charismatic in nature. The example of postcolonial Congo, as well as other African countries, is similar to the colonial era as far as local religious movements are concerned. During the colonial period, both Kimbanguist and Kitawala[27] "movements" illustrated the socio-political and cultural factors that influenced their initial emergence in Western and Eastern Congo. While these two religious groups are not the focus of this book, they are important to the study of Congolese religious and messianic "movements." Therefore, I briefly use the first one, Kimbanguism, for illustration purposes before moving to the case of the Église *Francophone Arche de l'Alliance* in Goma.

Many have observed that the first wave of the Congolese spiritual revival in Western Congo, and later throughout the central African region, emerged from two Congolese who promoted the Africanization of the Christian faith which strongly resonated among Congolese people in the late eighteenth century and early twentieth century: Prophetess Kimpa Vita Béatrice[28] and Prophet Simon Kimbangu (1887/9—1951)[29] respectively (Irvine 1974; Young 1965, 284–288). In fact, followers of Simon Kimbangu have described his ministry as "a great spiritual uplift and revival" (Martin 1975, 50). Kimbangu, whose name has been defined either as *celui qui révèle ce qui est caché* ("one who reveals what is hidden") or a contested word, "skill," grew up with his aunt Kinzembo after the death of both his mother (Luezi) and father (Kuyela).

A few years later, Kimbangu's aunt handed him over to the Baptist missionaries of the British Missionary Society (BMS), who, in the course of translating the Bible, taught him how to read and write by using the newly translated Kikongo Bible. In other words, he owes his early religious and intellectual experiences to BMS missionaries, from whom he received both baptism (along with his widow wife Marie Mwilu with whom he had three sons—Daniel Charles Kisolokele Lukelo [1914–1992], Salomon Dialungana Kinagana [1916–2002] and Joseph Ndiangienda Kuntima [1918–1992]) and biblical teachings, which he also taught as a catechist in Lukungu. These missionaries, esteeming him with high regard, described him as an exceptionally intelligent and diligent indigenous student who wittingly accomplished his assignments.

Kimbangu began his ministry activities as an evangelist in the Bas-Congo areas, more precisely in Nkamba's (district of Thysville, today [2019] Mbanza-Ngungu in the Kongo Central province) surroundings, in the early 1900s amidst an international context of war and period of drought and diverse pandemics (e.g., sleeping sickness, influenza, typhoid and smallpox). According to many scholars and witnesses, this period of economic and environmental hardships, coupled with famine, constitutes the premises of Kimbangu's divine call framed in a threefold mandate: (1) to feed God's sheep, (2) to share the gospel and (3) to be Christ's witness (Asch 1983, 19).

While Simon Kimbangu teachings—accompanied by healings and miracles—attracted the admiration of local populations[30], his fame encouraged additional schemes against him from both the colonial state authorities and missionaries (notably Catholics) (Nzongola-Ntalaja 2002, 49). Local populations did not only consider him to be a prophet, but they further compared him to a black savior (Jesus Christ). Unlike Protestant missionaries who under pressure from Belgian authorities chose to dissociate themselves from Simon Kimbangu and his movement on theological grounds, the colonial state coalesced with Catholic missionaries for his immediate arrest. This action posed a dilemma in part because of its unpredicted local consequences. Many, including Nzongola-Ntalaja (2002, 49), believe that Kimbangu was probably influenced by Pan-African movements during his journey to Kinshasa (1918–1920). This influence most likely contributed to his conflicts with Belgian authorities. Marie-Louise Martin addressed the socio-political and religious challenges Simon Kimbangu and his followers caused to both the Belgian colonial administration and missionaries, which resulted in his hastened arrest in the last quarter of 1921:

> Genuine and would-be prophets of Kimbangu spread the movement so rapidly in May 1921 that the Belgian administration began to be afraid. On 1 June 1921, it called a meeting of the leaders of Catholic and Protestant missions in Mbanza-Ngungu to repudiate Kimbangu and other prophetic movements. In the Belgian documents, there is special reference to the insistence on the immediate arrest of Kimbangu by one of the Catholic missionaries. The Protestants hesitated, wishing to dispel the movement not by force but by persuasion. The Belgian administration agreed with the Catholics, who wanted to intervene immediately because they were afraid that Kimbanguism could turn into a political movement. On 2 June the District Commissioner ordered that Kimbangu and his four assistants be arrested without delay. (Martin 1975, 58)

After an earlier escape and a three-month refuge from his pursuers, Simon Kimbangu finally handed himself over to the colonial authorities on 12 September 1921 in Nkamba. By this voluntary surrender, Marie-Louise Martin (1975, 60) explained that Kimbangu responded to God's instruction of returning to Nkamba in order to be arrested. On 3 October 1921, life imprisonment, instead of 120 strokes of the whip and the death penalty, was imposed on him following the Belgian king's commutation. Thus, he spent the next thirty (30) years of his life thousands of kilometres away from his family in the prison of Elizabethville (now Lubumbashi), until his death in October 1951. His wife and two youngest sons—five-year-old Salomon Dialungana and three-year-old Joseph Ndiangienda—were placed under house arrest in Nkamba, while the eldest son, Charles Kisolokele (seven years old at the time) was already relegated to Boma's *colonies scolaires* (Catholic school).

Kimbanguism, as well as other early (between the late 1800s and early 1900s) Congolese religious groups, may have been considered a peripheral movement when compared to mainline churches. However, more than a century later the reality is different. The protest letter of Joseph Diangienda to the Belgian Senate's president against their continuous discriminations and a demand for their official recognition was finally granted in 1959, the same year in which Simon Kimbangu's wife, Marie Mwilu, passed away. Not only was the indigenous religious movement that began thirty-eight (38) years earlier (i.e., 1921) officially recognized as the *Église de Jésus-Christ sur la Terre par son envoyé spécial Simon Kimbangu* (Church of Jesus Christ on the Earth by his sent one Simon Kimbangu, EJCSK), but since then it has continued to be one of the three main religious institutions in the Congolese post-colonial state, besides the Roman Catholic and Protestant churches (Église du Christ au Congo [Church in Christ in Congo], ECC), as well as being socially involved primarily in the areas of health and education (Martin 1975). In fact, with more than eight (8) million members, EJCSK has been ranked as the largest independent church in Africa (Cox 1995, 246).

Revival Churches in Congo: Emergence of the *Centre Évangélique Francophone Arche de l'Alliance* Goma

There is general consensus among researchers of African religious studies about the continuous growth, since the late 1970s, of both Pentecostal churches and charismatic movements, particularly in the Congo. In spite of the plurality of these groups, which actually complicates its (Pentecostalism) definition, the works of the Holy Spirit in the believer's life constitutes their common denominator. In an inclusive way, the British theologian Allan Anderson described Pentecostalism in his book *An Introduction to Pentecostalism: Global Charismatic Christianity* as "all churches and movements that emphasize the working of the gifts of the Spirit, on both phenomenological and theological grounds," and not on formal doctrinal considerations (Anderson 2004, 13–14). During my fieldwork in both Kinshasa and Goma, many religious leaders and adherents identified themselves as part of Revival churches while belonging to either an Evangelical, Pentecostal, or *Assemblées de Dieu* (Assemblies of God) denomination. As observed above, the Holy Spirit and its gifts are central to these denominations. In the context of my research and for the purpose of this book in particular, I do include Revival churches in the Pentecostal category. The global growth of these religious groups is recognized in the African socio-political context (Anderson 2004).

Although these forms of Pentecostal churches (Revival Churches), sometimes termed African Initiated Churches (AIC), are no longer at the margin of religious groups, or labelled as peripheral, they often continue to be marginalized when they are identified to certain demographic categories such as age, education level, gender and marital status that carry their own marginalization dynamics. Since the 1990s, many of these religious categorizations have no longer fit in the general African context and particularly in the Congo. For instance, the membership of Revival Churches is no longer exclusively dominated and associated with some stereotypes (youth, unemployment, female participants, etc.). On the contrary, Congolese elites, business owners and professors, to name but a few, are increasingly part of the contingent of these churches—irrespective of their motivations.

Whether in the Mobutu or in the two Kabila regimes (Laurent-Désiré and Joseph), political dignitaries have actively participated in the promotion of Pentecostalism. In the early 1990s, the former Mobutu information minister, Dominique Sakombi Inongo, also known as *frère* ("brother") Jacob (Nzongola-Ntalaja 2015, 301), founded his own church, *La Voix de Dieu* (The Voice of God) after his public repentance of magic practices. Another former Mobutu minister to have repented of his evil doing and to have opened his own church in Kinshasa is Honoré Ngbanda Nzambo Ko Atumba. Under Joseph Kabila's regime, the former Vice-President Azarias Ruberwa Manywa was also involved in Congolese Pentecostal churches as a pastor. These few dignitaries are merely illustrative of the ongoing active roles of Congolese political leaders in Pentecostal churches since the 1990s.

In 1987, the first branch of the Evangelical Church *La Borne*[31] (Kinshasa) started under the leadership of Pastor Israel N'Sembe Loyela. To the name *Centre*

Évangélique *Francophone*, like its mother church, was added *Arche de l'Alliance* (Arch of the Covenant) from which derived thirteen years later, in 2000, the Goma extension *Centre Évangelique Francophone Arche de l'Alliance* (Francophone Evangelical Centre Arch of the Covenant, CEF). Similar to many other Revival churches that emerged out of home meetings, termed "cell groups," some members of *Arche*/Masina who moved to Eastern Congo for professional purposes in the mid-1990s created *Arche*/Goma first as a cell group resulting in the establishment of an extension of *Arche*/Masina.[32]

Joining the group that was already meeting in Goma, Pastor Estone Kasereka Vutwire the current church leader, who was then working with Campus for Christ in Kindu, received the leadership of the church in the late 1990s.[33] When I asked him about his calling, he responded, "I received my pastoral ministry as early as 1998 and the church was officially commissioned on July 4, 1999."[34] He spoke of his pastoral calling in the form of a vision that was progressively unfolded in terms of direction and meaning: "the vision we received was progressively clear to us." It is important noting the use of the collective pronoun, which one may interpret as unwillingness and reticence to mention the names of some of the first participants of *Arche de l'Alliance*/Goma who left in order to start their own churches. There are reasons to agree with many observers who say that Revival churches follow almost the same pattern of emergence and a similar life cycle.

First, an initial phase consists of at least two situations. On the one hand, a testimony from an individual or a group of people who have experienced a supernatural encounter serves as a triggering element (potential) adherents rally around. On the other hand, social-political and economic factors initiate this first phase of emergence of Revival churches. In other words, social difficulties that are generally materially and often politically connected facilitate the emergence of these churches. In the two situations, potential members and adherents of these churches not only identify themselves with the core message they propagate, but they further feel concerned and compelled to get involved, as opposed to remaining passive observers. I do not imply that these factors alone triggered the emergence of Revival churches, although several observers give them a considerable place in their studies (Matangila 2006; Batende 1993–1994).

Moreover, the context in which initiators of Revival churches received their revelation (others use "vision" or "mission") and on which they do emphasize usually carries a supernatural connotation like visionary and audible appearances. Oftentimes, the core message of those revelations is to address a given problem and/or respond to a social need. It is also said that Beatrice Kimpa Vita and Simon Kimbangu had supernatural vision with an assignment to their people

(Congolese). Coming back to Pastor Kasereka Vutwire, although he did not have a supernatural manifestation, he shared with me how he responded to God's calling to start *Arche de l'Alliance*/Goma:

> We started here in Goma from nothing. We passed through many challenges to reach this particular location. To be in Goma is a response to a divine calling. Because, you know, ministry is not a personal initiative, it is a calling, a vocation; it is a divine direction. It is also about responding to a need…delicate social situations.
>
> God always speaks progressively. That is, he sheds his light, he gives a direction and instruction, which might sometimes be *brute* (raw) and later be clarified. So, we had it in our heart, in 1998, to start a church.[35]

These pioneers encountered tremendous challenges in the early stage of their ecclesial initiatives which were mainly financial and materials. As a result, they had to cope with various functioning costs. While these pioneers continued working as part-time workers, they also relied on the so-called *partenaires* (partners)—these supporters are not only locally based, but they are most of the time from abroad. Spiritual aspects of these churches generally overshadowed their financial hardships, particularly during their initial stages.[36] Consequently, early financial difficulties are often ignored by scholars of African religious and theological studies from both Western and Congolese backgrounds. The first phase of the emergence of Revival churches usually took up to four (4) years before their fruits began to show and thus allowed for the following phase.

The second phase following the emergence of Revival churches, as well as indigenous religious organizations, consisted of their legitimation. After the first phase has strengthened the core of Revival churches' founders usually through isolation and religious/spiritual activities (e.g. prayer and fasting[37]), they then focus on expanding their vision in their own local abode and in foreign lands. Pastor N'sembe and several members of *Arche de l'Alliance*/Masina opened satellite churches in countries like the US and Australia. Conversely, Pastor Kasereka opened branches in the neighbouring city of Goma, in Beni, and in Kampala, capital of Uganda as well. He equated churches that have expanded beyond their local places to *Églises fortes* (strong churches).

Besides opening satellite churches, another characteristic of strong churches, according to Pastor Kasereka, was their "participation in the mission" in following "the command of Jesus Christ to his apostles," as stated in the Gospel according to Matthew 28:19–20, which he quoted: "*Allez faire de toutes les nations les disciples, les baptisant au nom du Père, du Fils et du Saint-Esprit*" (Go and make disciples of all nations, baptizing them in the name of the Father, of the Son and of the Holy Spirit).

After a brief pause, he emphasized the last part of the verse: *"Enseignez-leur à observer tout ce que je vous ai prescrit"* (Teach them to observe all I have commanded you). The "needs of God as given to me," Pastor Kasereka pursued, were to "build churches in different *chef-lieu de provinces* [provincial capitals] and which will then radiate not only in the peripheries, but they will also reach out to foreign nations." This path to producing strong churches appeared very clear to him (Pastor Kasereka):

> We are still working on this first stage here in Goma, where we have started. We have already opened a satellite church in Beni. We continue to pray for other missions to be opened, but the next step will be abroad, in countries that are more in need of the Gospel. We are heading towards this vision: establishing strong churches for the mission.[38]

During my discussions with Pastor Kasereka, "building strong churches" seemed to be the guiding principle for *Arche de l'Alliance*/Goma as he unfolded some of their upcoming projects. The second phase of Revival Churches relates to his description of a strong church, which I call a legitimation phase.

While the legitimation phase serves to numerically grow the church, as new adherents join the church as well as enlarge its influence, emphasis is increasingly placed upon social aspects. This second phase centers on building infrastructures such as church facilities (e.g., schools, hospitals, and so on). One of the direct, or indirect, objectives is to enhance the church's visibility and social relevance within its own community. This social emphasis on local development also comes with economic and political implications.

Furthermore, during this phase of Revival churches their organizational structures, often non-existent or not clearly defined, were contested, resulting in leadership conflicts. Foremost, intense crises, motivated by the race for leadership positions, emerged within this particular phase. In other words, one faced a kind of a cleaning-up period, as a consequence of the disappointments of potential candidates for certain key positions. While few decided to endure the situation, many chose to leave the organization, to create their own church and thus establish a circle of splitting churches following the same pattern.

Three Kinds of Grassroots Pastoral Approaches: *Communautés* Ecclésiales *Vivantes de Base, Upendo* and Cell Groups

The end of the Second World War, coupled with a series of decolonization of many African colonies, marked a new era in international relations and the nature of relationships among religious actors. Since missionaries and colonizers worked in close collaboration, particularly Belgian colonists who operated according to their three pillars "State-Church-Capital", their works were mutually impacted. On the one hand, the power and authority held by colonial states (Belgian authorities in the Congo) had to be transferred to *indigènes* (indigenous) elites, who (for the majority) did not have the required skills and either lacked appropriate training and expertise or were limited in number to take on the kinds of responsibilities now being faced (Ngomo Okitembo 1998, 26). On the other hand, foreign missions had to hand over the leadership of ecclesial activities to the available local priests and laypeople.

Aware of the Congolese nationalist movements threatening the colonial order, foreign missions, chiefly Catholics and Protestants, operating in the Congo were already anticipating a transitional period, which was not only perceived as political, but spiritual as well, to a post-colonial era in at least three ways. First, the Catholic Church and its missionaries sought to distance themselves from Belgian authorities because they did not want to be accused of collaborating with colonizers or of competing with colonizers and other actors in the colony. In *Politics in the Congo,* the American political scientist Crawford Young wrote about the Catholic Church's sentiment:

> The Vatican was well aware of the dangers for the permanence of Christian communities in Africa if they remained identified with a moribund colonial system. The Church was rethinking its future, not only adapting its alliance with the colonial regime but accelerating the Africanization of its personnel and liturgy. And those in touch with the seminaries in the Congo knew that national sentiment was strong among the African clergy. (1994, 9, 139)

Indeed, as Young postulates, the church and missions in general were in a dilemma related to their close relationships with Belgian authorities in the Congo and, alternatively, to the pursuit of the Christian faith with natives. This process was elsewhere referred to as the indigenization of Christianity. The second strategy missionaries used was to carefully choose among local elites, predominantly graduates from Catholic seminaries (the so-called évolués) for key political positions. Both colonists and missionaries could rely on this first group of Congolese intellectuals to carry out their activities and at the same time serve their interests. The third way missionaries prepared themselves ahead of the political and religious shifting of power included the coalescence of different foreign religious groups despite their doctrinal differences and conflicts.

Following the independence of the Congo (1960), Catholic bishops operating in the former *État Indépendant du Congo* (Congo Independent State) gathered at the sixth (6th) *Assemblée Plénière* (plenary assembly) in Leopoldville for at least three reasons. First, Congolese socio-political turmoil that stemmed from both independence and anticlerical movements preoccupied the Catholic leadership mostly and the foreign missionaries in general. As a result, significant concerns arose in respect to the Catholic Church's status and its future prospects in the country. This preoccupation led them to assess their missionary work and influence in the Congo. Second, the 6th plenary assembly sought to emphasize the church's works with respect to laypeople, who viewed themselves (even today in 2017) as marginalized and ignored in ecclesial matters. The third reason for the 6th *Assemblée plénière* was to develop new ways of reaching out to local Congolese communities. The Congolese bishops at this meeting strongly encouraged making local grassroots communities a priority. In other words, the aim of the new pastoral approach was to establish "local Christian communities" who would uphold their faith's values in their respective communities in their day-to-day life (Église Catholique du Congo Belge 1961; Ugeux 1987; Ugeux 1988). In addition, this pastoral approach aimed to create more united and cohesive communities (*Koinonia,* communion) including the relationships between the church's hierarchy and laity (Église Catholique du Congo Belge 1961, 70–71, 163; Mugaruka 2008). Some other decisions of the 6th plenary assembly related to these new *communautés chrétiennes vivantes* (Living Christian Communities, CCV) included *l'abandon de la pastorale d'institution* (the abandonment of an institution-orientated pastoral care) for a more *pastorale de présence* (pastoral of proximity) and, alternatively, "the strengthening of apostolic efforts" in the CCV (preaching, liturgy, laity training and charity) (Église Catholique du Congo Belge 1961, 133).

Participants[39] in the 6th *Assemblée Plénière* included one of the first African bishops and the only Congolese ordinary bishop from the Kivu ecclesiastic province,[40] namely Joseph Mikararanga Busimba (from Goma's diocese). In Bishop Busimba's diocese, the first *communautés* ècclésiales *vivantes de base* (CEVB)[41] took off fairly quickly in the mid-70s with the arrival of the new bishop, Faustin Ngabu, who replaced Monseignor Busimba (Kaboy 1986; Tuungane 2013; Ugeux 1987, 282). Like other Catholic dioceses in the country, the pastoral image of Goma's Church was characterized by the same focus of its hierarchy, namely, the apostolate of laypeople in the CEVs (Kaboy 1986). The diocese of Goma articulated its CEVs' activities in three main corporate ecclesiastic areas, including (1) praying together, (2) evangelizing together and (3) working together (Kaboy

1986, 59–67). However, the pastoral orientation of the hierarchy did not always equate to what happened in the field.

The term "CEV" holds a different meaning for Goma's Catholic district than for other Catholic districts in other Congolese ecclesiastic provinces. For instance, many leaders in Goma pointed out that the so-called *quartiers* should actually be identified as CEVs. Both *quartiers* and CEVs are meeting places of Catholic parishioners, with two primary differences being that priests usually administer the Eucharist once per week in the former and believers gather twice in the latter. To put it differently, there is another layer between the parish and the CEV, which is a *quartier*. While leaders of the Goma Catholic Church officially launched the pastoral option of *communautés* écclésiales *vivantes* in the early 1970s, local members lacked clear direction about its definition and functions. One leader (a *Mutumishi*, leader of a CEVB), I call *Mutumishi* André, lamented the lack of a pastoral ministry for CEVBs as follows:

> There is no pastoral dedicated to CEVB. They [hierarchy] told us to put them in place [build][42] exclusively for prayers, turning rosaries—that's it. Besides turning rosaries, one is not permitted to talk about any other thing. Believers know that they have to build their own *Shirikas* (CEVBs), a little house of prayer. They meet there for that purpose. If a priest happens to be there, he does his liturgy. CEVB here are solely a place of prayer.

Early priests in the district testified that *Mutumishi* André further helped in establishing the first *Shirika*, but not according to the number of families (less than 50), as Bishop Faustin Ngabu suggested in his unpublished book (which I was able to access) in Kiswahili *Shirika za waKristu.* Instead, believers met according to the breakdown of sectors and streets (*Mutumishi* André 2013). In his pastoral letter "*Les communautés de base,*" Bishop Ngabu argued that "members of these families know each other, they can support each other, correct, live and work together in the plan of God" (cited in Ugeux 1987, 253). Similarly, one of the Xaverians' fathers, Zampese Franceso, later introduced a new program, which included masses. Therefore, Father Zampese organized the first weekly masses (including the Eucharist) where believers from different streets would meet (the aforementioned quartiers and also known as chapels) (*Mutumishi* André 2013). However, after Father Zampese Francesco's departure, further noted *Mutumishi* André noted that the CEVs' programs, particularly masses, had been lagging behind. For him, what would have been left out were the "*comités*"[43] (committees) or "*conseils de communautés*" (community councils) as Bernard Ugeux (1987, 328) called them, which mainly constituted a president, secretary and treasurer who managed to carry out the activities in both the CEVBs and *quartiers.*[44]

The Catholic Church was not the only religious organization to be affected by the Congolese socio-political instabilities of the 1960s and 1970s. The creation and emphasis of churches in local communities of the *3ème* CBCA and *Arche* materialized more precisely and respectively in the mid-1970s and late 1990s. The question that may arise is: "did these local communities generally exist in Protestant and Revival churches and particularly in *3ème* CBCA and *Arche?*" *3ème* CBCA local meetings were more similar to those of Catholics than *Arche* for a number of reasons. First, *3ème* CBCA and Catholic churches in the Congo share almost the same colonial and postcolonial histories. As religious institutions, they both participated in the transfer of missionary leadership to local ones, albeit violently in the case of the *3ème* CBCA. Second, one may equate the Catholic *quartiers* with *3ème* CBCA's *Kijiji* (chapel). Like *quartiers*, *3ème* CBCA parishioners meet once a week (usually on a Saturday) for an hour-long mass.

Third, unlike *Arche* and many Revival churches, where cell groups grew to become churches, the creation of what is either called *Upendo*s ("love" in English) or "cells" is the prerogative of *3ème* CBCA church leaders' initiatives. These *Upendos* can be likened to both Goma's *Arche*'s cell groups and the Catholic Church's CEVBs. One of the main differences that distinguished many *Upendos* from both Catholic CEVBs and *Arche de l'Alliance*'s cell groups was the meeting frequency: *Upendos* members meet early every morning except Saturdays for *Kijijis*. Programs in *Upendos* and *Arche de l'Alliance*'s cell groups are comparable in that worship, prayers and Bible readings are central. In the three local communities—CEVBs, *Upendos* and cell groups—many adherents have shared with me the importance and the value of their respective meetings. These meetings, according to many, strengthen their bonds of togetherness and a sense of solidarity, which they rarely experience in larger groups. In fact, I have even met some local members who attend two local communities (i.e., CEVBs and cell groups).

Conclusion

Initially, this chapter presented the context of the emergence of Goma as an important city bordering the Rwandan city of Gisenyi. In the first section, I attempted to position the socio-political and economic context of the research site. The city of Goma is variously ascribed as it is bestowed with both positive and negative meanings, such as "blessed" or "cursed" city. Following this first section, to understand the emergence of Christian communities in Goma in order to situate the three selected Churches for the case studies, I addressed the earlier history of encounters between Western missionaries and the Congolese, with regards to individuals and cultural interactions. The first encounters between colonists and missionaries and local populations occurred during two different evangelization periods, which lasted approximately five (5) centuries. Up until the Berlin Conference in 1885, when King Leopold II was given full and exclusive control over the Congolese territory where he personally ruled for more than two decades (1885–1908), fierce competition over the control of Congo's basin dominated Western powers' relationships. European missionaries, essentially of the Catholic tradition, advanced from both King Leopold II and the État Independent du Congo era. The second and third sections of this chapter thus focused specifically on issues related to the interrelationships between the state and the Catholic and Protestant churches in the Congo in general and particularly in Goma.

The final four sections of this chapter related to different contexts of the emergence of Goma's *3ème* CBCA and *Arche* Churches. While the first stemmed primarily from internal conflicts between members of the Baptist community in the Kivu province, the second emerged amidst the mid-1990s' contentious socio-political context. It was similarly in the same period that the city of Goma overflowed with an unprecedented number of Rwandan refugees, following 1994's genocide. Lastly, I addressed three local forms of churches rooted at the grassroots level, from three Christian traditions, namely the Catholic Church with their CEVBs, the *3ème* CBCA Church with *Upendos* and Revival churches with cell groups.

Endnotes

1. The name *Kivu* derives from the Hunde language *Kipfu* (Bipfu in the plural form), meaning "great cloud of lake." Four lakes surround the region: Albert and Édouard in the north; and Kivu and Tanganyika in the south.
2. A Wikipedia page, from which I was inspired, offers an interesting view of the different configurations of the Congo provinces since the colonial period. See https://en.wikipedia.org/wiki/Provinces_of_the_Democratic_Republic_of_the_Congo (last accessed in April 2019).
3. Some informants indicated to me that these tensions and competitiveness did not only happen in the Kivu province, it also occurred in other provinces (e.g., Kasaï) affected by the provincial subdivisions. While provinces that were already developed benefitted from the new configuration, other members of new provinces felt disadvantaged by their new territories. In addition, I was also told that inhabitants of provinces which had leaders in politics could have their voices heard when subdivisions

occurred. The ethnic character of the provincial subdivisions was often emphasized. Some even argued that President Mobutu decided his appointment of governors to counter ethnic influence in provincial administrations. As of January 1966, President Mobutu decided that governors were no longer elected by their constituencies, but they would be appointed and act as *commis de l'état* (state clerks). See for further details Kadari Mwene-Kabyana, "La politique étrangère du Zaïre (1965–1985): Illusion de puissance et clientelisme," Ph.D. Dissertation, Université Laval, 1999, 170–172.

4. See http://www.provincenordkivu.cd (last accessed in April 2019).
5. Despite the fact that some authors use the names *Kongo* (with a *k*) and *Congo* (with a *c*) interchangeably, their distinction needs to be highlighted here, mainly because of their attribution to different territories. The first, Kongo, refers to a kingdom that existed at least between the fourteenth and the sixteenth centuries within a geographic area that included the second (Congo). Many have indicated that the Kingdom of Kongo was established earlier than the fourteenth century. Even though its precise spatial configuration remains uncertain and contemporary notions of boundaries are different compared to then, some historians have argued that this kingdom's territory reached as far as modern-day northern Angola, the southern Congo Republic (Congo-Brazzaville) and the southwest of the Democratic Republic of Congo. For instance, regarding the issue of boundaries, the Congolese historian Isidore Ndaywel è Nziem claims that the notion of boundaries was inexistent and irrelevant because kings ruled over people and not over specific territories. Nonetheless, the Kingdom of Kongo had a nucleus of six provinces, namely Mbamba, Soyo, Mpangu, Mbata, Nsundi and Mpemba. Ndaywel è Nziem, *Histoire générale du Congo: de l'héritage ancien à la République démocratique*, Bruxelles: Duculot: De Boeck & Larsier: Afrique-Editions, 1998.
6. Most of the Arabs I refer to in this chapter are slave traders from the Zanzibar areas.
7. The American Henry Sanford replaced Sir Bartle Frere as an executive member of the AIA, while a diplomatic position was assigned to him in South Africa.
8. For further details on the negotiations between Leopold II and the Propaganda, see Marcel Benedictus Storme, "Engagement de la Propagande pour l'organisation territoriale des Missions au Congo," in Josef Metzler (ed.), *Sacrae Congregations de Propaganda Fide Memoria Rerum, Vol. III/1, 1815-1972*, Freiburg: Herder, 1975, pp. 274-279; Maurice Willaert, *Kivu redécouvert*, Bruxelles: M. Arnold, 1973, p. 71.
9. After Alessandro Franchi, Cardinal Giovanni Simeoni served as a prefect of the Congregation for the Propaganda of Faith during his last fifteen (15) years (March 1878 to January 1892).
10. Between 1890 and 1900, no less than ten Belgian Catholic congregations joined the Congo Independent State: Jesuits in the Lower Congo and Kwango (1893), Trappists of Westmalle in Bamania (1895), the priests of the Sacred Heart in Stanleyville (1897), the Premonstratensians of Tongerloo in Buta (1898) and the Redemptorists

in Matadi (1899). To these Fathers' congregations were added the women: the sisters of the Charity of Gang (1891), the Sisters of Notre-Dame of Namur (1894), the White Sisters (1895), the Franciscans of Mary (1896), the Sisters of Precious Blood (1898) and the Sisters of Immaculate Heart (1899) Louis Ngomo Okitembo, *L'engagement politique de l'Eglise catholique au Zaïre, 1960–1992*, Paris: L'Harmattan, 1998, p. 26. The number of Catholic missionaries continued to increase and spread throughout the Congolese territory.

11. Both Leopold II and Lavigerie envisioned building "kingdoms" in Africa. For instance, the former wished, among other things, to become an heir of the Pharaohs, while the latter, as Mudimbe seemed to indicate in *Idea of Africa*, dreamt of "building a Christian Kingdom in Central Africa." See V. Y. Mudimbe, *The Idea of Africa*, Bloomington: Indiana University Press, 1994, pp. 105–106. See also, Jean-Pierre Chrétien, *L'Afrique des Grands lacs: deux mille ans d'histoire*, Paris: Aubier, 2000, pp. 174–175; Adam Hochschild, *King Leopold's Ghost: A Story of Greed, Terror, and Heroism in Colonial Africa*, Boston: Houghton Mifflin, 1998, pp. 76–80; Ruth M. Slade, *English-speaking Missions in the Congo Independent State (1878–1908)*, Bruxelles: Academie Royale des Sciences Coloniales, 1959, p. 59.
12. The young abbot's name was suggested to occupy a vacant position at the *Tribunal Apostolicum Rotae Romanae* (Apostolic Tribunal of the Roman Rota). Even though his work was not essentially that of a judge, his assignments were similar to one: as chaplains to the pope, auditors to the Rota (around a table) consider cases sovereigns and nations bring to the attention of the Holy See. One may compare it to an ecclesial supreme court. See William Fanning, "Auditor," in C. George Herbermann, et al. (eds.), *The Catholic Encyclopedia: An International Work of Reference on the Constitution, Doctrine, Discipline, and History of the Catholic Church, Vol. 2*, New York: Robert Appleton Company, 1907, pp. 70–71; Richard F. Clarke, *Cardinal Lavigerie and the African Slave Trade*, New York: Green, 1889, p. 20.
13. Author's translation from the original in French.
14. Some of the surrounding circumstances of the new congregation and which many have argued to be its premise were critical situations the country was facing, e.g. drought, famine and outbreaks of cholera and typhus. In the midst of this unprecedented crisis, the Archbishop put in place structures to assist orphans, including Muslims, who were primarily offered shelter and education. Jean-Claude Ceillier points out that this situation was the trigger of Lavigerie's several initiatives and chief missions to Africa (and later in southern territories). W. Fanning, "Auditor," pp. 70–71.
15. The Sacred Congregation *de Propagande Fide* was a Catholic department designed to propagate the Catholic faith into non-Catholic regions. While commonly known as "Propaganda," its formal title was *sacra Congregatio christiano nomini propaganda*. Although it was officially founded in 1622, under Pope Gregory XV (February 9, 1621—July 16, 1623), the project progressively evolved over a period of time,

beginning with Pope Gregory XIII (May 13, 1572—April 10, 1582). The latter established an initial commission consisting of three cardinals (Caraffa, Medici and Santorio). After his death, seven of his successors were Sixtus V (April 24, 1585—August 27,1590), Urban VII (15–27, September 1590), Gregory XIV (December 5, 1590–October 16, 1591), Innocent IX (October 29–December 30, 1591), Clement VIII (February 2, 1592–March 3, 1605), Leo XI (April 1–27, 1605) and Paul V (May 16, 1605–January 28, 1621). Upon the release of bull "Inscrutabili Divinae," on 22 June 1622, the Propaganda was instituted conducted by seventeen members: thirteen (13) cardinals, two (2) prelates, one (1) secretary and one (1) consultor. See Jean-Claude Ceillier, *Histoire des missionnaires d'Afrique (Pères blancs): de la fondation par Mgr Lavigerie à la mort du fondateur, 1868–1892*, Paris: Karthala, 2008, p. 34; Umberto Benigni, "Propaganda," in C. George Herbermann, et al. (eds.), *The Catholic Encyclopedia: An International Work of Reference on the Constitution, Doctrine, Discipline, and History of the Catholic Church, Vol. 12*, New York: Robert Appleton Company, 1907, pp. 456–461.

16. Marcel Storme reproduced the complete report in his book *Rapports du Père Planque, de Mgr. Lavigerie et de Mgr. Comboni sur l'Association internationale africaine*, Bruxelles: 1957, pp. 75-137. Dated of 2 January 1878, Lavigerie's *Mémoire secrète* is a fifty-five (55) page document, which constitutes the longest of all reports the Propaganda ever received following Cardinal Franchi's request to the heads of congregations working in Africa. Cardinal Lavigerie, observed Paul Gantly, had a difficult relationship with Father Auguste Planque, successor of Bishop Melchior de Marion Brésillac (founder of the *Société des Missions Africaines*). See Patrick Gantly, *Histoire de la Société des missions africaines (SMA), 1856-1907 (Tome 1): De la fondation par Mgr de Marion Brésillac (1856), à la mort du père Planque (1907)*, Paris: Karthala, 2009.
17. Although the Propaganda entrusted, in September 1865, the evangelization of the western region of Central Africa to Father Prosper-Philippe Augouard's Holy Ghost congregation, it was only 15 years later that they established themselves in Boma and began to expand their mission in the area.
18. Local inhabitants not only opposed the first two missionaries, but the weather conditions were another constraint against them. Consequently, they decided to delay their Congolese penetration while sending a friendly letter to the *Manicongo*, the king of Kongo, Pedro V.
19. In 1910, the American Baptist Foreign Mission Society (ABFMS)—a missionary section of the society Northern Baptist Convention (NBC)—replaced the ABMU. Due to dissensions between the NBC's leaders, another missionary society, the Conservative Baptist Foreign Mission Society (CBFMS), emerged. The dissensions were basically twofold, on the one hand, some NBC members were bothered about their conservative doctrines being threatened by "libertarian" views; on the other hand, they felt that their political power was shifting toward their so-called "less conservative" colleagues. The creation of the CBFMS, as a new missionary society,

posed legal and practical questions. For instance, the CBFMS encountered great opposition when it sought to acquire the NBC capitals such as the ABFMS' assets. See Jack Edward Nelson, *Christian Missionizing and Social Transformation: A History of Conflict and Change in Eastern Zaïre*, New York: Praeger, 1992, p. 50; Philippe B. Kabongo-Mbaya, *L'Eglise du Christ au Zaïre: formation et adaptation d'un protestantisme en situation de dictature*, Paris: Karthala, 1992, p. 12.

20. Contrary to Catholic missionaries who had already been beneficiaries of state educational subsidies since the 1906 concordat with the Vatican, Protestants received their approval to such subsidies only after the Second World War. Even though they revised their view about the subsidies they once refused, they still encountered difficulties to be granted them. While the subsidies were not singularly financial, Belgian authorities attached conditions that aimed to support their desire to see Belgian religious actors replace foreign missionaries, chiefly Protestants. Some of the benefits from the Belgian administration included, for example, perpetual hectares of lands, while Belgian Catholic missionaries were to operate under the state jurisdiction and provide the state with their Congolese field research findings (e.g., geographical, ethnographical and linguistic studies). See Isidore Ndaywel è Nziem, *Nouvelle histoire du Congo: Des origines à la République Démocratique*, Kinshasa: Afrique éditions, 2008, p. 325; Marvin D. Markowitz, *Cross and Sword: The Political Role of Christian Missions in the Belgian Congo, 1908–1960*, Stanford, California: Hoover Institution Press, 1973, p. 7; Église Catholique du Congo Belge, *Actes de la VIe Assemblée plénière de l'Épiscopat du Congo (Léopoldville 20 novembre – 2 decembre 1961)*, Léopoldville, Congo: Secrétariat génèral de l'Épiscopat, 1961, pp. 29–34.
21. The state was one of the main providers of jobs in the Belgian Congo, establishing at the same time a new category of professionals, later known as the évolués (evolved), among which the Congolese Protestants in general sought in vein to become members. See J. E. Nelson, *Christian Missionizing and Social Transformation: A History of Conflict and Change in Eastern Zaïre*, pp. 69–76.
22. Even today (2017) the state's authorization, referred to as a *personnalité civile* (civil personality) is mandatory for any non-profit organization who were including churches, in order to legally operate in the Congo.
23. Unlike Catholic missionaries who were directly accountable to the Holy See, each Protestant mission operated under its sole hierarchical structure (missionary society). Eight of the Protestant societies working in the Congo decided, in 1902, to put in place an organizational body called the *Conférence générale des œuvres missionnaires protestantes* [General Conference of Protestant Missionaries]. Nine years later, in 1911, the organization was replaced with the *Conseil Protestant au Congo*. See Rudolf Heinrichs-Drinhaus, "L'influence de l'Eglise protestante: Aspects matériel et immateriél," in Manfred Schulz (ed.), *Les porteurs du développement durable en R.D.Congo: Évolutions récentes de la vie politique, économique, religieuse, culturelle et de la societé civile*, Kinshasa; Berlin: Cepas; Spektrum, 2010.

24. For further details, the book of the Congolese Protestant Pastor Philippe Kabongo-Mbaya documents key historical moments of the ECZ/ECC. See P. B. Kabongo-Mbaya, *L'Eglise du Christ au Zaïre: Formation et adaptation d'un protestantisme en situation de dictature*. Regarding the same subject, see also: R. Heinrichs-Drinhaus, "L'influence de l'Eglise protestante: Aspects matériel et immateriél."; Thomas Munayi Muntu-Monji, "Le rôle de l'Eglise protestante au cours des cinquante années d'independance 1960–2010," in Faustin-Jovite Mapwar Bashuth (ed.), *Eglise et Societé: Le discours socio-politique des éveques de la Conference epicospale nationale du Congo (CENCO)*, Kinshasa: Facultés catholiques de Kinshasa, 2007; Mambu-Lo Tsudi wa Kibuti, "L'Église du Christ au Congo (ECC) et son attitude face à la politique (1970–1997)," Diplôme d'études supérieures (D.E.S) en Sciences Historiques, Université de Kinshasa, 2003; Gaston Nkasa Yumba, "L'apport de l'Eglise Protestante au développement économique et social du Congo," in Centre de recherchers interdisciplinaires et de Publications Université Protestante au Congo (ed.), *L'Eglise dans la societé Congolaise: Hier, Aujourd'hui et Demain (Actes des journées scientifiques interfacultaires du 25 au 28 avril 2001)*, Kinshasa: Editions de l'Université Protestante au Congo (EDUPC), 2001.
25. Personal interview with "Atcha Shali," *3ème* CBCA Participant 2, Goma, 2013.
26. Personal interview with "Mamie," Arche Participant 1, Goma, 2013 (author's translation).
27. Inspired by the American Watch Tower, commonly known from 1934 onwards as Jehovah's Witnesses, the *Kitawala* movement spread mainly into Eastern Congo (first in the Katanga province) in 1923 from southern African countries (South Africa and both southern and northern Rhodesia). In a context of colonization, Kitawalists, who's religious "movement" had political repercussions, believed in the divine restorations of equality, chiefly between white colonists and black indigenous peoples, as well as their material riches. Consequently, the colonial state systematically repressed the religious group. On the one hand, it was banned in the Belgian Congo; on the other hand, any recalcitrant was relegated/deported, in accordance with the 5 July 1910 decree, in rural centres like Ekafera (Equator province), Belingo (Leopoldville province), Kasaji (Katanga) and Lubutu (Oriental province). The decree stipulates, "all indigenous disturbing the public quietness can be compelled, through a General Vice-governor's ordinance, to be removed from a location or be relocated to a determined place" Article 1 of the decree of "Droit de residence sur les territoires du Congo belge" quoted in Susan Asch, *L'Église du prophète Kimbangu: de ses origines à son rôle actuel au Zaïre, (1921–1981)*, Paris: Éditions Karthala, 1983, p. 18n16. See also Ndaywel è Nziem, *Nouvelle histoire du Congo: Des origines à la République Démocratique*, pp. 383–384; Michael G. Schatzberg, *The Dialectics of Oppression in Zaire*, Bloomington: Indiana University Press, 1988, pp. 125–132.
28. Born in the late seventeenth century, Kimpa Vita Nsimba, also known by her baptismal name, Dona Béatrice, claimed to be possessed by the spirit of a well-respected

Capuchin monk, Saint Antony, who appeared to her and took over her entire life, to henceforth restore the unity and pride of the Kongo Kingdom. Her preaching and teaching focused on God's judgment and, in several ways, targeted the Catholic Church. For instance, she challenged the Western portrait of Christianity that European missionaries brought to Africa and that was disconnected from Africans' realities; thus, her promotion for a black Christ, who is not only interested in Africans' issues, but can understand them and intervene for their sakes. For Kimpa Vita, the physical image of Christ (white or black) equated with the proximity to either white or blacks' problems. She allowed certain symbols of the Christian faith to encroach into her own environment, paralleling for example Bethlehem to San Salvador, Nazareth to Nsundi, or the Holy land to Kongo. The birth of her child, who she asserted to have been conceived by the Holy Spirit like Jesus Christ, culminated, with the approval of King Pedro IV under the strong influence of Capuchin missionaries, in her death sentence in 1706. Arrested in Bas-Kongo, Dona Béatrice was sent to Luanda in Angola where she was burnt alive holding her child. She died, as reported, with "the name of Jesus in her mouth." For further details and from which this section on both the Antonian and Kimbanguist movements came from: S. Asch, *L'Église du prophète Kimbangu: de ses origines à son rôle actuel au Zaïre, (1921–1981)*; Marie-Louise Martin, *Kimbangu: An African Prophet and his Church*, Great Britain: Basil Blackwell, 1975; Georges Balandier, *La vie quotidienne au royaume de Kongo du XVIe au XVIIIe siècle*, Paris: Hachette, 1965, pp. 261–268.

29. The birth date of Kimbangu is either indicated as either 1887 or 1889.
30. Kimbangu, now called *Ngouza* ("healer"), attracted on a daily basis as many as 5,000 Congolese from Bas-Congo and its surroundings who came from several sectors of activity and society (e.g., administration, religious organizations and the army). These people were either seeking answers to their predicaments or thronging for curiosity. The colonial state imposed measures that aimed to control and refrain migratory influx toward Nkamba. For instance, Congolese were required a state's authorization to change locations. S. Asch, *L'Église du prophète Kimbangu: de ses origines à son rôle actuel au Zaïre, (1921–1981)*, p. 22.
31. In 1965, Jacques André Vernaud (1930–2011), a Swiss evangelist who was posted in Congo-Brazzaville at the time, decided to establish his ministry in Congo-Leopoldville (Kinshasa) where he later initiated a network of Pentecostal churches and thus created, that same year, the 37th *Communauté des Assemblées de Dieu du Congo* (Community of the Assembly of God in Congo, CADC) to which Arche/Goma belongs, among other Pentecostal churches. Vernaud played a key role in the expansion of this new movement both in Kinshasa and in the countries' provinces. For example, four years later, in 1969, the 37th CADC organized in Kinshasa the first evangelistic crusade featuring the American Pentecostal evangelist Tommy Lee Osborn. Thousands of Congolese gathered and many of them became members of Pentecostal churches. This event enhanced the visibility of both Pentecostalism and CADC in the country.

See Kalombo Sebastien Kapuku, "La pentecôtisation du protestantisme à Kinshasa," *Afrique contemporaine* 4, (2014).

32. Personal interview with Israel Loyela N'sembe, Kinshasa, 2013.
33. *Ibid.;* Personal interview with Estone Vutwire Kasereka, Goma, 2013.
34. E. V. Kasereka.
35. *Ibid.*
36. Many, of course, argue that the issue is instead elsewhere, i.e. both financial ethics and literacy.
37. In the example of *Arche*/Goma, they spent more than twelve months in prayer and fasting in the early days in cell groups before the erection of the church. E. V. Kasereka.
38. Personal interview with Estone Vutwire Kasereka, Goma, 2013 (author's translation).
39. Among the 37 Catholic bishops operating in the Congo, only 4 were Congolese, while all 21 General Vicars were from the Congo. Marco Moerschbacher, *Les laïcs dans une Église d'Afrique: l'œuvre du cardinal Malula (1917–1989)*, Paris: Éditions Karthala, 2012.
40. The other four representatives of the ecclesiastic province of Kivu included, respectively, three ordinary bishops from Bukavu, Beni and Kasongo: (1) Monsignor L. Van Steene, (2) Monsignor Henri Piérard, (3) Monsignor Rich Cleire and (4) the apostolic administrator Danilo Cattarzi of Uvira. See Église Catholique du Congo Belge, *Actes de la VIe Assemblée plénière de l'*Épiscopat du Congo (Léopoldville 20 novembre *–2 decembre 1961).*
41. Other terms that mean the same thing are *communautés chrétiennes de base* (Base Christian Communities, CCB), *communautés chrétiennes vivantes* (Living Christian Communities, CCV) and *communautés ecclésiales vivantes* (Base Living Christian Communities, CEV).
42. See also Bernard Ugeux, "La pastorale des petites communautés chrétiennes dans quelques diocèses du Zaïre," Ph.D. Thesis, Institut Catholique de Paris, 1987, 348.
43. Although CEVB participants are mainly women, their committees are paradoxically dominated by men. On a few occasions, a woman may take the place of either a treasurer or a secretary. Except for the parish's involvement, who may impose his candidate in the position of a president, committees are generally elected.
44. Besides morning prayers in the *Shirika,* some do read the so-called "Ordo" where daily biblical scriptures are already indicated according to dates. Issues related to conflicts and peace are labelled as "politics" and therefore a taboo topic. In fact, *Mutumishi* André observed that CEVBs should be a place where peace and reconciliation emerge, but unfortunately conflict and suspicions are often nurtured there. Cf. Personal interview with "*Mutumishi* André," Catholic Participant 7, Goma, 2013.

    Another participant, a grassroots member, disagreed on another note, which concerned financial contributions (*quêtes*). For instance, he did not understand the reason why "Kinshasa" (capital of the Democratic Republic of Congo) should ask each CEVB in the country to contribute USD 10 for an assessment of its fiftieth anniversary.

Bibliography

Achebe, Chinua. *Hopes and Impediments: Selected Essays*. New York: Anchor Books, 1990.

Alfani, Roger Bantea. "Religion et transformation des conflits: le rôle des Églises à Goma en RD Congo (1990-2010). " In Dieng Moda (ed.), *Evolution politique en Afrique: Entre autoritarisme, démocratisation, construction de la paix et défis internes*. Louvain-la-Neuve, Belgique: Academia-L'Harmattan, 2015.

Anderson, Allan. *An Introduction to Pentecostalism: Global Charismatic Christianity*. New York, NY: Cambridge University Press, 2004.

Asch, Susan. *L'Église du prophète Kimbangu: de ses origines à son rôle actuel au Zaïre, (1921–1981)*. Paris: Éditions Karthala, 1983.

Balandier, Georges. *La vie quotidienne au royaume de Kongo du XVIe au XVIIIe siècle*. Paris: Hachette, 1965.

Batende, Mwene. "Les sectes: un signe des temps?, Essai d'une lecture sociologique des «religions nouvelles» issues du christianisme." *Cahiers des religions Africaines* 27–28, no. 53–56 (1993–1994): 25–43.

Beckford, A. James. "Introduction." In A. James Beckford (ed.), *New Religious Movements and Rapid Social Change*. Beverly Hills, California: Sage, 1986.

Benigni, Umberto. "Propaganda." In C. George Herbermann, A. Page Page, J. Thomas Shahan, Condé Pallen and J. John Wynne (eds.), *The Catholic Encyclopedia: An International Work of Reference on the Constitution, Doctrine, Discipline, and History of the Catholic Church, Vol. 12*. New York: Robert Appleton Company, 1907.

Bontinck, François. *Aux origines de l'*État Indépendant du Congo: documents tirés d*'archives américaines*. Louvain: Nauwelaerts, 1966.

Braekman, E. M. *Guy de Brès*. Bruxelles,: Librairie des Eclaireurs Unionistes, 1960.

———. *Histoire du protestantisme au Congo*. Bruxelles: Librairie des éclaireurs unionistes, 1961.

Ceillier, Jean-Claude. *Histoire des missionnaires d'Afrique (Pères blancs): De la fondation par Mgr Lavigerie à la mort du fondateur, 1868–1892*. Paris: Karthala, 2008.

Chrétien, Jean-Pierre. *L'Afrique des Grands lacs: deux mille ans d'histoire*. Paris: Aubier, 2000.

Clarke, Richard F. *Cardinal Lavigerie and the African Slave Trade*. New York, NY: Green, 1889.

Comby, Jean. *Deux mille ans d'*évangélisation histoire de l*'expansion chrétienne*. Paris: Desclée et Bégédis, 1992.

Conseil Pontifical. Justice et Paix. *Compendium de la doctrine sociale de l'Église*. Città del Vaticano: Libreria Editrice Vaticana, 2004.

Cox, Harvey. *Fire from Heaven: The Rise of Pentecostal Spirituality and the Reshaping of Religion in the Twenty-first Century*. Reading, MA: Addison-Wesley, 1995.

Église Catholique du Congo Belge. *Actes de la VIe Assemblée plénière de l'Épiscopat du Congo (Léopoldville 20 novembre–2 decembre 1961)*. Léopoldville, Congo: Secrétariat génèral du l'Épiscopat, 1961.

Eglise du Christ au Zaire. "Règlement d'ordre Intérieur de la Commission Justice, Paix et Sauvegarde de la Création (JPSC)," 1994.

Fanning, William, "Auditor." In C. George Herbermann, A. Page Page, J. Thomas Shahan, Condé Pallen, and J. John Wynne (eds.), *The Catholic Encyclopedia: An International Work of Reference on the Constitution, Doctrine, Discipline, and History of the Catholic Church, Vol. 2*. New York: Robert Appleton Company, 1907.

Freund, Bill. *The African City: A History*. New York: Cambridge University Press, 2007.

Gytambo Kibisari, Jean Willy. "La proliferation des églises de reveil à Kinshasa: interpellation de l'ECC et de l'état Congolais," Mémoire (Licence), Université Protestante au Congo, 2007.

Heinrichs-Drinhaus, Rudolf. "L'influence de l'Eglise protestante: Aspects matériel et immateriél." In Manfred Schulz (ed.), *Les porteurs du développement durable en R.D.Congo: Évolutions récentes de la vie politique, économique, religieuse, culturelle et de la societé civile*. Kinshasa; Berlin: Cepas; Spektrum, 2010.

Hermet, Guy. "Les fonctions politiques des organisations religieuses dans les régimes à pluralisme limité." *Revue française de science politique* 23, no. 3 (1973): 439–472.

Hochschild, Adam. *King Leopold's Ghost: A Story of Greed, Terror, and Heroism in Colonial Africa*. Boston: Houghton Mifflin, 1998.

Irvine, Cecilia. "The Birth of the Kimbanguist Movement in the Bas-Zaire, 1921." *Journal of Religion in Africa* 6 (1974): 23–76.

Kabongo-Mbaya, Philippe B. *L'Eglise du Christ au Zaïre: Formation et adaptation d'un protestantisme en situation de dictature*. Paris: Karthala, 1992.

Kaboy, Theophile Ruboneka. *Le diocèse de Goma: Un aperçu historique de ses origines et de son développement (1911–1985)*. Goma: Construire ensemble, 1986.

Kapuku, Kalombo Sebastien. "La pentecôtisation du protestantisme à Kinshasa." *Afrique contemporaine* 4, no. 252 (2014): 51–71.

Keith, Arthur Berriedale. *The Belgian Congo and the Berlin Act*. Oxford: Clarendon Press, 1919.

Kisangani, Emizet F. *Civil Wars in the Democratic Republic of Congo, 1960–2010*. Boulder: Lynne Rienner, 2012.

Kitumaini, Jean-Marie Vianney. *Nouveaux enjeux de l'agir socio-politique de l'Église face aux défis de la société en Afrique: Application* à *l'Archidiocèse de Bukavu (RDC) à travers ses magistères successifs: en marge du premier centenaire de l'*évangélisation de *l'Archidiocèse de Bukavu, 1906–2006*. Paris: Harmattan, 2011.

Lagergren, David. *Mission and State in the Congo: A study of the Relations between Protestant Missions and the Congo Independent State Authorities with Special Reference to the Equator district, 1885–1903*. Lund: Gleerup, 1970.

M'Bokolo, Elikia. *Des missionnaires aux explorateurs: les Européens en Afrique*. Paris: ABC, 1977.

Markowitz, Marvin D. *Cross and Sword: The Political Role of Christian Missions in the Belgian Congo, 1908–1960*. Stanford, CA: Hoover Institution Press, 1973.

Martin, Marie-Louise. *Kimbangu: An African Prophet and his Church*. Great Britain: Basil Blackwell, 1975.

Matangila, Alexis. "Pour une analyse du discours des Eglises de réveil à Kinshasa: Méthode et contexte." *Civilisations* 54, no. 1/2 (2006): 77–84.

Maurel, Auguste. *Le Congo de la colonisation belge à l'indépendance*. Paris: L'Harmattan, 1992.

McDonnell, Kilian. *Charismatic Renewal and the Churches*. New York: Seabury Press, 1976.

Mongo, Nomanyath Manyath Mwan-Awan-A, David. "Les églises de réveil dans l'histoire des réligions en République démocratique du Congo: questions de dialogue œcuménique et interreligieux." Doctorat, Université Lille III—Charles de Gaulle, 2005.

Mpisi, Jean. *Kivu, RDC: La paix à tout prix !: La Conférence de Goma (6–23 janvier 2008)*. Harmattan, 2008.

Mudimbe, V. Y. *The Idea of Africa*. Bloomington: Indiana University Press, 1994.

———. *L'odeur du père: essai sur des limites de la science et de la vie en Afrique noire*. Paris: Présence africaine, 1982.

Mudimbe, V. Y., and Mbula Susan Kilonzo. "Philosophy of Religion on African Ways of Believing." In Elias Kifon Bongmba (ed.), *The Wiley-Blackwell Companion to African Religions*. Malden, MA: Wiley-Blackwell, 2012.

Mugaruka, Richard. "L'experience des communautés écclesiales de base et les défis de l'après guerre dans l'est de la R.d. Congo." *L'Église catholique et l'éducation civique dans les communautés écclesiales vivantes de base, à l'aube du IIè synode sur l'afrique (du 21 au 25 avril 2008)*, Faculté Catholique de Kinshasa: 2008.

Munayi Muntu-Monji, Thomas. "Le rôle de l'Eglise protestante au cours des cinquante années d'independance 1960-2010," In Faustin-Jovite Mapwar Bashuth (ed.), *Eglise et Societé: Le discours socio-politique des éveques de la Conference epicospale nationale du Congo (CENCO)*. Kinshasa: Facultés catholiques de Kinshasa, 2007.

Mwene-Kabyana, Kadari. "La politique étrangère du Zaïre (1965–1985): Illusion de puissance et clientélisme." Ph.D. Dissertation, Université Laval, 1999.

Ndaywel è Nziem, Isidore. *Histoire générale du Congo: de l'héritage ancien à la République démocratique*. Bruxelles: Duculot: De Boeck & Larsier: Afrique-Editions, 1998.

———. *Nouvelle histoire du Congo: Des origines à la République Démocratique*. Kinshasa: Afrique éditions, 2008.

Neill, Stephen. *Colonialism and Christian Missions*. New York: McGraw-Hill, 1966.

Nelson, Jack Edward. *Christian Missionizing and Social Transformation: A History of Conflict and Change in Eastern Zaïre*. New York: Praeger, 1992.

Ngabu, Faustin. "Courage, n'ayez pas peur (Is 13:4)." *Pastoral Letter*, May 18th, 1996.

Ngomo Okitembo, Louis. *L'engagement politique de l'Eglise catholique au Zaïre, 1960–1992*. Paris: L'Harmattan, 1998.

Nkingi, Mweze Chirhulwire Dominique. "Eglise de réveil: Génese et modes opératoires." In Kinyamba Sylvain Shomba (ed.), *Les spiritualité du temps présent*. Kinshasa: Éditions M.E.S, 2012.

Nkomo, Stella M., and Hellicy Ngambi. "African Women in Leadership: Current Knowledge and a Framework for Future Studies." *International Journal of African Renaissance Studies—Multi-, Inter- and Transdisciplinarity* 4, no. 1 (2009): 49–68.

Nkunzi, Baciyunjuze Justin. *La naissance de l'*Église au Bushi: l èrе des pionniers 1906–*1908*. Rome: Gregorian University Press, 2005.

Nzongola-Ntalaja, Georges. *The Congo from Leopold to Kabila: A People's History*. London; New York: Zed Books, 2002.

———. *Faillite de la gouvernance et crise de la construction nationale au Congo-Kinshasa: une analyse des luttes pour la démocratie et la souveraineté*. Kinshasa; Montréal; Washington: ICREDES, 2015.

Oryang, John. "Can Peace Succeed in the Democratic Republic of Congo." *Peace News*, May 4, 2017 (https://www.peacenews.com/single-post/2017/05/04/Can-Peace-Succeed-in-the-Democratic-Republic-of-the-Congo).

Otite, Onigu. *Ethnic Pluralism and Ethnicity in Nigeria: With Comparative Materials*. Ibadan: Shaneson C. I., 1990.

Oyatambwe, Wamu. Église catholique et pouvoir politique au Congo-Zaire la quête démocratique. Paris: L'Harmattan, 1997.

Paffenholz, Thania. "Civil Society and Peacebuilding." In Thania Paffenholz (ed.), *Civil Society & Peacebuilding: A Critical Assessment*. Boulder: Lynne Rienner, 2010.

Pakenham, Thomas. *The Scramble for Africa: 1876–1912*. New York: Random House, 1991.

Palmer, Michael D., and Stanley M Burgess. "Introduction." In Michael D. Palmer and Stanley M. Burgess (eds.), *The Wiley-Blackwell Companion to Religion and Social Justice*. Chichester, West Sussex; Malden, MA: Wiley-Blackwell, 2012.

Paluck, Levy Elizabeth. "Methods and Ethics with Research Teams and NGOs: Comparing Experiences across the Border of Rwanda and Democratic Republic of Congo." In Chandra Lekha Sriram, John C. King, Julie A. Mertus, Olga Martin-Ortega, and Johanna Herman (eds.), *Surviving Field Research: Working in Violent and Difficult Situations*. London; New York: Routledge, 2009.

Parrinder, Edward Geoffrey. *African Traditional Religion*. (3rd ed.). London: Sheldon Press, 1974.

Paul VI. "Eucharistic Celebration at the Conclusion of the Symposium Organized by the Bishops of Africa: Homily of Paul VI." Kampala, Uganda, July 31st, 1969. https://w2.vatican.va/content/paul-vi/en/homilies/1969/documents/hf_p-vi_hom_19690731.html.

———. "Evangelii Nuntiandi." *Vatican Website*. December 8th, 1975.

———. "Populorum Progressio." *Vatican Website*. March 26, 1967.

Pourtier, Roland. "Le Kivu dans la guerre: acteurs et enjeux." *EchoGéo [online]*, 2009.

Prudhomme, Claude. "Le rôle des missions chrétiennes dans la formation des identités nationales: le point de vue catholique." In Claude Prudhomme and Jean-François Zorn (eds.), *Missions chrétiennes et formation des identités nationales hors d'Europe, XIX-XXe s*. Lyon: CREDIC, 1995.

———. *Stratégie missionnaire du Saint-Siège sous Léon XIII (1878–1903): Centralisation romaine et défis culturels*. Roma: Ecole française de Rome, 1994.

Randles, W. G. L. *L'ancien royaume du Congo des origines à la fin du XIXe siècle*. Paris: Mouton, 1968.

Renguet, Jacques. "Monseigneur Busimba et la paroisse du Chant d'oiseau." In Ntawihaye Gisamonyo Gonzalve Twose and Bucyalimwe Stanislas Mararo (eds.), *Mgr Joseph Busimba Mikararanga (1912–1974), premier prêtre et Èvêque noir du Kivu, fondateur et grand pasteur du Diocèse de Goma*. Goma, Congo (Democratic Republic): Association Les Amis de Goma, 2012.

Reybrouck, David Van. *Congo: The Epic History of a People*. London: Fourth Estate, 2014.

Reyntjens, Filip, and René Lemarchand. “Mass Murder in Eastern Congo, 1996–1997.” In René Lemarchand (eds.), *Forgotten Genocides: Oblivion, Denial, and Memory*. Philadelphia: University of Pennsylvania Press, 2011.

Roberts, Allen F. *A Dance of Assassins: Performing Early Colonial Hegemony in the Congo*. Bloomington; Indianapolis: Indiana University Press, 2013.

Roeykens, Auguste. *Les débuts de l'œuvre africaine de Léopold II*. Bruxelles: Académie royale des sciences coloniales, 1955.

Schatzberg, Michael G. *The Dialectics of Oppression in Zaire*. Bloomington: Indiana University Press, 1988.

Schreiter, Robert J. “The Catholic Social Imaginary and Peacebuilding.” In Robert J. Schreiter, R. Scott Appleby and Gerard F. Powers (eds.), *Peacebuilding: Catholic Theology, Ethics, and Praxis*. Maryknoll, NY: Orbis Books, 2010.

Schreiter, Robert J., R. Scott Appleby, and Gerard F. Powers. *Peacebuilding: Catholic Theology, Ethics, and Praxis*. Maryknoll, NY: Orbis Books, 2010.

Seay, Laura Elizabeth. “Authority at Twilight: Civil Society, Social Services, and the State in the Eastern Democratic Republic of Congo.” Ph.D. Dissertation, The University of Texas at Austin, 2009.

———. “Effective Responses: Protestants, Catholics and the Provision of Health Care in the Post-war Kivus.” *Review of African Political Economy* 40, no. 135 (2013): 83–97.

Sekanga, Freddy Bomay. “Les rôles d'un prophete: Regard sur les prophetisme des églises de reveil de Kinshasa.” Mémoire (Licence), Université Protestante au Congo, 2009.

Shorter, Aylward. *African Christian Theology: Adaptation or Incarnation?* London: G. Chapman, 1975a.

———. *Prayer in the Religious Traditions of Africa*. Nairobi: Oxford University Press, 1975b.

Slade, Ruth M. *English-speaking Missions in the Congo Independent State (1878–1908)*. Bruxelles: Academie Royale des Sciences Coloniales, 1959.

Smith, Donald Eugene. *Religion and Political Development: An Analytic Study*. Boston, MA: Little, Brown, 1970.

Smythe, Carlyle. *The Story of Belgium*. London: Hutchinson & Co., 1900.

Springs, Jason A. “Structural and Cultural Violence in Religion and Peacebuilding.” In Atalia Omer, R. Scott Appleby and David Little (eds.), *The Oxford Handbook of Religion, Conflict, and Peacebuilding*. New York, NY: Oxford University Press, 2015.

Stauffacher, Gladys. *Faster Beats the Drum*. Pearl River, NY: Africa Inland Mission, 1977.

Stenger, Friedrich. *White Fathers in Colonial Central Africa: A Critical Examination of V.Y. Mudimbe's Theories on Missionary Discourse in Africa*. Münster: Lit, 2001.

Storme, Marcel Benedictus. “Engagement de la Propagande pour l'organisation territoriale des Missions au Congo.” In Josef Metzler (ed.), *Sacrae Congregations de Propaganda Fide Memoria Rerum, Vol. III/1, 1815–1972*. Freiburg: Herder, 1975.

———. *Rapports du Père Planque, de Mgr. Lavigerie et de Mgr. Comboni sur l'Association internationale africaine*. Bruxelles, 1957.

Tsudi wa Kibuti, Mambu-Lo. “L'Église du Christ au Congo (ECC) et son attitude face à la politique (1970–1997),” Diplôme d'études supérieures (D.E.S) en Sciences Historiques, Université de Kinshasa, 2003.

Twose, Ntawihaye Gisamonyo Gonzalve, and Stanislas Bucyalimwe Mararo. *Mgr Joseph Busimba Mikararanga (1912–1974), premier prêtre et Èvêque noir du Kivu, fondateur et grand pasteur du Diocèse de Goma.* Goma, Congo (Democratic Republic): Association Les Amis de Goma, 2012.

Ugeux, Bernard. "La pastorale des petites communautés chrétiennes dans quelques diocèses du Zaïre." Ph.D. Thesis, Institut Catholique de Paris, 1987.

Ukiwo, Ukoha. "Hidden Agendas in Conflict Research: Informants' Interests and Research Objectivity in the Niger Delta." In Christopher Cramer, Laura Hammond, and Johan Pottier (eds.), *Researching Violence in Africa: Ethical and Methodological Challenges.* Leiden; Boston: Brill, 2011.

UN Department of Peacekeeping Operations. *United Nations Peacekeeping Operations: Principles and Guidelines.* New York: United Nations, 2008.

UN Security Council 6943rd Meeting. *Report S/RES/2098/ (2013).* March 28, 2013.

UN Security Council. *Special Report of the Secretary-General on the DRC and the Great Lakes region (S/2013/119).* February 27, 2013.

United States Conference of Catholic Bishops. "The Challenge of Peace: God's Promise and Our Response A Pastoral Letter on War and Peace," 1983.

Vaeyrynen, Raimo. *New Directions in Conflict Theory: Conflict Resolution and Conflict Transformation.* London: International Social Science Council ; Sage, 1991.

Vatican Council II. "Gaudium et Spes," December 7th, 1965.

Väyrynen, Raimo. "To Settle or to Transform? Perspectives on the Resolution of National and International Conflicts." In Raimo Väyrynen (ed.), *New Directions in Conflict Theory : Conflict Resolution and Conflict Transformation.* London: International Social Science Council ; Sage, 1991.

Vlassenroot, Koen, and Karen Büscher. "The City as a Frontier: Urban Development and Identity Processes in Goma." *Crisis States Working Paper 61 (Series 2),* London: London School of Economics, 2009.

———. "Humanitarian Presence and Urban Development: New Opportunities and Contrasts in Goma, DRC." *Disasters* 34, no. 2 (2010): 256–273.

Willaert, Maurice. *Kivu redécouvert.* Bruxelles: M. Arnold, 1973.

Willame, Jean-Claude. *Banyarwanda et Banyamulenge: Violences éthniques et gestion de l'identitaire au Kivu.* Bruxelles: CERAF, 1997.

Willame, Jean-Claude, and Benoit Verhaegen. *Les provinces du Congo: Structure et fonctionnement (Lomami – Kivu Central).* Léopoldville: Université Lovanium, 1964a.

———. *Les provinces du Congo: Structure et fonctionnement (Nord-Kivu – Lac Léopold II).* Léopoldville: Université Lovanium, 1964b.

Young, Crawford. *Politics in the Congo: Decolonization and Independence.* Princeton: Princeton University Press, 1965.

Yumba, Gaston Nkasa. "L'apport de l'Eglise Protestante au développement économique et social du Congo." In Centre de recherchers interdisciplinaires et de Publications Université Protestante au Congo (ed.), *L'Eglise dans la societé Congolaise: Hier, Aujourd'hui et Demain (Actes des journées scientifiques interfacultaires du 25 au 28 avril 2001).* Kinshasa: Editions de l'Université Protestante au Congo (EDUPC), 2001.

4 What Kinds of Peace?

Introduction

This case study-based research aimed to understand the role of the Roman Catholic, *3ème Communauté Baptiste au Centre de l'Afrique* and *Arche* Churches, with specific reference to religious peacebuilding, as well as general conflict transformation in Goma. These three churches were specifically selected due to the historical evolution of conflicts in that particular region of the world, as well as the role religious actors have played in them. Therefore, I explicitly sought to understand the dynamics of these religious actors, not purely from a top-down perspective, but also from the perspectives emerging from the voices and efforts of people who are typically neglected at the grassroots level, and who too often remain completely ignored in relation to their roles in peace initiatives. Some of my informants talked negatively about several peace-related activities. They complained that humanitarian projects were exclusively initiated both by those in leadership positions at the three churches and foreign actors. Meanwhile, the potential beneficiaries of these projects were rarely consulted and may not have seen their broader social impacts. These views have overshadowed the relatively good works of many other peacebuilders.

Despite some of my findings presented in preceding chapters, this chapter (Chapter Four) sequentially addresses the central research question, along with its four sub-questions. Since this is a qualitative research case study, I have purposely incorporated my own observations, as well as those of my research participants, to answer these questions. In this chapter, I attempt to share what the anthropologist Harry Wolcott (1994) called "raw data," as opposed to presenting "cooked" or "processed" data. However, the raw data presented below carry both ethical responsibilities and challenges.

Several ethical difficulties arise when reporting stories from individuals who have experienced violent conflicts, which are, at times, still latent. For instance, how do you faithfully share their experiences without causing them further harm? How do you preserve the confidentiality of sensitive information entrusted to you by those who are still involved in their respective churches? How do you reconcile conflicting information from informants with competing interests? Not only do these questions represent major challenges, but they further remind me of the care required in reporting these findings without censoring myself. Bearing in mind the aforementioned ethical considerations, this chapter is subdivided into four main sections.

First, in this chapter I explore various definitions of the two main concepts of this study (namely, peace and conflict), which I couple with the religious and spiritual aspects that this book entails, since the main actors come from religious contexts. In other words, the resulting question I seek to answer is, "How do these participants, both leaders and followers, relate to the issues of peace and conflict?" Second, I reflect on the causal factors of conflicts. From both a historical and chronological perspective, further grounded in the participants' viewpoints, I seek to capture their perspectives on the emerging causes of conflicts, particularly in the city of Goma. Among the causes which emerged from the fieldwork are issues of geographical location, identity-based exclusion and competition over natural resources. However, one needs to be cautious concerning some issues that are equally regarded as causes and consequences of conflicts, such as ethnicity and natural resources. Third, I explore the role of religious actors, including leaders and members at the grassroots level, with the aim of understanding their theology of peace. That is to say, this third set of questions intends to raise issues pertaining to their theology of peace. Although leaders and adherents of the Catholic, *3ème* CBCA and *Arche* Churches view peace as an ideal, and a condition for social and economic development, their approaches and their paths toward it differ for several reasons, which I likewise address in this third section. Fourth and finally, I examine the nature of relationships within and between the three churches. My objective here is to examine in more precise ways the dynamics of power within these religious organizations and their competitive relationships in the Goma religious market.

Different Kinds of Peace: Catholic, *3ème* CBCA and *Arche* Churches in Goma

A Semblant and a Soi-disant Peace: The Absence of War and Disharmony

Research participants opposed the terms *peace* and *conflict* in their attempts to define them. While some considered the first as the absence of the second, others nuanced both terms by echoing what scholars of peace and conflict studies have pointed out, namely, negative and positive peace. Research participants, from either leadership or membership positions, continuously made references to the spiritual aspects of the two concepts, in order to provide a better understanding of the role of religious actors in conflict transformation efforts. In addition, a cross-comparison of the three churches provides further insights into the evaluation of their definitions of *peace* and *conflict.* Some participants viewed peace as the mere absence of war (or violence) while others perceived it as a harmonious environment. Chuma—the pseudonym of a devout Catholic participant in his mid-forties—expressed his view of a *véritable paix* (true peace) in opposition to a "*semblant de paix*" (a semblance of peace). He was convinced and insisted that a collective group of people must live together. He considered that essential, and representative of the core element of true peace in North Kivu, and Goma in particular. In other words, according to him, "true peace" is a space or environment where people talk with one another, trust each other, protect each other's interests and eschew mutual jealousy. Chuma went on to say:

> I have chosen to begin with a negative definition of peace. That is, peace which is not synonymous with the "absence of weapons." For instance, as previously mentioned, between 1965 and 1993, there was a "semblance of peace" in the Masisi area. But that was not a true peace, because people were not truly reconciled…I can therefore only assert that peace is the will to live collectively. When people are willing to live together, they can talk to each other, as I said previously, and be sincere with one another. When each one is concerned and seeks to promote each other's interests and when the phenomenon of "why Roger progresses, and I do not" ends only then there can be peace. For from these jealousies emerge conflicts. As stated before, we need to reconcile with ourselves and with others and to accept living with others.

> The willingness to live together is a reigning principle in North Kivu's communities. Thus, living together is very important. As long as we cannot live together, we will never have true peace.[1]

Agreeing with Chuma on the definition of a negative kind of peace is Mayaliwa, pseudonym of another Catholic participant involved in peace-related programs in the diocese of Goma. He regretted that people in Goma often associate peace with the absence of war. One of the ways he explained the "peace equals absence of war" relationship was by making sense of the fact that the population has become so accustomed to war that its absence is celebrated, and other related issues dismissed.

> We in the East are somewhat accustomed to war; we easily associate peace with the absence of war. Its absence usually signifies the presence of peace. We can lack/miss peace, even in the absence of war! The security situation in the diocese [city of Goma] has never been stable. For several decades, the [Catholic] diocese has continued to encounter volatile security situations. Different wars [have come and gone]: whether for power conquest or between communities. Goma has always been the starting point. At least, [it has been] an extremely targeted geographical place. [We can name the following wars]: AFDL, RCD, recently CNDP and now the M23. Goma is always, one could say, a little geographic hub, which strongly feels the consequences of chronic regional instability. I would say that the security situation has been unstable since 1993. The East is yet to have a peaceful period. There has never been a time where one says, "Now it is peaceful, now we can breathe, now people can benefit from a lasting peaceful climate." Every time there has ever been a quiet time, it has always suddenly disappeared.[2]

This conversation with Mayaliwa reveals the volatility of the situation, particularly in Goma, a city that has suffered severely under armed conflicts over the past two decades. As a result, he suggested that the Gomatricians (inhabitants of Goma) have gotten used to inhabiting such a conflictual environment.

Chuma, who also lived in the small town of Masisi, made a correlation between conflicts in the town and their immediate humanitarian consequences in Goma. Although he now lives in North Kivu's capital, he continuously mentioned stories from Masisi, located about 70 km northwest of Goma. Undoubtedly, the humanitarian situation, which Chuma qualified as catastrophic, has impacted him negatively. "People have been completely destroyed; they are unrecognizable," he repeated in Kiswahili and paralleled the situation there (in Masisi) to that of the internally displaced population in Mugunga, a locality near Goma which acknowledged to now have a *soi-disant paix* (so-called "peace").[3] For him, like Mayaliwa, the temporary cease-fire between antagonists (essentially between the M23 rebels and the FARDC) was not the real peace. "How could one describe the situation in Mugunga, as a peaceful situation?" Chuma answered his own question: "Parentless children and women sleep in the open air; we are cultivating and reproducing the *Mayibobo* (street children) phenomenon."[4] And, "of course, these people are no longer under the M23's bombs, but how many women have been sexually violated? How many children have become *Mayibobo*? I tell you, these issues are time bombs waiting to explode."[5] Indeed, my observations in Mugunga's internally displaced camp resembled that which Chuma and other informants had shared with me. To return to the kind of habitats the population of Goma had been forced to live in, I make use of the following two examples.

Given that the city of Goma became a theater of bombshells[6] in the latter part of August 2013, I had received a call from a female informant, Furaha, who strongly reprimanded (not negatively, but as someone who is concerned for one's safety) me on the phone in Kiswahili: "Baba (father), are you still here?" She was astounded: "You better hurry-up and leave this our Goma, because as for us, we are already used to these wars," and the phone cut off.[7] Furaha was actually telling me that my presence, at that particular moment, was a problem—because unlike her, I had been away from Goma for over fifteen years, as I had told her previously. To her, my extended absence from Goma suggested that I had become estranged from that social *milieu*. I was a foreigner in her eyes and thus unfamiliar with the war and, therefore, she would have been held accountable should I have been harmed in any way. I do not think Furaha wanted to be responsible for me, which is fair enough, despite her seeming to consider my safety before her own.

Mapendo was another key informant who expressed much generosity and help during my fieldwork.[8] Not only did he assist me in introducing me to other key participants, but during that same period (August 2013), he kept calling and sending me text messages to ensure that I completed all my interviews and gathered all the necessary materials. He always reminded me to take precautionary safety measures (e.g., my movements, where and what to eat, etc.). In fact, Mapendo had already considered the possibility of my crossing over a border to a safer neighbouring country to escape the situation. I am sharing these two experiences in particular, not because I necessarily agree with all what Mayaliwa shared with me, but rather to support his view regarding the population becoming accustomed to conflict, specifically wars.

Lastly, in the opinion of Ukweli, another church leader, *paix injuste et incorrecte* (*unjust* and *incorrect peace*) can be described as a "group endangering the future of everybody until all of its conditions for peace are fully met, irrespective of others."[9] Even though Ukweli spoke in metaphorical terms several times during our one-on-one interview at his office and he refrained to explicitly mention in this particular example the group he was referring to, he made sure to emphasize that the so-called peace "they" seek on "their" own terms is an "unjust" and a "disrespectful" peace that disregards the views of others.[10]

Despite these characterizations of what may also be referred to as an *uneasy peace*, many informants continued to express their expectations for a more sustainable and lasting peace that responds to their immediate and future needs. In the next section, I address the other side of peace, portrayed as positive.

Véritable Peace: Individual and Collective Harmony

Contrary to both the *semblant* and *soi-disant* forms of peace, many brought up what I have coined as the positive side of the same concept (peace), which bears no form of violence. To some, it seems like an unattainable, or a utopic, form of peace, which keeps the population alive with a positive expectation while postponing current problems. The positive definition of peace, as aspired to by the majority of participants, remains an individual as well as a collective project for a harmonious lifestyle. This harmony arises from within individuals and it spreads all around us, including in our very nature. Sister Marie-Bernard Alima, former General Secretary of the ECJP (Episcopal Commission for Justice and Peace), summarizes it as the "capacity to live in harmony with God, with oneself, with one's brothers and sisters."[11]

Véritable Peace as a Threefold Project: Divine, Personal and Communal

A peace that is considered positive and viewed from a Christian perspective requires the interplay of at least three key prerogatives. These are not equally important; they are complementary to each other and uncompetitive. Firstly, it is a divine component that needs to be acknowledged by the second component, which is one of the two beneficiaries (the individual and the community). Secondly, peace is also an individual and a personal issue. Unless individuals make peace their own personal objective, the positive kind of peace does not manifest. Thirdly, positive peace is tied to the community and society at large.

Irrespective of the organizational level of the church, whether at the leadership or grassroots level, members of the three churches agreed on the divine embodiment of a true peace, which is sometimes called *shalom, shalom-total,* or *le bien-être comblé* (fulfilled wellbeing). While their understanding of peace generally appertains to the same Christian God and Bible, their activities aimed at attaining this kind of peace diverged, and oftentimes collided (particularly on doctrinal issues). In their understanding of peace, Catholic informants included prayers oriented to Mary, the mother of Jesus Christ and pastoral letters, which *Arche de l'Alliance* members never mentioned, except to disagree with their counterparts and focus attention on their activities relating to a Trinitarian God (God the Father, Jesus Christ and the Holy Spirit).[12] The *3ème* CBCA informants, on the other hand, rejected the importance given to Mary and the works of the Holy Spirit in their day-to-day lives, and instead placed more emphasis on biblical texts and personal effort. In contrast to most *Arche* and *3ème* CBCA members, who read peace-related biblical scriptures during services, only a few Catholics had Bibles. Instead, audiences silently agreed with the prayers of their leaders (bishops, priests, or laypeople).[13] One pastor, who I will call Sambela, captures the importance of this "divine pole" of peace as a vertical one that precedes the horizontal in the following terms:

> Peace is first of all vertical before becoming horizontal. Until Man [human] finds peace with God, even if there is a pretence of peace, it will not be peace. I call it a lull…There is a difference between peace and lull… The Bible calls Him "the God of Peace." It also calls Him the God of Love, etc. It does not mention his power first; it talks of a God of Peace and Justice. All these attributes of God are prerequisites for a horizontal peace.[14]

Sambela's dualistic understanding of peace lies in the significance of biblical texts, which firstly prioritize the God-human relationship: "Peace is first of all vertical."[15] This relationship, shaped in a mutual discovery between God and humankind, leads the second (humankind) to capture the first's attributes, thus resulting in a "horizontal peace." I subsequently explore the latter (horizontal peace) when I deal with the third element (community/society) of the threefold peace project.

The second element of positive peace rests on the role of individuals (in their singularities), who are also the first beneficiaries (of peace). Peace is essentially a matter of personal and inner transformation before it can be related to others. For the observed interviewees, it was essential that one be transformed with the same convictions of a positive peace. This is similar to the premise of the Catholic Commission for Peace and Justice. Many, according to the then-General Secretary of the ECJP (Episcopal Commission for Justice and Peace), Sister Marie-Bernard Alima, seek to transform others while their own transformation has yet to happen. Not only does she believe that real peace is embedded within spiritual virtues, in addition, she insists that people (mainly Christians) must be witnesses of peace (and justice) to others (interview with Alima 2013). The third element of the positive kind of peace is the "Other," which is not only recognized here in the sense of a community or a society but may further take on a plural form. The description of Ukweli, the informant we discussed earlier, encompasses this general idea of the "Other" in participatory and inclusive terms for the emergence and reproduction of peace. He described this other pole of peace as follows:

> Some people in this country…want it [the country] to assume and realize A, B, C and D before they can behave well or integrate into the society…Peace, this total-Shalom, involves everyone's participation as well as each other's respect…Respecting the society in which we live. Until we can all commit to respect our society, to respect others, to keep in mind that there are others besides ourselves in this environment, there will not be any peace. Because, there will not be any consideration for others. For the Bible says, "Let each esteem others as better than themselves." The Bible says, "Seek peace with all men, without which no man will see God." We need to have peace with all men. When the Bible says to be in peace with all men, it does not imply that X and Y should only be receivers of peace. We are all called to be producers or givers of peace. That is, peace stems from within the individual and radiates externally. We are not only making or benefitting from the peace others provide us; we must all diffuse peace. We must all provide peace. We must all spread peace around us.[16]

Peace, or "Total-Shalom," as Ukweli delineated to, is a collective/societal endeavor that requires the unconditional, deliberate and responsible involvement of its members. Despite the fact that the state holds an important place and plays a key role in society, citizens are not disengaged of their responsibilities for both right and correct actions. He was insistent about the respectful way in which these actions have to be taken before peace is reached: "Respecting the society in which we live. Until we can all commit to respect our society, to respect others, to mind that we are not ourselves in this environment, there will not be any peace." In fact, during our conversation, Ukweli cited several biblical texts, without necessarily giving their contexts and their references, to strengthen his case. I am not implying that they were out of context, which is not my role; however, I am saying that the Bible was used as an authoritative source. For instance, he continually repeated, "The Bible says…the Word declares…"

Causes of Conflict: Perspectives from the Catholic, *3ème* CBCA and *Arche* Churches in Goma

One of the most open-ended questions considered in this book, and the source of much debate, concerns the causes of conflict in Goma and, more broadly speaking, in the North Kivu province. This is not a new research question in studies with particular interests in the area, nor will the ongoing debates end anytime soon. The findings presented in this book and notably, this section, may contribute in some way to similar debates surrounding the fundamental causes of conflict, such as geographic space, land conflicts, natural resources and ethnicity. Allow me to illustrate this point using the last of the previous issues, i.e. ethnicity. Although my interviewees did not rank the causes of conflict in any particular order, I shall discuss them here in an order that emphasizes their frequency of occurrence. This classification does not mean that any causes are more important than others. As I will expand upon in the next section, both frequent and infrequent causes are contributing factors that generally operate in conjunction with each other, even if some occur more often than others.

My findings disagree with some scholars, such as Emizet Kisangani (2012), who for instance, in his book *Civil Wars in the Democratic Republic of Congo, 1960–2010,* claims that ethnicity is not the main cause of conflicts in Eastern Congo. Yet, in my findings, it is possible to concur with at least one of his conclusions, which states that various forms of ethnic discrimination play a role in the production and reproduction of conflicts. My position is to neither under- or overestimate any of the causes put forward by the interviewees. Rather, my intention is to view the ways in which they interrelate within the socio-political and economic contexts of Goma. My research findings are among the first steps to, understand the issue of conflicts from both the grassroots and church leadership perspectives, recognizing that subsequent research could include many other churches in the Congolese provinces.

Thus, the rest of this section will elaborate on what my findings suggest about the combination and mutations (transformations) of causes of, or explanations for, conflicts given by interviewees, not only in the city of Goma, but also in North and South Kivu provinces. The first part, given next, will address the internal uncontrollable and controllable causes of conflicts, such as urban space, natural resources, leadership failures and ethnicity. The second part will examine the external causes of these conflicts.

Urban Space as a Cause of Conflicts: Goma, a Mysterious City Prone to Violence and Leisure

The title of this section may confuse some due to the "mysterious" connotation given to an urban space. It displays the ambiguity and difficulty in attempting to describe the city of Goma. In fact, the mysterious attribute of this city may only astonish a few *Gomatraciens/Gomatraciennes* or *Gomatiens/Gomatiennes* (male/female inhabitants of Goma), since many people have this perception of the city. A quote from the book by Bill Freund, professor of Economic History at the University of KwaZulu-Natal, *The African City: A History*, which reads: "Cities attract friends and enemies," perfectly suits and describes the situation in Goma (Freund 2007). While some depict Goma as a conflict zone, others still paradoxically maintain, even though it applies to a limited category of the so-called "privileged" among the population, the historical name of the "Switzerland of Central Africa," mainly because of its favorable climate and proximity to Lake Kivu. At the same time, some view it as a "cursed" or a "mourning" city because of several tragedies it has suffered and continues to endure (such as volcanic destruction, sexual abuse and war), whilst others regard it as a place of refuge and compassion. Still others continue to perceive Goma as a place of socio-political and economic opportunities, or a "boomtown," as Silke Oldenburg (2016) recently put it and as Karen Büscher (2011) explored in her dissertation.

The common denominator of these perceptions is not simply their relative temporalities or volatilities; it also rests on the movement of people, goods (including natural resources) and capital in and/or out of the city. The intentions of these flows are not always clearly defined, particularly for the valuable goods (vehicles and natural resources) that cross over the Rwandan border during periods of intense conflict and violence, such as the last conflict in November 2012, the taking over of Goma by M23 rebels, or the previous rebellions (notably between September 1998 and August 1999).[17] Targeting an urban space like Goma highlights additional symbolic representations, by reason of its institutional embodiments.

Not only does Goma headquarter the North Kivu political and administrative institutions (governorate and parliament) and the United Nations peacekeeping mission called the *Intervention Brigade* (an unprecedented offensive mandate),[18] several NGOs (national and international) and representatives of both bilateral (Germany, the USA, France, Belgium, etc.) and multilateral cooperation (CEPGL, UNICEF, OMS, etc.) are also based in the city. The presence of these organizations and institutions, with the movement and the mobility they create, position Goma as a node or hub among its neighbouring cities and towns, both locally and regionally, resulting in a space of contestations, resistance and thus, of constant conflict (Vlassenroot and Büscher 2009, 2010). During my discussion with Mayaliwa, a Catholic participant I had mentioned earlier, I asked him "What is Goma all about?" He jokingly and concisely replied:

> How can I explain it to you? Curses and blessings attract, intentions notwithstanding, whether good or bad. We see all authorities and celebrities parading here: Angelina Jolie; the wife of Clinton [Hillary], I don't recall if he himself passed by; Ban Ki-moon. They all passed through here. Goma is a kind of a compulsory path. Only Obama remains. This is, in my view, political and economic tourism. Many feel sorry for the Congolese for their own personal interests. Not to mention the NGOs. They come in and go out like a depot. They swarm about without understanding. This is their capital. Unheard and unnoticed, [they come and go]. For instance, have you seen all the houses at the lake shore? Who are there? This is the reality of Goma. It is on the one hand a touristic capital and on the other, the capital of sexual abuse.[19]

Even though Mayaliwa's descriptions of the city of Goma may be viewed as extreme and pessimistic, they nonetheless coincide with those of many respondents. They gave meaning to their urban experiences in relation to this urban environment. The representations of what Mayaliwa calls "authorities," who are mainly foreigners, likewise included what some may call rumours; in this case, of a conspiracy theory for the Congo's Balkanization (Jacquemot 2009; Stephen Jackson and Médard 2001). The address of the French President, Nicolas Sarkozy, in January 2009 to diplomatic corps, further fueled such ideas of conspiracy against the security of Congo's borders. President Sarkozy suggested a solution to continuous conflicts in the Great Lakes region during his speech to diplomatic corps. His solution mainly consisted of the sharing of the Congolese space and natural resources with its neighboring countries and particularly with Rwanda. His comparative observations of the two countries' (Congo and Rwanda) demography, areas and natural resources led him to that suggestion. He said:

> For the Great Lakes region, violence has unleashed one more time. Military option would provide no solutions to root issues, which occur repetitively for more than ten years now.
>
> New approaches are required to reassure regional countries that their issues will be globally resolved. Therefore, the place and destiny of Rwanda, with which France has resumed bilateral relations, is to be reconsidered. A country [Rwanda] that has both a dynamic demography and a small surface area. This reality poses the question for the Democratic Republic of Congo, a country with an immense surface area and its strange border natural resources. It is important that at one time or another a structural dialogue takes place instead of a conjectural dialogue: how, in this region of the world, space is be shared, natural resources are shared, and we agree to understand that geography holds its laws, that countries rarely change their address and learn to live beside each other.[20]

Both Mayaliwa's remarks and other respondents' observations regarding the French President's speech overlap with what some Gomatricians still believe to be the motive of the Congo Balkanization project: an economic agenda. They justify this so-called "foreigners' project" as the final path that will facilitate access to Congolese natural resources which, according to them, began even before the country's independence. While very few made the link to regional events that occurred in the late 1950s, several others recalled the 1990s as being the era of conflict (mainly ethnic). For instance, some informants pointed out that the colonial authorities played a key role in exacerbating the conflicts between local communities, while others claimed ignorance of the stakes involved until the Rwandan genocide in 1994 and the aftermath of the arrival of the rebellion movement *Alliance des Forces Démocratiques pour la Libération du Congo* (Alliance of Democratic Forces for the Liberation of Congo, AFDL) in 1997. Whether for Chuma, who was born in the province, and Pascal, a long-time inhabitant of the province, they both recognized at least two main events that shaped the socio-political context of modern-day North Kivu. According to them, there are two historical events that caused, on the one hand, the reconfiguration of the political administrations and, on the other hand, widespread killing during the inter-community conflicts: the creation of the *Provincettes* and the *Kanyarwanda*[21] War. Chuma says:

> I want to tell you that security issues in this area go back to the independence years, around 1960. A few years after the national and international independence of Congo, around 1964, we had what was called the *Provincettes*, a dismantling of the *Grand Kivu*. It meant that North and South Kivus and Maniema were divided into small provinces and we thus had the so-called small governors. The first war, called the *Kanyarwanda* War, in the Masisi, also began in 1964. That war, which involved the Hutu and the Hunde communities, decimated many, many people.[22]

Even though other factors may contribute to the rise of conflicts, their premises are twofold. Namely, the form that they usually take—identity-based (ethnic)—and their points of departure (from abroad, Rwanda in particular). From Rwanda, the famines in the early 1900s and demographic concerns led to migration to Congo. In addition, the two main ethnic groups[23] in Rwanda (Hutu and Tutsi) were politically threatened at different periods, resulting in their flight and taking refuge in other places such as Eastern Congo. Chuma recalls that during the colonial era, Belgian authorities influenced the migration of some ethnic groups, probably for labour purposes (interview with Chuma 2013).

Mayaliwa and Pascal are two of the few who flatly disagreed with Chuma's view. Instead of seeking alibis and excuses, according to these two informants, governance and state performance lie at the root of conflict in the region. People not only become deeply worried after sunset—the period during which armed robbers often operate and violence occurs, though it also happens at noon—they feel stressed throughout the night because of potential theft and attack. Nor is the state justice system guaranteed to ordinary people of Goma. An issue of great concern to many in North Kivu remains the misappropriation of land, i.e., conflict over land. While the Congolese state fails to provide at least equal justice to everyone irrespective of socioeconomic status, churches, particularly the Catholic Church, fill such gaps with their para-justice organizations which operate at the grassroots level, such as the Justice and Peace Commissions.

The high densities of the North Kivu province (80 inhabitants/km^2) and its capital, Goma (14,474 inhabitants/km^2), the fertility of land and the endowment of natural resources are all additional ingredients that lead to conflicts in the area (Alfani 2015). They require a sub-section of their own, which is given below.

Land and Natural Resources as Factors of Conflict: Bulongo ya Baba and No NKunda no Job

Two of the main causes of conflicts that many interviewees reported to me are the control of the land and of its natural resources. While the scarcity of land seems to be a fuelling element of local conflicts, in addition to ongoing population growth, the abundance and variety of natural resources in the "African Far West" (Stephen Jackson and Médard 2001) appear to be a further driver of conflict. These two causes of conflicts are interconnected in such a way that the profits from natural resources are used to invest in land acquisitions, especially for elites, who are the primary beneficiaries of conflict (Oldenburg 2016, 187). For others, land not only secures one's natural resources, it also represents a constituent of survival that enables its owner to support his or her family (Autesserre 2010, 131).

In Goma, as well as elsewhere in the North Kivu province such as the Masisi region, the control of land is the main cause of conflict. Nevertheless, looking at this element alone does not convey its full manifestation in generating conflicts. Not only is it crucial to examine the issue across time and space, examining the socio-political dynamics of the province is also important. Issues of land tenure are not recent in the socio-political lives of Gomatricians and Congo's easterners, in general. Many have argued that the policies of Belgian authorities during the colonial period have severely exacerbated conflicts, chiefly in Eastern Congo. Although implemented during the colonial state era, the consequences of their policies are still evident in contemporary Congo (Autesserre 2010; Mamdani 2001; Mararo 1990, 1997).

Belgian authorities introduced two kinds of citizenships in the *État Indépendant du Congo*: (1) civic or political and (2) ethnic (Autesserre 2010; Mamdani

2001). At first, the former was exclusively reserved for Belgian residents, before being given to the so-called évolués (evolved, civilized or developed). Local Congolese, those who were considered "indigenous," were granted the latter (ethnic citizenship) in accordance with their ethnic or tribal association, which entitled them to rights and privileges such as using land. One was qualified as a nonindigenous citizen once he or she did not belong to a given ethnic group and, as a result, was "denied 'customary' access to land" for lacking "native authority." The only option left for nonindigenous citizens to access land, failing their own native authority, was to pay tribute to "customary" authorities (Mamdani 2001, 238). Therefore, conflicts over land are grounded in the definition given to the identity terms "indigenous" and "nonindigenous," which tie individuals to either one or the two groups and all that relates to them. One participant from the Kinyarwanda-speaking origins strongly critiqued what he called the phenomenon of *Bulongo ya Baba,* ("Fathers' land"), according to which, in his interpretation, some communities continue to regard land as belonging to the "autochthonous." Another person, from the Hunde ethnic group, decried the fact that the Banyarwanda refuse to accept their "true identity" as newcomers (immigrants), which, would in some way disqualify them of the right to land access, since they are foreigners. Although these two parties keep pointing fingers at each other, they both agree on the state's incapacity to enforce the law. This issue of land access as a driver of conflict is similarly tied to the economic aspect of natural resources, as previously mentioned.

Contrary to many who believe that conflicts are essentially interpersonal, others think that they mainly stem from political and economic interests. The mismanagement of economic interest entices both individuals and groups at the local, regional and international levels to use divisive social behaviors that generate and sustain conflicts. For instance, one church leader observed that natural resources constitute one of the pillars, if not the main one, of conflicts in Eastern Congo. While natural resources are not directly extracted in Goma, this provincial capital is a meeting point, or a node, for buyers and sellers where the main *comptoirs*[24] are located (Stephen Jackson and Médard 2001, 127). Rachid, a 22-year-old inhabitant of Walikale, travelled to Goma for a one-week mission to sell his few grams of yellowish mineral he called cassiterite (tin ore). For Rachid, despite the tremendous negative consequences of conflicts in the province, they offer some benefits, such as business opportunities for people like him.

> I had to leave school in grade 12 and find *Ka kilaka*[25] (a means of living) and to support my little brothers who are still in school. We don't have any jobs and everyone *se débrouille*

> (we are fending for ourselves) here. We are encountering some issues of selling [these minerals] with the current government law, but we still manage to sell them. Without this disorder, it would have been much harder. (interview with Rachid, fictitious name, 2013)

Rachid's observations shed light on another aspect of conflict that many of my interviewees also observed, namely, the profitability of conflicts in areas rich in natural resources, both for local populations and foreigners. In addition, mining in the eastern Congo sector is basically done either informally or formally. While informal mining is the most common practice in the area, formal mining is also common.[26] It was in the early 1980s that the mining sector was "informalized" with the "liberalization of trade and the exploitation of gold, diamonds and precious materials" (Kennes 2005). Like Rachid, many young miners (or *creuseurs*) from Walikale and Goma's other hinterlands organize themselves to mine minerals informally to meet their daily needs, making it difficult for the government to control revenue produced from the minerals (Stephen Jackson and Médard 2001). Trading raw minerals represents an alternative to unemployment for many young people (Jacquemot 2009). The character of the resources—cassiterite (tin ore), gold, coltan, wolframite, pyrochlore and diamonds—in the North and South Kivu provinces also contributes to the type of exploitation (informal mining). The aforementioned minerals—to which Le Billon adds "alluvial gems and timber"—are termed *diffuse resources* because of their high accessibility through production, "high lootability," ease of exploitation (one needs only a "shovel and a bucket" to extract them) and the fact that they may simply be transported by individuals on foot (Kennes 2005, 170–171; Le Billon 2003, 32–33). Nathalie Pauwels argues that informal networks, which are part of a "survival economy," are a result of "poor governance" (2007, 167). For Pauwels, informal networks have, for a long time, sustained the exchange of weapons and minerals (2007, 168). Whether to critique or to justify their situation, my informants in Goma often referred to the popular saying of a MONUC's peacekeeper: "No Nkunda, no job."[27] Besides the negative humanitarian consequences, natural resources continue to fuel conflicts, which, according to many, are sustained by local and external role players to whom they are beneficial. Not only do natural resources and dependence upon them shape an environment that leads to conflict, but their accessibility by either the state or rebel groups may also determine the rise of conflicts. In addition, relatively easy access and the inability (whether willingly or not) of the Congolese state to control some of the remote places in the country also further facilitates conflicts in Eastern Congo.

Thus, the cycle of conflict, constituted by various interests that directly or indirectly encourage conflict, in turn creates an environment that facilitates the trade of minerals. While natural resources and their mismanagement shape and maintain conflict-prone environments, another salient factor that characterizes conflict in Goma is ethnicity.

Ethnicity as a Factor of Conflicts: Ubaguzi na Ukabila, Two Interrelated Phenomena

Addressing the issue of ethnicity in relation to religious organizations is important for at least two reasons. First, ethnic identity has been a contributing factor to the regional history of violent conflict and continues to be an important one even within religious groups. Second, evidence from the field demonstrates that this phenomenon of ethnicity creates a sense of discomfort or even fear within individuals, to the extent that many avoid discussing the issue.[28] In other words, the politicization of ethnicity as a social phenomenon has led many to censor themselves for protective purposes. For instance, many mentioned to me that they did not want to talk about ethnicity because it was too closely linked to politics, which they also did not want to talk about. Others approached the subject of ethnicity in a different way: they first demonstrated their ignorance about the matter and then, as they became familiar with me and trusted me enough, they started discussing issues related to ethnicity. Therefore, ethnicity remains both a salient, "silent," "indirectly censured" and thorny issue in Goma, and in the North Kivu province in general. There often seems to be a taboo surrounding the issue.

Like religion, ethnicity is a mobilizing element in the African context and the Great Lakes region in particular. Ethnicity continues to be, in the Central African region, a fertile and controversial subject among scholars, practitioners and different interest groups. Although ethnicity concerns individuals, it stems from organizations such as political parties, administrations, rebel groups, schools, universities and churches (Cf. Brubaker 2006; Ekeh 1975). From a normative point of view, the phenomenon of ethnicity is hardly conceived as being a part of religious organizations, especially churches, from which one would expect both neutrality and impartiality, at least from a moral perspective. Others may consider such an expectation naive. Yet, religious organizations and, notably, churches, do influence social interactions. In fact, this relationship is tightly interwoven and the elements are supportive of each other. They are also the subject of competition in religious arenas. Generally, in Goma and elsewhere in the North Kivu province, churches and their affiliated organizations such as schools, hospitals and humanitarian organizations are often tainted by religious and ethnic connotations. Membership identification, especially with respect to the Catholic and the *3ème* CBCA Churches, is dominated by ethnic affiliations. Church members, as well as non-members, will note their ethnic group before their religious identity. In other words, ethnic identification overrides any other form of identification. The Nigerian sociologist, Onigu Otite makes the same points in the Nigerian context (Otite 1990). He writes, in his book *Ethnic Pluralism and Ethnicity in Nigeria*:

> A Hausa [M]oslem or Angas [C]hristian, for example, may not trust a Yoruba or Igbo [M]oslem or [C]hristian particularly at moments of national crises and competitions. Thus, although all [M]oslems or Christians belong to the same universalistic religion, some regard themselves or believers from their ethnic group as the pure, more reliable [M]oslems or Christians. (1990, 62)

Returning to the Congolese context and comparing the importance given to ethnic or religious identity, my research shows that *Arche* members valued and emphasized church or spiritual belonging more than members of the other two churches. Meanwhile, they downplayed other forms of identification associated with, for instance, ethnicity, skin colour, race, language and even gender. This is not to say that *Arche* is more inclusive and multicultural than any of the other churches in Goma. What is true, however, is that these characteristics were the least mentioned during my fieldwork in that church. Nonetheless, on several occasions, naming one of the city's churches made a connection and reference to an ethnic group. While this kind of ethnic labeling applied to the Goma Catholic Church and *3ème* CBCA Churches, gender and demographic labels were also used in the *Arche* Church. Speaking about the latter, for instance, a participant noted "the church of young people" or "a place where ladies attend." Therefore, I acknowledge the complexity of analyzing the demographics of each church, and the difficulty of defining this phenomenon in the socio-political context of Goma.

The ongoing social transformations of the previous decades in the Great Lakes region, especially since the 1990s, are a result of the intensity of cyclic violent conflict, which in turn further complicates this task. Therefore, the meaning and the significance of this social phenomenon may vary according to the immediate issues at stake (Prunier 2001, 157). Even though its manifestation carries both negative and positive meanings, the negative connotation has attracted greater attention than the positive one. Supporters of ethnicity argue that it provides a sense of belonging and an essential component for networking and solidarity in times of need, especially for minority groups. Nevertheless, its opponents claim that it erects boundaries between groups and promotes social inequality, which sequentially and ultimately lead to violence. On the one hand, ethnicity is a social phenomenon that relates to groups larger than kinship groups whose members share common interests, characteristics and attributes (e.g., phenotypes, faith, language, origin, ancestry [real or putative] and class issues) (Brubaker 2006). On the other hand, each ethnic group recognizes its own distinctiveness, and applies its own criteria in defining their counterparts. Mutual ascriptions, though they may be rejected, serve as boundaries between ethnic groups in various inter-relationships and interactions (Longman 2010; Nzongola-Ntalaja 1999; Samba 1982). These characteristics of ethnicity are part and parcel of the definition of ethnicity. In my attempt to define this phenomenon, I will include at least two interchangeable notions from the field, namely *Ubaguzi* and *Ukabila*, which are commonly rendered into English as *tribalism* and *discrimination*.[29] Ethnicity may thus be defined as inborn, owned or acquired characteristics which a group of individuals attributes to themselves and others for the purposes of inclusion and exclusion. This definition provides two views of the same phenomenon, namely (1) static and (2) dynamic.

The first view may be described as the rigid and the intangible characteristics of ethnicity. It can be neither chosen nor easily rejected, nor be contested as an ethnic membership, because one is born with it and need not subscribe to it. That is, ethnic affiliation is inherited or ancestry-based. This side of the definition somewhat coincides with primordialism, which asserts that society has primitive groupings in itself that are either biological, cultural or racial (Szayna, Tellis, and Winnefeld 2000, 18). Boundaries between groups are founded on these internal and external definitions (Jenkins 2008). However, the latter is a common explanation for social solidarity which is grounded in superficial human similarities. However, in the midst of egocentric interests, what ought to represent strength (superficial human characteristics) can no longer be embraced. Primordialists Pierre Englebert and Kevin Dunn pointed out that ethnic affiliation is placed above any other group criteria, in that members will show loyalty to their ethnic group in order to maximize their communal interests, even at the expense of other communities (2013, 68). Writing from the Nigerian and post-colonial African contexts, Peter Ekeh, in his article "Colonialism and the Two Publics in Africa: A Theoretical Statement," examines the dialectical relationship between what he names on the one hand a "primordial public," which relates to primordialism and, on the other, a "civic public," which may be comprised of mainline churches. This is still in accordance with Ekeh regard to either close association of mainline churches (Catholic and Protestant) with colonial administrations or the sharing of the "colonial ideologies" (Ekeh 1975, 92, 96).

Ekeh further observes that, belonging to a civic public from which leaders of ethnic groups draw capital without necessarily investing in it (civic public), fellow members expect their ethnic leaders to make generous contributions to their primordial public.[30] He writes that ethnicity or tribalism:

> [arises] where there is conflict between segments of the African bourgeoisie regarding the proportionate share of the resources of the civic public to differentiated primordial publics. The leaders of the primordial public...want to channel as great a share of these resources from the civic public to individuals who are in the same primordial public as they are—in part, one suspects, because a significant proportion of them will eventually find their way into the coffers of the primordial public. (Ekeh 1975, 109)

The other side of the definition of ethnicity is a dynamic one, and one that is more subjective and flexible regarding situational circumstances. Contrary to the primordialist view, supporters of a dynamic ethnicity believe that it is not only triggered by other factors such as religion, political and economic opportunities, but that it is also further influenced by time and geography (Englebert and Dunn 2013). Constructivism and ascriptivism are two of the other perspectives of ethnicity, which may relate to the second view of my definition of ethnicity. An ascriptive approach goes beyond the primordial approach to ethnicity. Ethnicity is described as a "subjective belief" of a given group that entertains their similarities for both socio-political and economical (power and domination) purposes (Szayna et al., 2000, 24–30).

While many have linked this phenomenon to groups or social status, few have investigated its institutionalization, that is, how it manifests itself and how it is perceived in established religious organizations. Scholars from different disciplines, like the US sociologist Rogers Brubaker and political scientist Crawford Young, have argued that ethnic groups are not protagonists of ethnic conflicts or violence *per se* (Brubaker 2006; Young 1998, 6). Instead, conflict and violence are facilitated and executed by various kinds of organizations, including religious ones. That is, as a social phenomenon, ethnicity by itself does not lead to conflict and violence. To put it differently, ethnicity is neither bad nor good; it only reveals how an individual or group consciously, or unconsciously, acts based on the way in which they imagine themselves, or according to their perceptions of what has been imagined for them (Juteau 1999, 9).

Institutions and organizational structures, such as churches, are two arenas where ethnicity plays a role and in which social inequalities are compounded. Religious institutions and hierarchal organizations are thus conducive to perpetuating inequality based on ethnic identity. In fact, many believe that discrimination based on ethnic identity is the primary cause of conflict in the North Kivu province. Many of my respondents claimed to have either been directly discriminated against or witnessed discrimination at some point in various social contexts of interrelations, especially secular and clerical. Their claims were mostly made in relation to competition for socio-political and economic resources.

Jean-Francois Bayart has pointed out that ethnicity plays a role in "accumulation, both of wealth and of political power," while tribalism is a "channel through which competition for the acquisition of wealth, power or status is expressed" (2009, 55). My empirical evidence, largely from the Catholic Church, illustrates that church hierarchies in Goma embody these features or types of capital, which many pursue whilst others ensure its preservation once it has been attained. As a result of the benefits these positions embodied, in Goma and elsewhere in the Congo, they were vernacularly called names such as *postes juteux* (*juicy* or *key* positions), *Ligablo,* or *dépanneur* (convenience store). These benefits can be organized into two categories. The first category encompasses positions closely associated with ecclesial functions, or the curia in the Catholic structure, namely (1) diocesan bishop, (2) legal representative, (3) finance officer and (4) chancellor.

The second category pertains to pastoral or diocesan services, such as school administration, seminary rectorate, humanitarian officers, Caritas' direction and clergy in "privileged" parishes. The importance of these two categories of *postes juteux* lies in the fact that they mobilize resources, in addition to providing symbolic, statutory, cultural, social and economic capital. While these two categories serve as bargaining features for their distributors, they allure potential beneficiaries to compete for their acquisition. African clergies and Congolese clergymen in particular (e.g., Ignace Maduku Ndongala 2012 and Godefroid Munima 1996) have, at times, to their detriment, expressed how ethnic factors have influenced the acquisition of the above types of capital. These two Congolese clergymen have expressed their resentment of protests regarding the asymmetrical relationships between diocesan bishops—who have the power both to appoint and to dismiss—and priests. Ndongala argues that the relationship between the two ordained clergies is asymmetric (Ndongala 2012). As a result, it has produced a monological (*monologale*), as opposed to a dialogical (*dialogale*) kind of relationship in many sub-Saharan African countries. This is analogous to Protestant and Revival Churches, where the will of legal representatives and presiding pastors is rarely contested. However, some dioceses have advisory committees (*la Consulte*). Ndongala further expressed that very few are consulted on diocesan issues in Catholic Churches. In fact, a handful of *Consultes* are ethnically diverse. As I considered the notion of nominations to illustrate how the instrumentalization of ethnicity plays a negative role, Ndongala's article is suitably enlightening:

> In many dioceses, nominations are not preceded with genuine and frank dialogue between the bishop and priests. Some rather choose pseudo-consultations and often a pro forma consultation. Once nominations are rendered public, they impose themselves as the irrefutable and non-negotiable will of the bishop…It is in a cooing of satisfaction that priests are required to accept them, under penalty of being sent into families or banished in extreme zones of the diocese or abandoned to their fate where they are condemned to vegetate without any posting. The unthinkable substrate underlying these uncriticised speculations can be attributed to the system of nominations to seniority or ethnic affinity or tribalism (2012).

The illustration by Ndongala coincides with my evidence from the field, in that it expresses the ubiquity of the phenomenon of ethnicity in religious organizations, particularly in the Catholic Diocese of Goma. The selection of the curia has been described not only as ethnic-based; in addition, many have pointed out that it also operates in the distribution of diocesan service posts. In fact, others have indicated that "phantom positions" (i.e., a position deprived of power and authority of performance) have been created in order to obscure or to camouflage its existence. Bourdieu's symbolic violence concept generally fits well in the context of Goma because of the silence that is observed by many people around markers of ethnicity. Churches in Goma and elsewhere provide favourable environments in which *Ubaguzi* and *Ukabila* are able to flourish. *Ukabila* does not solely manifest itself in the form of competition for positions. However, it takes various linguistic and symbolic forms, while an open conflict may catalyze the ethnic component in group mobilizations. In this regard, churches function as places of political recruitment and networking.

In fact, cleavages over ethnic groups are so common in Goma that the identities of congregations are shaped by ethnic boundaries.[31] It is common to hear people name some of these religious institutions according to an ethnic group like *Kanisa ya Banyarwanda* (Church of the people of Rwanda or those who speak Kinyarwanda), *Kanisa ya Banande* (Church of those who speak Ki Nande) or *Kanisa ya ba BanyaMulenge* (Church of the Banyamulenge, people, who come from the territory of Mulenge[32]). Despite the lack of objective statistics, and although some leaders and congregants acknowledge the existence of congregational ethnic labelling, churches were labelled according to the ethnicity of their main leader, or the majority of their supporters, or their dominant language (which all tended to coincide with one another). However, these so-called "ethnic churches" are far from being homogeneous, in that internal ethnic subdivisions still occur among them due to criteria such as linguistic differences and members' village of origin.

In summary, *Ubaguzi* and *Ukabila* in North Kivu and in its capital Goma, are an important part of relationships, both at social and ecclesial levels. Although occasionally dormant, they are regularly exacerbated during periods of conflict. Among other factors identified as causes of conflict, ethnic identity-based inequality, and discrimination within religious institutions, whether open or dissimilated, contribute to the perpetuation of *Ubaguzi* and *Ukabila*. The contributory roles of ordained and laymen leaders in either fighting or perpetuating these phenomena were demonstrated in many ways in Goma. In the subsequent section, I will address this issue in terms of bad governance and ecclesial failures.

Leadership as a Factor of Conflicts: Bad Governance and Ecclesial Failures

Leadership roles both at the state and church levels cannot be ignored when examining causes of conflict. On the one hand, the failure of the representatives of state authority, nationally and locally, reflects what many identified as bad governance. Leaders of the Catholic Church in Goma raised the issue of Congolese governance failure, explicitly and consistently, as one of the underlying causes of conflict in Eastern Congo. I once thought that this was a common response enforced among the Catholic leadership, both in Kinshasa and Goma. For them, any other causes of conflict would be tantamount to bad governance by the Congolese state authority. They hammered home the fact that the absence of state authority in some Congolese territories facilitates the proliferation of armed groups, particularly in Eastern Congo. The Congolese state's inefficiency, according to Mayaliwa—who equates insecurity with bad governance—appears to be intentionally maintained.[33] Although wars and rebellions weakened the Congolese state's capacity, many people such as Mayaliwa (a local Catholic leader) challenge the Congolese state's intention to fulfill the population's basic needs, such as employment, material goods and human security. For him, other factors presented as causes of conflict, like ethnic discrimination, were simply consequences of bad governance. The flaws in the Congolese state that Mayaliwa identified can are echoed by several authors (specifically political scientists) who have described the Congolese state as "soft," "fragile," "shadow," "weak," "failed," or "collapsed,"[34] or even as a "quasi-state"[35] (Robert H. Jackson 1990). The common denominator of these attributes, which pertain mainly to Third World countries, mostly in Sub-Saharan Africa, including the Congo, is their incapacity[36] to provide political goods and fundamental services to their citizens. Many, however, have regarded the above qualifying adjectives with scepticism, in large part because their criteria and indicators are considered vague and subjective (Alfani 2015, 89; Lavoix 2007). For instance, in *Business of Civil War: New Forms of Life in the Debris of the Democratic Republic of Congo,* Patience Kabamba states that this rhetoric does not consider local contexts or the views of local populations who are directly affected and generally neglected (2013). Other institutions find their primary roles increased as they fill the gaps created by these states' flaws. Churches are on the top list of actors lured to fill the "vacuum." Religious organizations seem to follow the same pattern of attributes and breaches of social contract as the above states. Such patterns contribute to conflict in many countries south of the Sahara.

While some link governance to statehood, others do associate it with the way that churches, and particularly their leadership, are governed, whether it is done efficiently or not. Although churches deal primarily with ecclesial issues while states are more concerned with political matters, both grapple with social problems, nonetheless. While church leaders of all denominations have suggested there is a strong connection between bad governance and conflict, several others—predominantly Catholics and mostly from the grassroots level—have pointed out that Congolese churches are another factor affecting conflicts. This is an idea that has rarely been addressed. The principal critique of church leaders regards their prophetic leadership roles.

For many of those I interviewed in Goma, the separation between church and state means that bishops, priests and pastors have the freedom and courage to raise their voices and challenge societal injustices and other issues facing the Congolese population. However, according to these interviewees, whether church leaders have "resigned" from their prophetic leadership role or have "corrupted" it, the result in the Goma context is still the same: church leaders have chosen to please and to integrate themselves with any incumbent state's authority (colonial, Congolese or rebel). As such, they constitute a state arm or pillar, like that of missionaries in the colonial period. In other words, there seems to be a continuation of a kind of church co-optation by the post-colonial Congolese state that is strikingly similar to that of colonial missionaries and the Belgian colonial authorities.

By assuming a prophetic leadership role, which religious leaders incarnate, church members expected them to speak out for the population against injustices, their religious and ethnic identities notwithstanding. According to its prophetic leadership role, the Church *vis-à-vis* the state is to serve as a counter-power and should not condone injustice or other anti-values. However, speaking out against such behaviours can be confrontational and conflictual, and many church leaders avoid it (Boyle 1992).

A Congolese priest and professor at the Catholic University of Congo, who recently passed away (November 6, 2016), Richard Mugaruka notes three aspects concerning the prophetic role of the church (2011, 166–168). First, it embodies the denunciation of character. Pastors and church leaders in general are to denounce social injustice and all forms of hatred, irrespective of the perpetrators (Muyombi 2006, 211–212; Vatican Council II, 1965, No. 75). These denunciations seem to be selective and partial for many. For instance, leaders will either take the side of protagonists, or keep quiet (Lusiensie Mulongo 2006, 62–64; Oyatambwe 1997; Tull 2005, 234–235). Instead of being at the service of the nation, church leaders use their positions to serve themselves with temporal conveniences (Mbembé 1988, 176–177; Paul VI, 1975, Nos. 32 and 35). Many have described this attitude of church leaders as an abandonment of the prophetic mission—thus the vernacular tag of *Église démissionnaire* (laid-off church)—and an embrace of the temporal dimensions of life.

The second aspect of the Church's prophetic role concerns the proclamation of the truth. The Church's main objective supersedes that of denunciation—it is to proclaim the transforming Gospel of Jesus Christ, for example, the Good News. What kind of good does this Good News offer but a shell, at least in the day-to-day lives of common Congolese people, particularly those in Goma? It has been reduced, as argued by Richard Mugaruka, to theoretical discourses and vain hopes that never materialize.

Third, the prophetic role of the Church encompasses that of education. One of its primary roles is to educate. Mugaruka has pointed out that the church cannot run away from this important task, which not only benefits its members but also society in general. Practical education which an individual may use in daily life can only improve the lives of Congolese people. Furthermore, to cultivate human conscience and enlighten the lives of its members, the church should also teach subjects such as peace, justice and human dignity (Mugaruka 2011, 77).

This kind of a double expectation (of representation and of accountability) from the grassroots level indicates a relatively difficult relationship (or bond) between leaders and the rest of society in the Congolese political and religious spheres. While this section addressed a vertical relationship between the top and grassroots levels, the next section will focus on a similar vertical dynamic between followers and God, and how this affects horizontal relationships.

Theologies of Peace from the Catholic, 3ème CBCA and *Arche* Churches in Goma

Addressing the concept of peace in religious settings such as those of the Catholic, *3ème* CBCA and *Arche* Churches in Goma led me to consider another concept that is both indirectly and directly related, namely the "theology of peace." In the context of this research, peace and theology may be indirectly related to each other, on the one hand, due to the type of actors involved in this study. On the other hand, the theology of peace is related to the ecclesiastical environment, the site and the fieldwork conducted. The concepts of peace and theology can be directly associated with each other on the grounds of claims that respondents made which carried theological meaning (Lederach 2010, 26). To phrase it differently, not only did their faith or religious tradition influence their understanding of peace and conflict, but this understanding was equally impacted by their personal relationship with God. When probed, for instance, on issues related to peace and conflict, as already reported in the beginning of this chapter, many bridged their day-to-day experiences with their corresponding faith, which I subsequently categorize in terms of theological principles.

Christianity and other religious traditions, provides one with principles and core values that nurture peace. The underlying principles and core values are built on the spiritual dimension they offer to opposing parties, which is usually one of the missing dimensions that many now consider when dealing with conflicts (Schreiter, Appleby, and Powers 2010). A spiritual dimension deals with the heart's issues. The principles and core values of a Christian peacebuilding approach are primarily drawn from the Scriptures.[37] Though the latter may be individually expressed, ecclesiastical structures and organizations further strive to demonstrate and to promote such principles.

Theological Principles/Values: Perspectives of the Catholic, 3ème CBCA and Arche *Churches in Goma*

During my discussions with followers of the Catholic, *3ème* CBCA and *Arche* Churches in Goma, both the concepts of *conflict* and *peace* carried theological meanings, doctrinal stands and various religious connotations. In explaining the reasons for conflict in their city and more broadly in the Congo, they constantly mentioned what they called the "evil condition of people's heart" as the core of self-identity and driver of one's actions. In the same vein, others defined this core of self-identity in terms of an individual's conscience that has been contaminated by evil. Nevertheless, others, advancing a sort of Christological model, described war and violent conflict as expressions of humankind's sinful nature. According to them, the only person who can "change/transform" or "heal" conflict is Jesus Christ, as the American theologian and bioethicist Lisa Sowle Cahill posited in her book chapter "A Theology for Peacebuilding" (2010, 303).

In conflicting contexts, and to foster the theology of peace, Cahill stresses the importance of including the notion of corporate redemption from sin through Christ. While this corporate redemption does not grant one a licence to commit reckless acts, nor does it require perfection from people. It offers to this "new creation," (to use the words of the main pastor of *Arche de l'Alliance/Masina,* Reverend Israel N'sembe, a sense of responsibility and humility in respect to one's own actions. Pastor N'sembe sums the actions of this new creation as a representation of, and conformity to, the "Prince of Peace." In accordance with the themes of "creation" and "redemption," Cahill (2010, 310) argues that the Bible offers, particularly to Christians, an opportunity to pursue peace with all peoples irrespective of their differences, either within their own faith, or beyond it. Both N'sembe and Cahill's views converge, though from two different Christian perspectives (Pentecostal and Catholic, respectively), towards positive social change caused by the theology of peace. Cahill observes, for instance, that "Catholic social tradition is committed to working confidently for social change. It is true that injustice will never be eradicated within history. But then again change is possible; greater—if not perfect—peace is within reach" (Cahill 2010, 316).

Yet, these positive expectations and hopes for a possible peace do not reflect the realities of many people living at the grassroots level in Goma, who interpret them as theoretical, utopic and futuristic. These Christians from Goma, as well as many others in the Kivu provinces, would disagree with Cahill's definition of hope as a "practical virtue," in the sense that several of them have yet to experience it (Cahill 2010). In fact, one Christian respondent, a Congolese professor in Kinshasa, opposed this kind of theology, which he associated with Revival Churches that are proliferating in many cities in the DRC:

> Many of these pastors from Revival Churches take advantage of the socio-political situation in the country [DRC]. They are just selling hope to suffering people, who are desperate and probably have no other opportunities in life. Hope has never changed a situation; it does not change anything and it will not start with us now in the Congo. The one thing it might do is to change one's attitude amidst difficulties while enduring them.

Of course, this professor's assertions, with which a leader in *Arche* agreed to, bear some truth. However, the latter nuanced his remarks, noting that not all "non-denominational" churches perform the same way. He remained steadfast on the importance of what he called "the message of faith" as he outlined some questions to me:

> Without our messages on the subjects of hope, faith and prayer, many Congolese would not have survived, and the rate of suicide would be increasingly high. "What would one offer to someone who has lost his or her parents and does not have abiding place?" In America [Canada] you have a state that cares about traumatized people. You probably have psychologists and psychiatrists who assist people. We do play all those roles here. I even wonder if your specialists can handle similar cases as we do. For instance, you have children who were born in rebellions and all they know is war. It is easier to criticize.

Although there is not a general consensus among the three churches on the theme of hope in circumstances of conflict, and the degree of emphasis is a divisive issue, many followers still agree on its valuable and indispensable place in Christian life and Congolese society. In addition to the above themes (heart/self-identity, redemption and hope), other theological principles were also raised in the pursuit of peace initiatives, namely, love, reconciliation and justice.

When asked about the cause of conflicts in Goma and the Congo overall, one of the overwhelming responses from members of CEVB, *Kijiji* and cell groups was *kukosa mapendo* (lack of love). Despite the fact that they did not distinguish between Christians and non-Christians, for these local members of the Catholic, *3ème* CBCA and *Arche* Churches, love was key to the promotion of peace. The importance of Christian love, *agape*, lies in its unlimited capacity to reach out to "others" (Alfani 2009, 104–109). In *Théologie de la paix*, the French theologian René Coste sums up this love in terms of a new and unique law: "the axial dynamic of a kind of love that knows no boundary and is able to sacrifice oneself" (1997, 100).

Similar to the theme of self-identity, love is rooted in the heart of Christians. Claude (fictitious name), a local leader of one of the cell groups of *Arche de l'Alliance* in Goma thinks that "when love finds its place in the heart of a *Mondimi* [believer/Christian in Lingala]" all these wars and rebellions will no longer take place. Believers, continues Claude, "will not promote them (wars and rebellions), just as several leaders of the main rebellions in the East have been pastors." Claude, a self-confessed *vrai Mondimi* (true/strong believer) in his early forties, distinguishes between *bolingo ya mutu* (intellectual love or literally love of the head) and *bolingo ya molimo* [divine/spiritual love or literally love of the heart]. While he describes the first as "calculated" and "intellectual" in nature, arguing that it promotes one's self and is primarily self-seeking, the second is quite the opposite. Claude pointed out that only "spiritual" love—which does not have gender and earthly identification such as ethnic groups—can guarantee *shalom* (peace). Many authors, predominantly Christian theologians from the Catholic tradition, formulate this love in at least two sacraments, namely the Eucharist and reconciliation (e.g., Cahill 2010; Coste 1997; Schreiter 2010).

However, the first practice, the Eucharist, does not fully resonate at the grassroots levels (i.e. CEVB, *Upendo* and cell groups) in neither of the three churches in Goma (Catholic, *3ème* CBCA and *Arche*). In fact, although many mentioned to me that clergies were the sole administrators of the Eucharist, they also said many of them rarely show up at their local masses and services. For instance, at three visits to one particular grassroot meeting-place, I can attest that the clergy was absent (I am not implying this was unjustified). Furthermore, no one ever reported to me that they had an ecumenical experience of the Eucharist as fellow Christian communities. According to Lederach (2010), since theologians have suggested that taking the Eucharist in an ecumenical context encourages unity in conflict-prone societies, its absence in Goma seems to be an area for further improvement of intra-Christian collaboration, and peacebuilding through shared ecumenical practices.

Ecclesiastical Structures for the Promotion of Peace

Unlike the Catholic and *3ème* CBCA Churches, which have officially implemented services or departments that specifically aim to resolve conflicts, the *Arche*/Goma Church does not. The Catholics have the *Commission Justice et Paix*, with representations at the local (*Commission Diocésaine/Paroissiale Justice et Paix*, CD/PJP), national (*Commission Épiscopale Justice et Paix*, CEJP) and regional levels (*Association des Conférences Épiscopales de l'Afrique Centrale* [Association of Episcopal Conferences of Central Africa], ACEAC).[38] Meanwhile, the *3ème* CBCA Church is quite similar. Stemming from the national structure of the Église du Christ au Congo (ECC), it exists locally under the name of *Commission Justice, Paix et Sauvegarde de la Création* (JPSC).[39] Although all ECC-affiliated churches do not have such a peace program, the *3ème* CBCA possesses one, even though it still is in its "infancy." Both commissions offer alternatives to the Congolese State justice program in Goma as well as other areas in the North Kivu province. While the Catholic Church workers officially refer their peace-related activities to the Catholic social teachings (Conseil Pontifical. Justice et Paix 2004) that explicitly promote human dignity, the *3ème* CBCA and *Arche*/Goma Churches do not have such internal written materials for religious peacebuilding efforts. Just as Catholic teachings include references from the Bible, they rely on biblical texts. However, many at the Catholic Church of Goma signified that some written materials, including social teachings, were only accessible to church leaders. Ultimately, at the grassroots level, the three churches demonstrated a lack of peace-related documentation.

On a different note related to the role of the Congolese state in the delivery of judicial services, some leaders of the two mainline churches agree on the failure of the state to function effectively at the local level. They complain that justice services are not equally rendered in Goma. The two leaders concur on the partiality of the state legal system, which according to them continues to impoverish the lower classes of Congolese society. It does not matter whether you are right or wrong, one informant observed, "*La justice c'est au plus donnant et aux mieux connectés*" (Justice is reserved to the higher payers and to the well-connected). Despite flaws in the training of the *Commission Diocésaine Justice et Paix* (Diocesan Justice and Peace Commission, CDJP) and *Commission Justice, Paix et Sauvegarde de la Création* (Justice, Peace, and Protection of Creation, JPSC) officers and their potential biases, state justice officials still encouraged people to amicably settle their disputes within the churches' structures. Undoubtedly, the reputation of the Catholic Justice Commission is recognized by many, primarily because of the experience it has gained over the years and its diversified and well-established source of financial support. In addition, the proximity of these justice commissioners to local populations offers them advantages over other judiciary systems (national and international). This advantage seems to be explained in at least two ways. On the one hand, the issues at stake are better understood by the justice commission's agents, who are very close to affected populations. On the other hand, offering practical solutions rather than theoretical propositions makes more sense to beneficiaries, who often have relatively limited intellectual capacities. Not only is it important to share different peacebuilding techniques with traumatized people, as argued by Sister Alima, it is much more important, practical and beneficial for these people to experience those techniques for themselves.[40] She strongly believes that peacemakers need to be more practical when community-based approaches are implemented, such as those supported in the ECJP:

> As long as people do not relate with those techniques in our *milieu,* they will remain techniques of the books. However, when you put people together, they discover each other, they discover positive sides of others, they learn to appreciate each other, not based on what books say, not because of what someone told me, but based on their own experience with one another. We [Congolese people] lived together, she [victims of conflicts] demonstrated how she is able to do good for me, thus people are now able to trust each

> other. Then, living together, working together, lay the ground for trust; in that a new positive perception of the other emerges.[41]

While Sister Alima does not deny the importance of theoretical contributions to peace studies, she critiques intellectual overemphasis regarding day-to-day activities and people's realities. For her, the problem lies in the way in which solutions and programs are delivered, especially when they are too intellectual in their presentation and disconnected from practical applications. The practicality and simplicity of peacebuilding approaches are reinforced by the stand of Revival Churches, despite the fact that they usually lack organizational structures, such as the justice commissions of their counterparts.

Perceptions of Relationships within and between the Catholic, *3ème* CBCA and *Arche* Churches

Perceptions of Relationships within the Catholic, 3ème CBCA and Arche Churches

The question that churches' internal relationships pose may be summed up as religious power relations between leadership hierarchies and followers (at the grassroots level). In other words, it relates, on the one hand, to the power relations between clergies themselves and, on the other hand, it concerns relations between clergies and laities. While the nature of these relations may vary from one church to another, both their organizational structures and their individual histories not only influence the nature of their internal relationships, but they balanced out by their counterparts. An investigation of their historical structures demonstrates that all three churches have experienced various forms of internal conflict, ranging from political interference and doctrinal issues to identity disputes. With reference to the latter issue, for instance, the dominance of ethnic over religious identity raises tensions and conflicts among members. Indeed, among sources of conflict both within and between churches, ethnicity tops the list for the Catholic and *3ème* CBCA Churches.

Similarly, the race for positions in religious institutions and organizations, and doctrinal differences, are catalysts for conflict, not only within *Arche*/Goma, but also within the Catholic and *3ème* CBCA Churches. How are power and roles distributed within the various ecclesial structures of the three churches? To put it differently, how are the levers of power controlled in these churches?

As the heirs of the European and American missions, which established stations in the eastern Congo region in the 1900s, the Catholic and *3ème* CBCA Churches inherited not only assets such as land, but they also received, along with political independence in the 1960s, the responsibility for, and autonomy over, their own religious activities. To many local people, these socio-political and ecclesial changes and transitions were superficial. Though the leadership was African, the economic and decision-making capacities remained abroad. Although these mainline churches were now led by Africans, they remained, in some respect, accountable and dependant on their headquarters, whether in Rome for Catholics or the United States for the *3ème* CBCA followers. On the other hand, like many African states, the first post-independence decades proved to be extremely conflict-ridden and violent.

In the late 1950s, on the eve of the Congo's independence, the Catholic and the *3ème* CBCA Churches (stations, at the time) in Eastern Congo underwent profound leadership changes that exacerbated existing conflicts, which were principally identity-based. We can use the selection process of the first African leader of North Kivu's Catholic Church, and its subsequent consequences, as an example of difficult internal church interactions. The direction of this church—which became a diocese on the 1st of March 1960—was handed over to Joseph Mkararanga Busimba, who acquired, as one of the first Congolese Catholic bishops, the label of "Bishop of the Independence." The appointment and bishopric consecration of this Hutu abbot by Pope John XXIII on May 8, 1960 raised ethnic contentions, especially from the Tutsis (Kaboy 1986, 12; Mujynya and Sebisogo 2012; Murairi 2008). Bishop Busimba was conscious of these identity dynamics that were dominated by ethnic rivalries within his own diocese.

Commenting on his episcopacy and the kind of leadership perception that prevailed within the diocese, one long-time Catholic clergyman mentioned this to me: "He [bishop Busimba] was a very wise man who was appreciated by many, especially by his close collaborates, who were in majority whites and Banyarwanda."[42] Similarly, Mararo notes that "Many services were in the hands of [white] missionaries…the Hutu, particularly from Bwisha/Rutshuru,…held key positions in Busimba's episcopacy" (2014a, 97). Following the same pattern, key positions in the diocese were rapidly taken over by the other ethnic groups, whom Mararo (2014a, 98) calls "non-natives," which remains a controversial and rejected (even if often used) term in North Kivu in particular. Among these so-called non-native members of the diocese was Patient Kanyamachumbi Semivumbi, a Tutsi from Rutshuru. Semivumbi was an associate of Bishop Busimba, whom he served for six years (1968—1974) in the capacity of General Vicar

(Mararo 2005b).[43] With the deterioration of Bishop Busimba's physical health, questions related to his succession further endangered the fragile unity and peace in the diocese. He was particularly preoccupied with perceptible conflicts and infighting among his potential successors, notably between two ethnic factions of clergymen: Tutsi and Hutu.

In fact, one priest told me that the bishop was deeply weakened, partly because of the ethnic conflict in the diocese. Even the few words at his deathbed expressed these same concerns about ethnicity: "…to all I recommend charity, never tribalism" (Kaboy 1986, 14; Twose and Mararo 2012, 50). According to my informants, the choice of a "neutral" clergyman, such as Bishop Faustin Ngabu, as Bishop Busimba's successor, was strongly encouraged. Jacques Renguet (2012, 302) from Chant d'Oiseau parish in Belgium confirms that Bishop Ngabu, then-rector of the Murhesa major seminary, was Bishop Busimba's choice for his successor:

> Conscious of his condition, he gathered all his strength for a trip to Rome. He returned appeased and serene: He was able to propose the choice of his successor, Faustin Ngabu, whose value he was aware of.

For many, the episcopacy of Bishop Busimba's successor, Faustin Ngabu (1974–2010), not only exposed the deep-rooted ethnicity-based favoritism and its reach. Ethnicity also became an increasingly violent matter in North Kivu's Catholic diocese (Mararo 2014a & b). Mararo (2014a, 98) went further to describe the situation as a kind of "Tutsization" of this religious institution, that is, a hegemony of one ethnic group (Tutsi). Other churches in Goma and North Kivu, in general, reflect similar internal ethnicized relationships, which was more common at the upper (leadership) level rather than at the grassroots. Another internal issue regarded the participation of the masses in decision-making processes. Even ordinary people within the diocese who were immediately concerned were not included in decision-making processes.

Church leaders rarely include adherents' views in their decision-making processes, even in matters that directly concern them. Many at the grassroots level complained to me that their leaders had never consulted them—not on ecclesiastical directions nor for their contributions to addressing problems. For example, the majority of my grassroots' respondents observed, through interviews and questionnaires, that it was their first time they could be heard and share their viewpoints on such critical issues as conflicts in their churches and in the country at large. Even though they were initially reluctant to accept my request for an interview (for their own personal security reasons, confidentiality purposes, and afraid to lose their jobs), I noticed a sort of relief, and expectation of positive returns, as they shared their stories. Furthermore, this exercise allowed them a further, unprecedented, retrospective opportunity within their own religious contexts. This was particularly true since, as one of the respondents told me, it was often the local religious leaders who answered questionnaires addressed to grassroots members. In this case, they appreciated my coming to talk to them directly and for the opportunity to answer the questionnaire themselves.

Tuungane, a pseudonym of a Catholic parishioner in his early fifties, lamented that seldom were pastoral issues, chiefly in CEVBs, ever dealt with in consultative or participative ways. In fact, they were often addressed directively, i.e., from the top-down rather than the bottom-up. While leaders of the church, according to Tuungane, "meet in Kinshasa [capital of Congo] to discuss issues that concern us with no prior consultations in CEVBs, they then bring us 'ready-made solutions' that do not suit our day-to-day realities in CEVBs and which we barely follow." For this parishioner, who had been actively involved in different parishes as a local leader, and in several CEVBs in North Kivu, the gap between the leadership and local members was so wide that he could not see how to bridge it or even reduce it, unless a radical change occurred from the top.

Drawing from his experience of several decades in Catholic churches in North Kivu, Tuungane believes that people at the grassroots level of churches are purposely left out for two main reasons. First, leaders (both ecclesial and secular) prefer to "keep members in ignorance" for their "own personal" gains. The second reason is related to the first and occurs primarily within the Catholic Church. It regards the lack of courage of leaders to challenge what Tuungane calls the Church's "structure of status-quo." For him, there are consequences attached to breaking the established ecclesial institutions, especially when it is done openly and encroaches on the Congolese state's interests. To illustrate his case, he described with sadness the case of two bishops, Christophe Muzirirwa and Emanuel Kataliko, who lost their lives during a political rebellion while trying to challenge the situation in the Archdiocese of Bukavu from the grassroots level (Kitumaini 2011). The same critiques Tuungane raised for his own religious institution, i.e., the Catholic Church in Goma, also apply to the other two churches.

However, my findings demonstrate that flaws in the relationships between leadership and grassroots members are particularly less present in *Arche*/Goma. Only two grassroots members in this church negatively evoked the issue of their interaction with the top leadership. The paucity of such remarks may be explained by the fact that this church is relatively new. In addition, it may be because the

Arche leaders come mainly from mainline churches, and they understand the importance of proximity with adherents.

Perceptions of Mutual Relationships: Catholic, 3ème CBCA and Arche Churches

Relationships between churches can occur either at the leadership or grassroots levels, or a combination of both. While church leaders generally set the direction of their religious organizations, followers tend to follow that direction without any form of consultation with their leaders. One can categorize at least three kinds of relationships between the Catholic, *3ème* CBCA and *Arche* Churches. The first kind of relationship is indifference, which churches adopt both at the leadership and grassroots levels (although it is rare in the latter). Second, churches can also build and maintain a competitive and/or rivalrous kind of relationship. Third, a cooperative relationship (complicit), as the word itself indicates, occurs when churches are not only willing to support each other, but their actions demonstrate support both privately and officially. These relationships are not static but are dynamic in terms of their flexibility, meaning they evolve in any of the three directions. In addition, they can also be combined and operate simultaneously depending on several factors, which I will address subsequently.

I define the first type of relationship between the three churches as "opaque," in that there are no interactions between religious groups. This does not necessary imply they are confrontational. It may, however, mean that they simply avoid each other in their respective activities while operating in the same territory, and that they acknowledge their mutual differences (e.g., doctrinal, theological, visionary, etc.). Despite the fact that some may have bemoaned the situation, they would not go as far as to negatively condemn the other religious group while mentioning that, as Christian leaders, they rarely meet. For instance, when I asked about the nature of their relations with the Catholic Church, the general consensus among the heads of the *3ème* CBCA Church was that they were difficult. One of them said:

> We do not have much cooperation with the Catholic Church. I really regret the situation. People are confined to their own corners. People are not eager to work together. Problems raised in other social contexts affect our relationships.

What seemed to bring different religions and denominations together, including Muslims, this leader continued, were crisis situations whereby leaders try to at least demonstrate unity. In fact, according to him, *3ème* CBCA youth are more likely to meet with their Muslim counterparts during interreligious dialogue efforts than Catholics are. Though rare, he did acknowledge the few occasions they have met as leaders:

> When the country is threatened by conflicts, leaders of different religions and denominations meet. We also gather as one religious body to contact political authorities for peace issues: Revival, Protestant and Catholic Churches, all inclusive. However, this is rare. We are more motivated to gather in crises situations, rather than making it our lifestyle.

Similarly, Catholic leaders stated that they also have close relationships with Muslim members, as opposed to Protestants in general. However, *Arche*'s members demonstrated reticence for cooperation except in their "evangelization" period, during which they reached out to Muslims with the aim of converting them to Christianity. In a nutshell, it is possible to conclude that for all three churches, ecumenical relations are difficult, and in the case of two out of these three churches, their relations are more difficult than their interreligious ones with Muslims.

Competition-driven and *rivalry-oriented* are words that characterize the second kind of relationship between the Catholic, *3ème* CBCA and *Arche* Churches. In other words, these two components galvanize their relationships, particularly at the leadership level. Their competitions are largely over political issues and membership appeals (see the next chapter for more analysis on this topic). Those attracted to these churches make rational choices, in terms, for instance, of returns before joining or appearing with any group. For instance, it would be more beneficial to a political leader to attend an important event, while sending a representative to another event with less political impact. Furthermore, a member will leave a church out of frustration, dissatisfaction or lack of fulfillment for another one that adequately responds to his or her needs. In addition, as indicated previously and supported by some scholars like the Ivorian anthropologist Bony Guiblehon (2011), the attribute of a failed nation-state plays a key role in determining the reaction of the masses, whose needs are yet to be met.

In addition, theological and doctrinal concerns top the reasons for church shifting. Several members of *Arche* in Goma justified leaving the Catholic Churches because "they were not properly fed spiritually," which they explained as "to read the Bible and understand it, as well as to 'vibrantly/powerfully' pray." A study by the Belgian historian Leon de St-Moulin conducted in Kinshasa in 2002[44] shows that the majority of respondents gave the following three main reasons for the success of the Revival Churches:

> 34.5 % "people seek [from Revival Churches] truths that are hidden in mainline churches"; (2) 24.7% "people expect to receive miracles by attending [Revival Churches] without subscribing to their credo"; (3) 21.3% "people go for the healings that take place there." (Léon 2010)

The "understanding of the Bible" and "positive" results of prayers (healing, deliverance) as incarnated by leaders of the Revival Churches are the two important "agendas" which are largely sought after by their (future) followers and further constitute the targets of strong criticisms from other churches and scholars, who argue that the leaders of the Revival Churches lack theological correctness (Angang 1993–1994; Djongongele 1993–1994; Gytambo Kibisari 2007; Mongo 2005; Ntumba 2010). One of such fierce critique was from Nkingi Mweze Chirhulwire Dominique's claims, who perceives Revival Churches as a public danger:

> The issue is not about religious expression, which would have been normal, but it regards alienating religious expression. The evils described above are extremely serious. Speeches of the so-called Revival Churches do not embody salvation. It is merely a commercial show, a mass hysteria with destructive consequences which result to easily perceptible inflation.
>
> Without necessarily being prophets of doom, we need to be afraid that in a decade the Congolese nation would be made up of unrecoverable abnormal and alienated people. Dementia knocks at our doors: some pastors and their members are already carrying it. (Nkingi 2012, 227)

Like Nkingi and several other authors, church leaders in Goma have concerns about Revival Churches' theologies, of which they strongly disapprove, primarily because of the Revival leaders' improvisation in pastoral positions. For example, they criticized their theological illiteracy and disapproved of their sole focus on intangible things at the expense of concrete issues. One leader commented, for example, on a question related to his perceptions of Revival Churches:

> We have some problems over there also, because we have the impression that Revival churches focus essentially on prayer, on deliverance, on the works of the Holy Spirit, even though we still believe that these things must manifest themselves in daily concrete issues. Human beings are not solely made of the spirit, but they are also made of substance. We want to focus our ministry on spiritual matters, and on substance also. We really want a balance of the two.[45]

Amidst the above criticisms, Revival Churches in particular have been working on various strategies in an attempt to counter-attack these "severe" attacks. Thus, the last kind of relationship that many are conscious of, and invest time and energy in, is the building of strong connections, and coalitions of pastors that share their same beliefs, both locally and internationally. One of the purposes of creating the Église du Christ au Congo [Church of Christ in Congo, ECC], as illustrated in Chapter Three, was not only to counter-attack a well-established Catholic Church, but to demonstrate the support of local Congolese churches against "foreign missionaries." In the same vein, one pastor noted that pastors in Goma created an organization that brought together pastors from Goma (KIPAGO) in the late 1990s. This kind of cooperative relationship is much more present among *3ème* CBCA and *Arche* Church leaders and members. One may argue that the two organizations are led by pastors of the same ethnic groups. Though ethnic identification also plays a role, though this was not confirmed during my fieldwork.

Conclusion

The peacebuilding role of non-state actors like the Catholic, *3ème* CBCA and *Arche* Churches in transforming a social context such as Goma is of utmost importance, especially if lasting peace is to be realised. The inclusion of a third church (*Arche*) alongside the two mainline churches demonstrates how, over the long-term, religious institutions have not only established themselves, but have also evolved alongside the people of North Kivu and Goma.

This chapter began by highlighting the understandings and definitions of *peace* and *conflict* that members of the Catholic, *3ème* CBCA and *Arche* Churches hold. Although some argued that peace was a combination of inner and then outer harmony, others nuanced it as being between a *semblance* and a *véritable* peace. However, others perceived peace as an ongoing project that individuals should pursue both vertically (with the divine) and horizontally (with the community).

The causes of conflict were then further examined. I presented a repertoire of five main causes of conflict raised by interviewees. Though none of the five appeared to be a root cause of conflict in the city of Goma, their combinations proved to be a determining factor. For instance, ethnicity was significant only within structures such as churches and organizations. Another important cause of conflict was associated with natural resources such as land and minerals, especially in places where the state's presence was limited (or absent). Not only did the Congolese state's failure in providing goods and services contribute to conflict, but the failure of religious leaders in fulfilling their prophetic leadership role was equally interpreted as a cause. From the elaboration of different causes of conflict, the notion of the theology of peace was examined.

The theology of peace, from the perspective of the three churches, was examined in a preceding section, "Theological Principles/Values" (*p. 139*). This helped to identify the importance of faith and its potential for religious peacebuilding and conflict transformation. Given that this study concerned three Christian Churches, the concept of and belief in Jesus Christ was the foundation of their theologies of peace. However, as in the definition of peace and conflict, differences existed between what the literature proposed and what fieldwork revealed. One instance may illustrate this: ecumenical Eucharist[46], as observed elsewhere, is yet to take place in Goma (at least at the three churches under investigation).

While the above theological beliefs and stances regarding the role of Christian Churches in religious peacebuilding and conflict transformation are well articulated, their translation to daily activities did not always occur. This was particularly the case when it came to relationships between leadership and grassroots membership in the Catholic, *3ème* CBCA and *Arche* Churches. These issues of mutual relationships were explored in the last section of this chapter.

Endnotes

1. Personal interview with "Chuma," Catholic Participant 2, Goma, 2013.
2. Personal interview with "Mayaliwa," Catholic Participant 5, Goma, 2013.
3. A camp for displaced populations was located in Mugunga.
4. "Chuma," Catholic Participant 2, Goma, 2013.
5. *Ibid.*
6. Bombshells were falling in the city and killed some and destroying some properties. I witnessed a young lady who was killed, and her body was carried in the city towards the city hall.
7. Personal interview with "Furaha," Participant A3, 2013.
8. Personal interview with "Mapendo," Participant A4, 2013.
9. Personal interview with "Ukweli," Participant A2, 2013.
10. *Ibid.* The use of third person pronouns without disclosing the subject was a common practice among my informants.
11. Personal interview with Marie-Bernard Mbalula Alima, Kinshasa, 2013.
12. The Catholic Church also organized novena prayers with peace as the principal theme. Examples of prayer requests to Mary can be found in the pastoral letter from Bishop Faustin Ngabu following the post-Rwandan genocide and an influx of refugees in Goma. He writes: Let us, therefore, unite with the Virgin Mary in seeking

Jesus; when we find him, he will welcome us into his mystery of salvation…That is why in the face of our current dangers, I invite you to fill your cups of water with prayer and fasting…In this month of the virgin Mary, we will unite with her to fervently pray. I especially invite you to unite with her in prayer between the 23 to the 31 of May, which is the Visitation Feast of Mary to her cousin Elizabeth. I also invite you to enter into communion with her in shared thanksgivings and a shared faith.) See Faustin Ngabu, "Courage, n'ayez pas peur (Is 13:4)," *Pastoral Letter*, May 18th, 1996.

13. On a similar subject, Paul Gifford initiated a conversation on the importance of the Bible in Pentecostal churches in general and in African faith churches in particular, using Kenya's Winners Chapel, for illustrative purposes. He clearly distinguishes the use of the Bible in mainline churches from Pentecostal-Evangelical churches. For instance, he points out that in mainline churches, the Bible is "occasionally referred to," while biblical texts in Pentecostal-Evangelical churches are "ritualized." Paul Gifford, "The Ritual Use of the Bible in African Pentecostalism," in Martin Lindhardt (ed.), *Practicing the Faith: The Ritual Life of Pentecostal-Charismatic Christians*, New York: Berghahn Books, 2011, p. 182. Elsewhere, a Congolese Professor at the Catholic University in Kinshasa Angang, Dosithée Atal Sa, though using the term "sects," shows the ever-presence of the Bible in the lives of non-mainline churches' believers. Angang presents a book (the Bible) which its users self-administer to dissipate their present predicaments without any form of prescription. For instance, he worries for the believers-patients in the hands of uncertified pastors-physicians:

    The use of the Bible risks…finally to be an arsenal of rescue or a pharmaceutical recipe, which is administered for the relief of pains. We then rely on biblical verses for that purpose. As a result, an intellectual slothfulness is developed and opens the reader to easy solutions. Sects lead astray…God is manipulated in his providence and his action (Cf. *Cahiers des religions Africaines* 27–28, (1993–1994): 447.

14. Personal interview with "Sambela," Participant A1, 2013.
15. *Ibid.*
16. Personal interview with Ukweli 2013 (author's translation).
17. Informants shared with me that besides violence perpetrated on Goma's population during the official few days of the M23 occupation of the city, many luxurious vehicles loaded with plundered valuable goods crossed over the border on a daily basis. Similar practices were also implemented during previous rebellions. Bernard Leloup illustrates, for instance, two sequential strategies put in place by the Rwandan-backed RCD:

    In the first place, between September 1998 and August 1999, the systematic looting of all stocks of minerals, stocks, softwood lumber, agriculture products, as well as funds and livestock in the conquered territories; secondly, once those stocks run out, the occupying forces and their allies actively began to exploit the country's resources (minerals and forestry).

See Bernard Leloup, "Le Rwanda et ses voisins," in Stefaan Marysse and Filip Reyntjens (eds.), *L'Afrique des grands lacs: annuaire 2004–2005*, Paris: L' Harmattan, 2005, p. 153.

18. Contrary to one of the three basic principles (consent of the parties, impartiality, non-use of force except in self-defense) that limits the mandate of UN peacekeepers to the use of force except in situations of self-defense, the FIB (initially composed of more than 3,000 forces) was mandated to operate either unilaterally or jointly with the FARDC's targeted offensive operations against armed groups in the DRC. Cf. UN Security Council, *Special Report of the Secretary-General on the DRC and the Great Lakes region (S/2013/119)*, February 27, 2013; UN Security Council 6943rd Meeting, *Report S/RES/2098/ (2013)*, March 28, 2013; UN Department of Peacekeeping Operations, *United Nations Peacekeeping Operations: Principles and Guidelines*, New York: United Nations, 2008, pp. 31–43.
19. Personal interview with Mayaliwa 2013 (author's translation).
20. Address of the French President Nicolas Sarkozy to diplomatic corps in Paris, France on January 16, 2009. See the entire speech on http://discours.vie-publique.fr/notices/097000169.html; Natalie Nougayrède, "La France prépare une initiative de paix pour l'est de la République démocratique du Congo," *Le Monde*, (19 janvier 2009).
21. The Kanyarwanda War was a reaction of the autochthonous against the arrival of a large number of people from Rwanda.
22. Personal interview with Chuma 2013 (author's translation).
23. Besides Hutu and the Tutsi, a third ethnic group exist in Rwanda, namely, Twa.
24. *Comptoirs* are places where minerals are either bought or sold.
25. *Kilaka* in Kiswahili means a piece of material (tissue or leather) that covers a hole. I still remember how, as a child, my mother had to sew such pieces of material to cover the holes in our worn-out clothes and bring our shoes to shoemakers. We also had to cover our soccer balls with such material when they were pierced. This is the picture many are now using in reference to the innovative and resourcefulness of jobless people.
26. Informal mining activities are done at the mercy of artisanal miners' wellbeing and, ultimately, their lives. They dig the mines barehanded, with no protection. Cf. Witness, Global, "Faced with a Gun, What Can You Do?: War and the Militarisation of Mining in Eastern Congo," London: Global Witness, 2009.
27. Laurent Nkundabatware (commonly known as Nkunda), a former FARDC officer who rebelled against the Congolese army to head the rebel movement CNDP (*Congrès National pour la Defense du People*) [National Congress for the Defense of the People] from 2006 until early 2009. For the majority of my informants, these Rwandan-backed rebel movements (including AFDL, RCD and M23) were not only perceived as a continuation of the Rwandan invasion, but also as another form of the Tutsi domination over other ethnic groups. Hence the ethnic explanation given by

many for the conflict. See also Stanislas Bucyalimwe Mararo, *Maneuvering for Ethnic Hegemony: A Thorny Issue in the North Kivu Peace Process (DR Congo), Volume I: The 1959–1997 History of North Kivu*, Bruxelles: Éditions Scribe, 2014a.

28. Similar discomfort was interestingly noted in a recent publication (2017) by Tale Steen-Johnson in Ethiopia. Ethnicity is also viewed as a political and sensitive subject. See Steen-Johnsen Tale, *State and Politics in Religious Peacebuilding*, London: Palgrave Macmillan, 2017, pp. 104–107.
29. The current (2016) Catholic Diocesan Bishop of Goma, Theophile Ruboneka Kaboy, among others, calls *Ubaguzi* a "virus" or a "second AIDS." Even though bishop Kaboy does not explicitly specify the sphere of activity of *Ubaguzi*, my findings show that it is expressed both in secular and ecclesiastical organizations. Théophile Ruboneka Kaboy, Homily at the Jubilee celebration of the Saint-Esprit parish in Goma, August 4, 2013. The term *tribalism* has occasioned strong debates among scholars, mainly because of its pejorative connotations. Thus, scholars have the tendency to use *ethnic group* over *tribe*. See Ndaywel è Nziem, *Histoire générale du Congo: de l'héritage ancien à la République démocratique*, p. 271.
30. Still speaking of the Nigerian context, though similar cases occur in the Congo as well, Ekeh regrets that ethnicity or tribalism are pervasive in his countries' universities.
31. Scott Appleby observes that oftentimes religion strengthens ethnic boundaries. See R. Scott Appleby, *The Ambivalence of the Sacred: Religion, Violence, and Reconciliation*, Lanham, MD: Rowman & Littlefield Publishers, 2000, p. 62.
32. The Banyamulenge issue has been a subject of debates in Congolese politics in that their claims to citizenship and autochthony have been contested mainly because, as their contenders argue, in Congo such claims are always related to a given territory. Honoré N'gbanda, a former minister of the Mobutu regime and a current strong political exiled opponent to the Kabila regimes and a chairman of an association/platform called APARECO, writes: "*Toutes les études historiques et ethnologiques sur le Congo ne montrent nulle part trace d'un people du Congo dénommé Banyamulenge. Les études scientifiques le plus sérieuses ont démontré que dans cette région du Congo et un peu partout ailleurs, les peuples s'identifiaient généralement aux langues qu'ils utilisent et non aux lieux où ils résident.*"

    All historical and ethnographic studies on the Congo do not refer to a population called the *Banyamulenge*. Serious scientific studies have shown that in this region of the Congo and elsewhere people generally identify themselves with their language and not with their place of residence. See Honoré N'Gbanda Nzambo-ko-Atumba, *Crimes organisés en Afrique centrale: révélations sur les réseaux rwandais et occidentaux*, Paris: Duboiris, 2004, p. 192.
33. "Mayaliwa," Catholic Participant 5, Goma, 2013.
34. See for instance, Roger B. Alfani, "Religion et transformation des conflits: le rôle des Églises à Goma en RD Congo (1990–2010)," In Moda Dieng (ed.), *Évolution*

politique en Afrique: Entre autoritarisme, démocratisation, construction de la paix et défis internes, Louvain-la-Neuve, Belgique: Academia-L'Harmattan, 2015; Jean-Francois Bayart, "Africa in the World: A History of Extraversion," *African Affairs* 99, no. 395 (2000): 217–267; Pierre Englebert, "A Research Note on Congo's National Paradox," *Review of African Political Economy* 29, no. 93 (2002): 591–594; Tobias Hagmann, and Hoehne Markus V., "Failures of the State Failure Debate: Evidence from the Somali Territories," *Journal of International Development* 21, no. 1 (2009): 42–57; Joel, Migdal S., *Strong Societies and Weak States: State-society Relations and State Capabilities in the Third World*, Princeton, NJ: Princeton University Press, 1988; Caryn Peiffer and Pierre Englebert, "Extraversion, Vulnerability to Donors, and Political Liberalization in Africa," *African Affairs* 111, no. 444 (2012): 355–378; Daniel Posner, "Civil Society and the Reconstruction of Failed States," In Robert I. Rotberg (ed.), *When States Fail: Causes and Consequences*, Princeton, NJ: Princeton University Press, 2004; Denis Tull, *The Reconfiguration of Political Order in Africa: A Case Study of North Kivu (DR Congo)*, Hamburg: Institute of African Affairs, 2005; and William Zartman I., "Introduction: Posing the Problem of State Collapse," In I. William Zartman (ed.), *Elusive Peace: Negotiating an End to Civil Wars*, Washington, D.C.: Brookings Institution, 1995.

35. Cf. Jackson Robert H., *Quasi-States: Sovereignty, International Relations, and the Third World*, New York: Cambridge University Press, 1990.
36. Joel Migdal uses four criteria based on a states' capability to determine its degrees of strength (weakness) in its given socio-political environments: (1) the capacity to penetrate a society; (2) the capacity to regulate social relationships; (3) the capacity to extract resources; and (4) the capacity to appropriately use resources. While a strong state, according to Migdal, demonstrates a higher degree of capacities, a weak state is situated on the opposite end of the scale. Joel S. Migdal, *Strong Societies and Weak States: State-society Relations and State Capabilities in the Third World*, Princeton, NJ: Princeton University Press, 1988, pp. 4–5.
37. I am conscious of the fact that some have put forward certain values or principles—such as violence, war and just-war—to theologically justify their actions. These actions often reflect their belief systems which do not contribute to peace (non-violent) and the promotion of life. I will not be dealing, in this particular work with that particular approach for two main reasons. First, that approach was not part of my corpus; however, Coste explores, among other issues, concepts that pertain to a "violence God" and "wars of God" in the First (Old) Testament. Secondly, the peace I preconize is a non-violent one. See R. Coste, *Théologie de la paix*, pp. 41–80.
38. The Association of Episcopal Conferences of Central Africa (ACEAC) gathers the Episcopal Conferences of (1) Congo (Conférence Épiscopale Nationale du Congo, CENCO), (2) Burundi (Conférence Épiscopale des Évêques du Burundi, CECAB) and (3) Rwanda (Conférence Épiscopale du Rwanda, CEPR), which is headquartered

in Kinshasa, cf. Art. 1 and 2, ACEAC Statutes, "Association Sans But Lucratif 'Association des Conférences Épiscopales de l'Afrique'," 1984.

39. Eglise du Christ au Zaire, "Règlement d'ordre Intérieur de la Commission Justice, Paix et Sauvegarde de la Création (JPSC)," 1994. This structure is similar to the program proposed by the World Council of Churches to which some members (also known as communities; e.g., the Mennonite Community in Congo and the Baptist Community of Congo) of the ECC are affiliated to (Cf. http://www.ecunet.de/fra.root/index.html; http://www.oikoumene.org/en).
40. M.-B. M. Alima.
41. Personal interview with Alima 2013 (author's translation).
42. Author's interview in Goma, August 2013. Top clergymen leaders of the Goma's diocese, according to Bucyalimwe Mararo, also included a Hutu Gaspard Kajiga, two Tutsis (Frederic Rwamahina and Patient Kanyamachumbi) and a Hunde (Ladislas Kanane). Cf. S. B. Mararo, *Maneuvering for Ethnic Hegemony: A Thorny Issue in the North Kivu Peace Process (DR Congo), Volume I: The 1959–1997 History of North Kivu*, p. 97n344.
43. Bishop Kanyamachumbi occupied, among other key positions, the rectorate of both the minor seminary of Saint-Joseph of Buhimba for 3 years (1965–1968) and the major seminary of Murhesa for five years (1979–1984).
44. The study was conducted between March and April 2002 among 474 subjects (244 men and 230 women) with a majority of non-Catholics (307), who were born outside of Kinshasa (193), 356 of them high school graduates.
45. Personal interview with Siku Nzuri, Goma, 2013 (author's translation).
46. While some argue that an inter-denominational Eucharist may contribute to building peace between believers of different denominations, other observers point out that its failure should not be equated to people not wanting to work together, in part because of theological reasons. In addition, mutual respect over each other's rituals and their respective meanings need to be considered (this is also an important component in fostering peace).

Bibliography

Abble, A. *Des prêtres noirs s'interrogent.* (2e éd.). Paris: Éditions du Cerf, 1957.

Abu-Nimer, Mohammed. "Building Peace in the Pursuit of Social Justice." In Michael D. Palmer and Stanley M. Burgess (eds.), *The Wiley-Blackwell Companion to Religion and Social Justice.* Chichester, West Sussex; Malden, MA: Wiley-Blackwell, 2012.

———. "The Miracles of Transformation through Interfaith Dialogue: Are you a Believer?" In David Smock (ed.), *Interfaith Dialogue and Peacebuilding.* Washington, D.C.: United States Institute of Peace Press, 2002.

ACEAC Statutes. "Association Sans But Lucratif 'Association des Conférences Épiscopales de l'Afrique, '" 1984.

Achebe, Chinua. *Hopes and Impediments: Selected Essays*. New York: Anchor Books, 1990.

Acker, Joan. "Hierarchies, Jobs, Bodies: A Theory of Gendered Organzations." *Gender & Society* 4, no. 2 (1990): 139–158.

African Rights. *The Cycle of Conflict: Which Way Out in the Kivus*. London: African Rights, December 2000.

Albarello, Luc. *Choisir l'*étude de cas comme méthode de recherche. Bruxelles: De Boeck, 2011.

Alfani, Roger Bantea. "Religion et transformation des conflits: le rôle des Églises à Goma en RD Congo (1990–2010)." In Dieng Moda (ed.), *Evolution politique en Afrique: Entre autoritarisme, démocratisation, construction de la paix et défis internes*. Louvain-la-Neuve, Belgique: Academia-L'Harmattan, 2015.

———. "The Role of the Ruah YHWH in Creative Transformation: A Process Theology Perspective Applied to Judges 14." M.A., Université de Montréal, 2009.

Allan, Pierre. "Measuring International Ethics: A Moral Scale of War, Peace, Justice, and Global Care." In Pierre Allan and Alexis Keller (eds.), *What is a Just Peace?* Oxford: Oxford University Press, 2006.

———, and Keller, Alexis. "Introduction: Rethinking Peace and Justice Conceptually." In Pierre Allan and Alexis Keller (eds.), *What is a Just Peace?* Oxford: Oxford University Press, 2006.

Anderson, Allan. *An Introduction to Pentecostalism: Global Charismatic Christianity*. New York: Cambridge University Press, 2004.

Anderson, B. Mary, and Lara Olson. *Confronting War: Critical Lessons for Peace Practitioners*. Cambridge, MA: Reflecting on Peace Practice Project, Collaborative Development Action, 2003.

Angang, Dosithée Atal Sa. "L'utilisation de la Bible par et dans les sectes religieuses de Kinshasa." *Cahiers des religions Africaines* 27–28, no. 53–56 (1993–1994): 431–451.

Appleby, R. Scott. *The Ambivalence of the Sacred: Religion, Violence, and Reconciliation*. Lanham, MD: Rowman & Littlefield, 2000.

———."Religion, Conflict Transformation, and Peacebuilding." In Chester A. Crocker, Fen Osler Hampson, and Pamela R. Aall (eds.), *Turbulent Peace: The Challenges of Managing International Conflict*. Washington, D.C.: United States Institute of Peace Press, 2001.

———. "Religious Violence: The Strong, the Weak, and the Pathological." In Atalia Omer, R. Scott Appleby, and David Little (eds.), *The Oxford Handbook of Religion, Conflict, and Peacebuilding*. New York, NY: Oxford University Press, 2015.

Asch, Susan. *L'Église du prophète Kimbangu: de ses origines à son rôle actuel au Zaïre, (1921–1981)*. Paris: Éditions Karthala, 1983.

Autesserre, Séverine. "Hobbes and the Congo: Frames, Local Violence, and International Intervention." *International Organization* 63, no. 2 (2009): 249–280.

———. *Peaceland: Conflict Resolution and the Everyday Politics of International Intervention*. New York: Cambridge University Press, 2014.

———. *The Trouble with the Congo: Local Violence and the Failure of International Peacebuilding*. Cambridge; New York: Cambridge University Press, 2010.

Azar, Edward E. *The Management of Protracted Social Conflict: Theory and Cases*. Aldershot: Dartmouth, 1990.

———, and Burton, John W. *International Conflict Resolution: Theory and Practice*. Boulder, CO: Lynne Rienner, 1986.

Balandier, Georges. *La vie quotidienne au royaume de Kongo du XVIe au XVIIIe siècle*. Paris: Hachette, 1965.

Barash, David P. *Approaches to Peace: A Reader in Peace Studies*. (2nd ed.). Oxford, NY: Oxford University Press, 2010.

———., and Webel, Charles. *Peace and Conflict Studies*. Thousand Oaks CA: Sage Publications, 2002.

Barnett, Michael, Hunjoon Kim, Madalene O'Donnel, and Laura Sitea. "Peacebuilding: What is in a Name?," *Global Governance* 13, no. 1 (2007): 35–58.

Barnett, Michael, and Christoph Zürcher. "The Peacebuilder's Contract: How External Statebuilding Reinforces Weak Statehood." In Roland Paris and Timothy Sisk (eds.), *The Dilemmas of Statebuilding: Confronting the Contradictions of Postwar Peace Operations*. Abingdon, UK: Routledge, 2009.

Batende, Mwene. "Les sectes: un signe des temps?, Essai d'une lecture sociologique des 'religions nouvelles' issues du christianisme." *Cahiers des religions Africaines* 27–28, no. 53–56 (1993–1994): 25–43.

Bayart, Jean-Francois. "Africa in the World: A History of Extraversion." *African Affairs* 99, no. 395 (2000): 217–267.

———. "Les Églises chrétiennes et la politique du ventre: le partage du gâteau écclesial." *Politique Africaine* 39 (1989): 3–26.

———. *The State in Africa: The Politics of the Belly*. (2nd ed.). Cambridge; Malden, MA: Polity Press, 2009.

Beaud, Jean-Pierre. "L'échantillonnage." In Benoît Gauthier (ed.), *Recherche sociale: de la problématique à la collecte des données*, Québec: Presses de l'Université du Québec, 2006.

Beaud, Stéphane, and Florence Weber. *Guide de l'enquête de terrain: produire et analyser des données ethnographiques*. (4e ed.). Paris: La Découverte, 2010.

Beckford, A. James. "Introduction." In James A. Beckford (ed.), *New Religious Movements and Rapid Social Change*. Beverly Hills, CA: Sage Publications, 1986.

Beilin, Yossi. "Justice Peace: A Dangerous Objective." In Pierre Allan and Alexis Keller (eds.), *What is a Just Peace?* Oxford: Oxford University Press, 2006.

Benigni, Umberto. "Propaganda." In Charles George Herbermann, Edward Aloysius Pace, Thomas J. Shahan, Condé Bénoist Pallen, and John J. Wynne (eds.), *The Catholic Encyclopedia: An International Work of Reference on the Constitution, Doctrine, Discipline, and History of the Catholic Church, Vol. 12*, New York: Robert Appleton, 1907.

Benney, Mark, and Everett C. Hughes. "Of Sociology and the Interview: Editorial Preface." *American Journal of Sociology* 62, no. 2 (1956): 137–142.

Berger, Peter L. *The Sacred Canopy: Elements of a Sociological Theory of Religion*. Garden City, NY: Doubleday, 1969.

Bernard, H. Russell, and Gery Wayne Ryan. *Analyzing Qualitative Data: Systematic Approaches*. Thousand Oaks, CA: Sage, 2010.

Bock, Joseph G. *Sharpening Conflict Management: Religious Leadership and the Double-edged Sword*. Westport, CT: Praeger, 2001.

Boeije, Hennie. *Analysis in Qualitative Research*. Los Angeles: Sage, 2010.

Bontinck, François. *Aux origines de l'*État Indépendant du Congo: documents tirés d*'archives américaines*. Louvain: Nauwelaerts, 1966.

Boutros-Ghali, Boutros. *An Agenda for Peace: Preventive Diplomacy, Peacemaking and Peace-keeping*. New York: United Nations, 1992.

———. *An Agenda for Peace: With the New Supplement and Related UN Documents*. (2nd ed.). New York: United Nations, 1995.

Boyle, Patrick M. "Beyond Self-Protection to Prophecy: The Catholic Church and Political Change in Zaire." *Africa Today* 39, no. 3 (1992): 49–66.

Braekman, E. M. *Guy de Brès*. Bruxelles: Librairie des Eclaireurs Unionistes, 1960.

———. *Histoire du protestantisme au Congo*. Bruxelles: Librairie des éclaireurs unionistes, 1961.

Brewer, John D., Gareth I. Higgins, and Francis Teeney. "Religion and Peacemaking: A Conceptualization." *Sociology* 44, no. 6 (2010): 1019–1037.

Brubaker, Rogers. *Ethnicity without Groups*. Cambridge, MA: Harvard University Press, 2006.

Brun, Cathrine. "'I Love My Soldier': Developing Responsible and Ethically Sound Research Strategies in a Militarized Society." In Dyan Mazurana, Karen Jacobsen, and Lacey Andrews Gale (eds.), *Research Methods in Conflict Settings: A View from Below*. New York: Cambridge University Press, 2013.

Büscher, Karen. "Conflict, State Failure and Urban Transformation in the Eastern Congolese Periphery: The Case of Goma." Ph.D., University of Ghent, 2011.

Bujo, Bénézet. *Introduction à la théologie africaine*. Fribourg: Academic Press, 2008.

———, et Muya, Juvénal Ilunga *Théologie africaine au XXIè siècle, Volume II*. Fribourg: Editions universitaires, 2002a.

———., and Muya, Juvénal Ilunga. *Théologie africaine au XXIe siècle, quelques figures Volume I*. Fribourg, Suisse: Éditions universitaires, 2002b.

Cahill, Sowle Lisa. "A Theology for Peacebuilding." In Robert J. Schreiter, R. Scott Appleby, and Gerard F. Powers (eds.), *Peacebuilding: Catholic Theology, Ethics, and Praxis*. Maryknoll, NY: Orbis Books, 2010.

Ceillier, Jean-Claude. *Histoire des missionnaires d'Afrique (Pères blancs): De la fondation par Mgr Lavigerie à la mort du fondateur, 1868–1892*. Paris: Karthala, 2008.

Chad, Perry. "Processes of a Case Study Methodology for Postgraduate Research in Marketing." *European Journal of Marketing* 32, no. 9–10 (1998): 785–802.

Charmaz, Kathy. *Constructing Grounded Theory: A Practical Guide Through Qualitative Analysis*. London; Thousand Oaks, CA: Sage Publications, 2006.

Chesterman, Simon. "Ownership in Theory and in Practice: Transfer of Authority in UN Statebuilding Operations." *Journal of Intervention and Statebuilding* 1, no. 1 (March 2007): 1–24.

Chrétien, Jean-Pierre. *L'Afrique des Grands lacs: deux mille ans d'histoire*. Paris: Aubier, 2000.

Clarke, Richard F. *Cardinal Lavigerie and the African Slave Trade*. New York: Longmans, Green, 1889.

Coghlan, Benjamin, Pascal Ngoy, Flavien Mulumba, Colleen Hardy, Valerie Nkamgang Bemo, Tony Stewart, Jennifer Lewis, and Richard Brennan. "Mortality in the Democratic Republic of Congo: An Ongoing Crisis." *International Rescue Committee and Burnet Institute, New York and Melbourne* (2008).

Comby, Jean. *Deux mille ans d'*évangélisation histoire de l'*expansion chrétienne*. Paris: Desclée et Bégédis, 1992.

Conseil Pontifical. Justice et Paix. *Compendium de la doctrine sociale de l'*Église. Città del Vaticano: Libreria Editrice Vaticana, 2004.

Cooley, Alexander, and James Ron. "The NGO Scramble: Organizational Insecurity and the Political Economy of Transnational Action." *International Security* 27, no. 1 (2002): 5–39.

Corbin, Juliet M., and Anselm L. Strauss. *Basics of Qualitative Research: Techniques and Procedures for Developing Grounded Theory*. (3rd ed.). Los Angeles, CA: Sage, 2008.

Coste, René. *Théologie de la paix*. Paris: Éditions du Cerf, 1997.

Cousens, Elizabeth M. "Introduction." In Elizabeth M. Cousens, Chetan Kumar, and Karin Wermester (eds.), *Peacebuilding as Politics: Cultivating Peace in Fragile Societies*. Boulder, CO: Lynne Rienner, 2001.

Cox, Harvey. *Fire from Heaven: The Rise of Pentecostal Spirituality and the Reshaping of Religion in the Twenty-first Century*. Reading, MA: Addison-Wesley, 1995.

Creswell, John W. *Qualitative Inquiry & Research Design: Choosing Among Five Approaches*. (2nd ed.). Thousand Oaks, CA: Sage Publications, 2007.

———. *Research Design: Qualitative, Quantitative, and Mixed Methods Approaches*. (4th ed.). Thousand Oaks: SAGE Publications, 2014.

Curtis, Devon. "Introduction: The Contested Politics of Peacebuilding." In Devon Curtis and Gwinyayi Albert Dzinesa (eds.), *Peacebuilding, Power, and Politics in Africa*. Athens: Ohio University Press, 2012.

Cusimano, Maryann K. "God and Global Governance: Resurgent Religion in World Politics." In Maryann K. Cusimano (ed.), *Beyond Sovereignty: Issues for a Global Agenda*. Boston, NY: Wadsworth, 2009.

David, Charles-Philippe. "Does Peacebuilding Build Peace." In Ho-Won Jeong (ed.), *Approaches to Peacebuilding*. New York: Palgrave Macmillan, 2002.

———, and Toureille, Julien. "La consolidation de la paix: un concept à consolider." In Yvan Conoir and Gérard Verna (eds.), *Faire la paix: concepts et pratiques de la consolidation de la paix*. Québec: Les Presses de l'Université Laval, 2005.

Demart, Sarah. "Le 'combat pour l'intégration' des églises issues du Réveil congolais (RDC)." *Revue européenne des migrations internationales* 24, no. 3 (2008): 147–165.

———. "Les territoires de la délivrance: mises en perspectives historique et plurilocalisée du Réveil congolais (Bruxelles, Kinshasa, Paris, Toulouse)." Doctorat, Université Toulouse-Le-Mirail and Université catholique de Louvain-La-Neuve, 2010.

Denzin, Norman K. *The Research Act: A Theoretical Introduction to Sociological Methods*. (3rd ed.). Englewood Cliffs, NJ: Prentice Hall, 1989.

Djongongele, Damse Oshudi. "Le culte de la personne du chef spirituel dans les sectes." *Cahiers des religions Africaines* 27–28, no. 53–56 (1993–1994): 175–192.

Donais, Timothy. "Empowerment or imposition? Dilemmas of local ownership in post-conflict peacebuilding processes." *Peace and Change* 34, no. 1 (2009): 3–26.

Doyle, Michael W., and Nicholas Sambanis. *Making War and Building Peace: United Nations Peace Operations*. Princeton, NJ: Princeton University Press, 2006.

DuBois, Heather M., and Janna Hunter-Bowman. "The Intersection of Christian Theology and Peacebuilding" In Atalia Omer, R. Scott Appleby, and David Little (eds.), *The Oxford Handbook of Religion, Conflict, and Peacebuilding*. New York, NY: Oxford University Press, 2015.

D'Errico, Nicole C., Christopher M. Wake, and Rachel M. Wake. "Healing Africa? Reflections on the Peace-building Role of a Health-based Non Governmental Organization Operating in Eastern Democratic Republic of Congo." *Medicine, Conflict and Survival* 26, no. 2 (2010): 145–159.

Eggers, Nicole. "Kitawala in the Congo: Religion, Politics, and Healing in 20th–21st Century Central African History." Ph.D. Dissertation, University of Wisconsin-Madison 2013.

Église Catholique du Congo Belge. *Actes de la VIe Assemblée plénière de l'Épiscopat du Congo (Léopoldville 20 novembre–2 decembre 1961)*. Léopoldville, Congo: Secrétariat génèral de l'Épiscopat, 1961.

Eglise du Christ au Zaire. "Règlement d'ordre Intérieur de la Commission Justice, Paix et Sauvegarde de la Création (JPSC)." Eglise du Christ au Zaire,1994.

Eisenhardt, Kathleen M. "Building Theories from Case Study Research." *The Academy of Management Review* 14, no. 4 (1989): 532–550.

Ekeh, Peter. "Colonialism and the Two Publics in Africa: A Theoretical Statement." *Comparative Studies in Society and History* 17, no. 1 (1975): 91–112.

Ellis, Stephen, and Gerrie ter Haar. "Religion and Politics in Sub-saharan Africa." *Journal of Modern African Studies* 45, no. 3 (1998): 175–201.

———. "Religion and Politics: Taking African Epistemologies Seriously." *Journal of Modern African Studies* 45, no. 3 (2007): 385–401.

———. *Worlds of Power: Religious Thought and Political Practice in Africa*. Oxford, NY: Oxford University Press, 2004.

Englebert, Pierre. "A Research Note on Congo's National Paradox." *Review of African Political Economy* 29, no. 93 (2002): 591–594.

Englebert, Pierre, and Kevin C. Dunn. *Inside African Politics*. Boulder, CO: Lynne Rienner, 2013.

Englund, Harri. *Prisoners of Freedom: Human Rights and the African Poor*. Berkeley: University of California Press, 2006.

Esman, Milton Jacob. *An Introduction to Ethnic Conflict*. Cambridge; Malden, MA: Polity Press, 2004.

Fanning, William. "Auditor." In Charles George Herbermann, Edward Aloysius Pace, Thomas J. Shahan, Condé Bénoist Pallen and John J. Wynne (eds.), *The Catholic Encyclopedia: An International Work of Reference on the Constitution, Doctrine, Discipline, and History of the Catholic Church, Vol. 2*. New York: Robert Appleton, 1907.

Farrimond, Hannah. *Doing Ethical Research*. Houndmills, Basingstoke, Hampshire: Palgrave Macmillan, 2013.

Filoramo, Giovanni. *Qu'est-ce que la religion?: Thèmes, méthodes, problèmes*. Paris: Éditions du Cerf, 2007.

Fisher, Simon, Dekha Ibrahim Abdi, Jawed Ludin, Richard Smith, Steve Williams, and Sue Williams. *Working with Conflict: Skills and Strategies for Action*. London; New York: Zed Books, 2000.

Fixdal, Mona. *Just Peace: How Wars Should End*. New York: Palgrave Macmillan, 2012.

Fox, Jonathan. "Introduction." In Jonathan Fox (ed.), *Religion, Politics, Society, and the State*. New York: Oxford University Press, 2012.

Francis, Diana. *People, Peace and Power: Conflict Transformation in Action*. London: Pluto Press, 2002.

Freund, Bill. *The African city: A History*. New York: Cambridge University Press, 2007.

Gagnon, Yves-Chantal. *L'étude de cas comme méthode de recherche*. (2e ed.). Québec: Presses de l'Université du Québec, 2012.

———. *L'étude de cas comme méthode de recherche: Guide de réalisation*. Sainte-Foy: Presses de l'Université du Québec, 2005.

Galtung, Johan. "An Editorial." *Journal of Peace Research* 1, no. 1 (1964): 1–4.

———. "Violence, Peace, and Peace Research." *Journal of Peace Research* 6, no. 3 (1969): 167–191.

———. *Peace by Peaceful Means: Peace and Conflict, Development and Civilization*. Oslo: International Peace Research Institute, 1996.

———. "Religions, Hard and Soft." *Cross Currents* 47, no. 4 (1997): 437–450.

Gantly, Patrick. *Histoire de la Société des missions africaines (SMA), 1856–1907 (Tome 1): de la fondation par Mgr de Marion Brésillac (1856), à la mort du père Planque (1907)*. Paris: Karthala, 2009.

Gazibo, Mamoudou, and Jane Jenson. *La politique comparée: fondements, enjeux et approches théoriques*. Montréal: Presses de l'Université de Montréal, 2004.

George, Alexander L., and Andrew Bennett. *Case Studies and Theory Development in the Social Sciences*. Cambridge, MA: MIT Press, 2005.

Gerring, John. "What is a Case Study and What Is it Good for?" *American Political Science Review* 98, no. 2 (2004): 341–354.

Gifford, Paul. *Ghana's New Christianity: Pentecostalism in a Globalising African Economy*. London: Hurst, 2004.

———."The Ritual Use of the Bible in African Pentecostalism." In Martin Lindhardt (ed.), *Practicing the Faith: The Ritual Life of Pentecostal-Charismatic Christians*. New York: Berghahn Books, 2011.

Gillham, Bill. *Case Study Research Methods*. London; New York: Continuum, 2000.

Gopin, Marc. *Between Eden and Armageddon: The Future of World Religions, Violence, and Peacemaking*. Oxford, NY: Oxford University Press, 2000.

Gray, David E. *Doing Research in the Real World*. (3rd ed.). Los Angeles; London: Sage, 2014.

Guiblehon, Bony. "Laurent Gbagbo and the Evangelical Church in Côte d'Ivoire: Ambiguous Political Affinities." *International Journal of Religious Freedom* 4, no. 2 (2011): 37–59.

Guillemin, Marilys, and Lynn Gillam. "Ethics, Reflexivity, and 'Ethically Important Moments' in Research." *Qualitative Inquiry* 10, no. 2 (2004): 261–280.

Gytambo Kibisari, Jean Willy. "La proliferation des églises de reveil à Kinshasa: interpellation de l'ECC et de l'état Congolais." Mémoire (Licence), Université Protestante au Congo, 2007.

Hagmann, Tobias, and Markus V. Hoehne. "Failures of the State Failure Debate: Evidence from the Somali Territories." *Journal of International Development* 21, no. 1 (2009): 42–57.

Haynes, Jeffrey. *Religion, Politics and International Relations: Selected Essays*. New York: Routledge, 2011.

Heinrichs-Drinhaus, Rudolf. "L'influence de l'Eglise protestante: Aspects matériel et immateriél." In Manfred Schulz (ed.), *Les porteurs du développement durable en R.D.Congo: Évolutions récentes de la vie politique, économique, religieuse, culturelle et de la societé civile*, Kinshasa; Berlin: Cepas; Spektrum, 2010.

Herbst, Jeffrey. *State and Power in Africa: Comparative Lessons in Authority and Control.* Princeton, NJ: Princeton University Press, 2000.

Hermet, Guy. "Les fonctions politiques des organisations religieuses dans les régimes à pluralisme limité." *Revue française de science politique* 23, no. 3 (1973): 439–472.

Hertog, Katrien. *The Complex Reality of Religious Peacebuilding Conceptual Contributions and Critical Analysis.* Lanham, MD: Lexington Books, 2010.

Hochschild, Adam. *King Leopold's Ghost: A Story of Greed, Terror, and Heroism in Colonial Africa.* Boston: Houghton Mifflin, 1998.

Hufford, David. "The Scholarly Voice and the Personal Voice: Reflexibility in Belief Studies." In Russell T. McCutcheon (ed.), *The Insider/Outsider Problem in the Study of Religion: A Reader.* New York: Cassell, 1999.

Idowu, E. Bolaji. *African Traditional Religion: A Definition.* London: SCM Press, 1973.

Irvine, Cecilia. "The Birth of the Kimbanguist Movement in the Bas-Zaire, 1921." *Journal of Religion in Africa* 6 (1974): 23–76.

Jackson, Robert H. *Quasi-States: Sovereignty, International Relations, and the Third World.* New York: Cambridge University Press, 1990.

Jackson, Stephen, and Claire Médard. "'Nos richesses sont pillées!' Economies de guerre et rumeurs de crime au Kivu." *Politique africaine* 84, no. 4 (2001): 117–135.

Jacquemot, Pierre. "Ressources minérales, armes et violences dans les Kivus (RDC)." *Hérodote* 3, no. 134 (2009): 38–62.

Jenkins, Richard. *Rethinking Ethnicity.* (2nd ed.). London: Sage Publications, 2008.

Jeong, Ho-Won. "Peacebuilding Design: A Synergetic Approach." In Ho-Won Jeong (ed.), *Approaches to Peacebuilding.* New York: Palgrave Macmillan, 2002.

John Paul II. "Centesimus Annus." *Vatican Website.* May 1st, 1991.

———."Redemptoris Missio." *Vatican Website.* December 7th, 1990.

———."Slavorum Apostoli." *Vatican Website.* June 2nd, 1985.

Johnston, Douglas. "Faith Based Organizations: The Religious Dimensions of Peacebuilding." In Paul van Tongeren, Malin Brenk, Marte Hellema, and Juliette Verhoeven (eds.), *People Building Peace II: Successful Stories of Civil Society.* Boulder, CO: Lynne Rienner, 2005.

———. "Introduction: Beyond Power Politics." In Douglas Johnston and Cynthia Sampson (eds.), *Religion, the Missing Dimension of Statecraft.* New York: Oxford University Press, 1994.

Johnston, Douglas, and Cynthia Sampson, eds. *Religion, the Missing Dimension of Statecraft.* New York: Oxford University Press, 1994.

Jorgensen, Danny L. *Participant Observation: A Methodology for Human Studies.* Newbury Park, CA: Sage Publications, 1989.

Juteau, Danielle. *L'ethnicité et ses frontières.* Montréal: Presses de l'Université de Montréal, 1999.

Kabamba, Patience. *Business of Civil War: New Forms of Life in the Debris of the Democratic Republic of Congo.* Dakar: Codesria, 2013.

———. "Trading On War: New Forms of Life in the Debris of the State." Ph.D. Dissertation, Columbia University, 2008.

Kabasele Lumbala, François. *Le christianisme et l'Afrique une chance réciproque.* Paris: Karthala, 1993.

Kabongo-Mbaya, Philippe B. *L'Eglise du Christ au Zaïre: formation et adaptation d'un protestantisme en situation de dictature.* Paris: Karthala, 1992.

Kaboy, Theophile Ruboneka. *Le diocèse de Goma: Un aperçu historique de ses origines et de son développement (1911–1985).* Goma: Construire ensemble, 1986.

Kapuku, Kalombo Sebastien. "La pentecôtisation du protestantisme à Kinshasa." *Afrique contemporaine* 4, no. 252 (2014): 51–71.

Keith, Arthur Berriedale. *The Belgian Congo and the Berlin Act.* Oxford: Clarendon Press, 1919.

Kennes, Eric. "The Democratic Republic of Congo: Structures of Greed, Networks of Need." In Cynthia Arnson and I. William Zartman (eds.), *Rethinking the Economics of War: The Intersection of Need, Creed, and Greed.* Washington, D.C., Baltimore: Woodrow Wilson Center Press; Johns Hopkins University Press, 2005.

Kirk, Jerome, and Marc L. Miller. *Reliability and Validity in Qualitative Research.* Beverly Hills: Sage Publications, 1986.

Kisangani, Emizet F. *Civil Wars in the Democratic Republic of Congo, 1960–2010.* Boulder, CO: Lynne Rienner, 2012.

Kitumaini, Jean-Marie Vianney. *Nouveaux enjeux de l'agir socio-politique de l'Église face aux défis de la société en Afrique: application à l'Archidiocèse de Bukavu (RDC) à travers ses magistères successifs: en marge du premier centenaire de l'évangélisation* de *l'Archidiocèse de Bukavu, 1906–2006.* Paris: Harmattan, 2011.

Kwibeshya, Cyprien. "L'église et la promotion de la paix dans un monde en conflits: cas des Pays des grands Lacs." Travail de fin de cycle, Université Libre des Pays de Grands Lacs, 2003.

Lagergren, David. *Mission and State in the Congo: A Study of the Relations between Protestant Missions and the Congo Independent State Authorities with Special Reference to the Equator district, 1885–1903.* Lund: Gleerup, 1970.

Lavoix, Hélène. "Identifier l'État fragile avant l'heure: Le rôle des indicateurs de prévision." In Jean-Marc Châtaigner and Hervé Magro (eds.), États et sociétés fragiles: entre conflits, reconstitution et développement. Paris: Karthala, 2007.

Le Billon, Philippe. *Fuelling War: Natural Resources and Armed Conflicts.* Oxford: Oxford University Press, 2003.

Lederach, John Paul. *Building Peace: Sustainable Reconciliation in Divided Societies.* Washington, D.C.: United States Institute of Peace Press, 1997.

———. "Conflict Transformation in Protracted Internal Conflicts: The Case for a Comprehensive Framework." In Kumar Rupesinghe (ed.), *Conflict Transformation.* Houndmills, Basingstoke, Hampshire: Macmillan, 1995.

———. "Justpeace: The Challenge of the 21st Century." In Paul van Tongeren (ed.), *People Building Peace: 35 Inspiring Stories from Around the World.* Utrecht, Netherlands: European Centre for Conflict Prevention, 1999.

———. *The Little Book of Conflict Transformation.* Philadelphia: Good Books, Intercourse, 2003.

———. "The Long Journey Back to Humanity." In Robert J. Schreiter, R. Scott Appleby, and Gerard F. Powers (eds.), *Peacebuilding: Catholic Theology, Ethics, and Praxis*. Maryknoll, NY: Orbis Books, 2010.

Lederach, John Paul, and R. Scott Appleby. "Strategic Peacebuilding: An Overview." In Daniel Philpott and Gerard F. Powers (eds.), *Strategies of Peace: Transforming Conflict in a Violent World*. Oxford, NY: Oxford University Press, 2010.

Leloup, Bernard. "Le Rwanda et ses voisins." In Stefaan Marysse and Filip Reyntjens (eds.), *L'Afrique des grands lacs: annuaire 2004–2005*. Paris: L' Harmattan, 2005.

Lemarchand, René. "Burundi 1972: Genocide Denied, Revised, and Remembered." In René Lemarchand and Filip Reyntjens (eds.), *Forgotten Genocides: Oblivion, Denial, and Memory*. Philadelphia: University of Pennsylvania Press, 2011.

———. *The Dynamics of Violence in Central Africa*. Philadelphia: University of Pennsylvania Press, 2009.

Lemarchand, René, and Filip Reyntjens. "Mass Murder in Eastern Congo, 1996–1997." In René Lemarchand and Filip Reyntjens (eds.), *Forgotten Genocides: Oblivion, Denial, and Memory*. Philadelphia: University of Pennsylvania Press, 2011.

Léon, de Saint Moulin (SJ). "Le rôle de l'Église catholique dans la societé en RDC." In Manfred Schulz (ed.), *Les porteurs du développement durable en R.D.Congo: Évolutions récentes de la vie politique, économique, religieuse, culturelle et de la societé civile*. Kinshasa; Berlin: Cepas; Spektrum, 2010.

Lincoln, Yvonna S., and Egon G. Guba. *Naturalistic Inquiry*. Beverly Hills, CA: Sage Publications, 1985.

Little, David. "Religion, Violent Conflict, and Peacemaking." In David Little (ed.), *Peacemakers in Action: Profiles of Religion in Conflict Resolution*. Cambridge; New York: Cambridge University Press, 2007.

Little, David, and R. Scott Appleby. "A Moment of Opportunity?: The Promise of Religious Peacebuilding in an Era of Religious and Ethnic Conflict." In Harold G. Coward and Gordon S. Smith (eds.), *Religion and Peacebuilding*. Albany: State University of New York Press, 2004.

Longman, Timothy Paul. *Christianity and Genocide in Rwanda*. Cambridge, England; New York: Cambridge University Press, 2010.

Luboloko, Francois Luyeye. *Les sectes: interpellations et discernement*. Kinshasa: Éditions Le Sénévé, 2013.

M'Bokolo, Elikia. *Des missionnaires aux explorateurs: les Européens en Afrique*. Paris: ABC, 1977.

Mahoney, James. "Path Dependence in Historical Sociology." *Theory and Society* 29, no. 4 (2000): 507–548.

Malula, Joseph-Albert. "Essai de profil des prêtres de l'an 2000 au Zaïre: Message du Cardinal Malula," *in Documentation Catholique*, no. 1961 (1er mai 1988): 463–469.

Mamdani, Mahmood. *When Victims Become Killers: Colonialism, Nativism, and the Genocide in Rwanda*. Princeton, NJ: Princeton University Press, 2001.

Mana, Kä. *La nouvelle évangélisation en Afrique*. Paris; Yaoundé: Karthala; Clé, 2000.

Mararo, Stanislas Bucyalimwe. "Kinshasa et le Kivu depuis 1987: une histoire ambigue." In Stefaan Marysse and Filip Reyntjens (eds.), *L'Afrique des grands lacs: annuaire 2004–2005*. Paris: L' Harmattan, 2005a.

———. "Kivu and Ituri in the Congo War: The Roots and Nature of a Linkage." In Stefaan Marysse and Filip Reyntjens (eds.), *The Political Economy of the Great Lakes Region in Africa: The Pitfalls of Enforced Democracy and Globalization.* New York: Palgrave Macmillan, 2005b.

———. "La societé civile du Kivu: une dynamique en panne?" In Stefaan Marysse and Filip Reyntjens (eds.), *L'Afrique des grands lacs: Annuaire 1998–1999.* Paris: L'Harmattan, 1999.

———. "Land Conflicts in Masisi, Eastern Zaire: The Impact and aftermath of Belgian Colonial Policy (1920–1989)." Ph.D., Indiana University, 1990.

———. "Land, Power, and Ethnic Conflict in Masisi (Congo-Kinshasa), 1940s–1994." *The International Journal of African Historical Studies* 30, no. 3 (1997): 503–538.

———. *Maneuvering for Ethnic Hegemony: A Thorny Issue in the North Kivu Peace Process (DR Congo), Volume I: The 1959–1997 History of North Kivu.* Bruxelles: Éditions Scribe, 2014a.

———. *Maneuvering for Ethnic Hegemony: A Thorny Issue in the North Kivu Peace Process (DR Congo), Volume II: The 1996–1997 invasion of the "Tutsi without borders" and the remote reconciliation in North Kivu.* Bruxelles: Éditions Scribe, 2014b.

Markowitz, Marvin D. *Cross and Sword: The Political Role of Christian Missions in the Belgian Congo, 1908–1960.* Stanford, CA: Hoover Institution Press, 1973.

Marshall, Catherine, and Gretchen B. Rossman. *Designing Qualitative Research.* (5th ed.). Los Angeles: Sage, 2011.

Marshall, Katherine. *Global Institutions of Religion: Ancient Movers, Modern Shakers.* Abingdon, Oxon; New York: Routledge, 2013.

Martin, Marie-Louise. *Kimbangu: An African Prophet and his Church.* Great Britain: Basil Blackwell, 1975.

Marvel, Tom. *Le nouveau Congo.* Bruxelles: Cuypers, 1948.

Matangila, Alexis. "Pour une analyse du discours des Eglises de réveil à Kinshasa: Méthode et contexte." *Civilisations* 54, no. 1–2 (2006): 77–84.

Maurel, Auguste. *Le Congo de la colonisation belge à l'indépendance.* Paris: L'Harmattan, 1992.

Maxwell, Joseph Alex. *Qualitative Research Design: An Interactive Approach.* (3rd ed.). Thousand Oaks, CA: Sage Publications, 2013.

Mayrargue, Cédric. "Dynamiques religieuses et démocratisation au Bénin: Pentecôtisme et formation d'un espace public." Doctorat, Montesquieu–Bordeaux, 2002.

Mbanzulu, Kinkasa Salomon. "Problematique de succession dans les églises de reveil: crise de la mission." Mémoire (Licence), Université Protestante au Congo, 2009.

Mbembé, J. Achille. *Afriques indociles: christianisme, pouvoir et État en sociéte postcoloniale.* Paris: Karthala, 1988.

———. *De la postcolonie: essai sur l'imagination politique dans l'Afrique contemporaine.* Paris: Karthala, 2000.

Mbiti, John S. *African Religions & Philosophy.* (2nd ed.). Oxford: Heinemann, 1990.

McCann, Joseph F. *Church and Organization: A Sociological and Theological Enquiry.* Scranton: University of Scranton Press, 1993.

McDonnell, Kilian. *Charismatic Renewal and the Churches.* New York: Seabury Press, 1976.

Mendeloff, David. "Trauma and Vengeance: Assessing the Psychological and Emotional Effects of Post-Conflict Justice." *Human Rights Quarterly* 31, no. 3 (2009): 592–623.

Merdjanova, Ina, and Patrice Brodeur. *Religion as a Conversation Starter: Interreligious Dialogue for Peacebuilding in the Balkans.* New York: Continuum International Publishing Group, 2009.

Merriam, Sharan B. *Qualitative Research: A Guide to Design and Implementation.* San Francisco: Jossey-Bass, 2009.

Miall, Hugh. "Conflict Transformation: A Multi-Dimensional Task." *Berghof Research Center for Constructive Conflict Management* (2004).

Migdal, Joel S. *Strong Societies and Weak States: State-society Relations and State Capabilities in the Third World.* Princeton, NJ: Princeton University Press, 1988.

Miles, Matthew B., and Michael A. Huberman. *Qualitative Data Analysis: An Expanded Sourcebook.* (2nd ed.). Thousand Oaks: Sage Publications, 1994.

Moerschbacher, Marco. "La mission catholique en RDC et sa contribution au développement." In Manfred Schulz (ed.), *Les porteurs du développement durable en R.D.Congo: Évolutions récentes de la vie politique, économique, religieuse, culturelle et de la societé civile.* Kinshasa; Berlin: Cepas; Spektrum, 2010.

———. *Les laïcs dans une Église d'Afrique: l'*œuvre du cardinal Malula (1917–*1989).* Paris: Éditions Karthala, 2012.

Mongo, Nomanyath Manyath Mwan-Awan-A, David. "Les églises de réveil dans l'histoire des réligions en République démocratique du Congo: questions de dialogue œcuménique et interreligieux." Doctorat, Université Lille III—Charles de Gaulle, 2005.

Moore, Barrington. *Injustice: The Social Bases of Obedience and Revolt.* White Plains, NY: M.E. Sharpe, 1978.

Morse, Janice M., and Lyn Richards. *Readme First for a User's Guide to Qualitative Methods.* Thousand Oaks, CA: Sage, 2002.

Mossière, Géraldine. "Églises de réveil, ONG confessionnelles et transnationalisme congolais: une théologie du développement." *Canadian Journal of Development Studies/Revue canadienne d'*études du développement 34, no. 2 (2013): 257–274.

Moulin, Léon de Saint, and Z. Modio. "La signification sociale des sectes au Zaïre." *Cahiers des religions Africaines* 27–28, no. 53–56 (1993–1994): 247–268.

Mpisi, Jean. *Kivu, RDC: La paix à tout prix !: La Conférence de Goma (6–23 janvier 2008).* Paris: L'Harmattan, 2008.

Mudimbe, V. Y. *The Idea of Africa.* Bloomington: Indiana University Press, 1994.

———. *The invention of Africa: Gnosis, Philosophy, and the Order of Knowledge.* Bloomington: Indiana University Press, 1988.

———. *L'odeur du père: essai sur des limites de la science et de la vie en Afrique noire.* Paris: Présence africaine, 1982.

Mudimbe, V. Y., and Mbula Susan Kilonzo. "Philosophy of Religion on African Ways of Believing." In Elias Kifon Bongmba (ed.), *The Wiley-Blackwell Companion to African Religions.* Malden, MA: Wiley-Blackwell, 2012.

Mugaruka, Richard. "L'experience des communautés écclesiales de base et les défis de l'après guerre dans l'est de la R.D. Congo." *L'Église catholique et l'éducation civique dans les communautés écclesiales vivantes de base, à l'aube du IIè synode sur l'afrique (du 21 au 25 avril 2008).* Kinshasa: Faculté Catholique de Kinshasa, 2008.

———. *Reflexions pastorales: le rôle des églises dans la refondation de l'*État congolais, cinquante ans après son indépendance. Kinshasa: Feu Torrent, 2011.

Mujynya, Edmond, and Laurent Sebisogo. "Monseigneur Joseph Busimba: Pionnier, pasteur et homme de Dieu." In Gonzalve Gisamonyo Ntawihaye Twose and Stanislas Bucyalimwe Mararo (eds.), *Mgr Joseph Busimba Mikararanga (1912–1974), premier prêtre et Èvêque noir du Kivu, fondateur et grand pasteur du Diocèse de Goma.* Goma, Congo (Democratic Republic): Association Les Amis de Goma, 2012.

Mulongo, Freddy. "Dix questions à Kä Mana." *Reveil Net,* 8 avril 2009 (http://reveil-fm.com/index.php/reveil-fm.com2009/04/08/336-10-questions-a-ka-mana).

Mulongo, Lusiensie. "La contribution du diocèse de Goma au processus électoral en R.D.C pendant la transition (1990–2006)." Travail de fin de cycle (Licence), Université de Goma, 2006.

Munayi Muntu-Monji, Thomas. "Le rôle de l'Eglise protestante au cours des cinquante années d'independance 1960–2010." In Faustin-Jovite Mapwar Bashuth (ed.), *Eglise et Societé: Le discours socio-politique des éveques de la Conference epicospale nationale du Congo (CENCO).* Kinshasa: Facultés catholiques de Kinshasa, 2007.

Munima, Godefroid Mashie. *Prêtre prisonnier de la tribu.* Kinshasa: Editions Baobab, 1996.

Murairi, Jean-Baptiste Mitima. *Les Bahunde aux pieds des volcans Virunga (R-D Congo) Histoire et Culture.* Paris: L'Harmattan, 2005.

———. *Parlons Kihunde: Kivu, R-D.Congo, Langue et culture.* Paris: L'Harmattan, 2008.

Mushete, Ngindu. "Simon Kimbangu et le Kimbanguisme: une lecture historique à propos d'un colloque recent." *Cahiers des religions Africaines* 6 (1972): 91–103.

———. "Le propos du recours à l'authenticité et le christianisme au Zaïre." *Cahiers des religions Africaines* 8, no. 16 (1974): 209–230.

Muyombi, Anicet Mutonkole. *L'engagement de l'Église catholique dans le processus de démocratisation en République Démocratique du Congo.* Berlin: Peter Lang, 2006.

Muzorewa, Gwinyai H. *The Origins and Development of African Theology.* Maryknoll, NY: Orbis Books, 1985.

Mwene-Kabyana, Kadari. "La politique étrangère du Zaïre (1965–1985): illusion de puissance et clientelisme." Ph.D. Dissertation, Université Laval, 1999.

N'Gbanda Nzambo-ko-Atumba, Honoré. *Crimes organisés en Afrique centrale: révélations sur les réseaux rwandais et occidentaux.* Paris: Duboiris, 2004.

Ndaywel è Nziem, Isidore. *Histoire générale du Congo: de l'héritage ancien à la République démocratique.* Bruxelles; Duculot: De Boeck & Larsier: Afrique-Editions, 1998.

———. *Nouvelle histoire du Congo: Des origines à la République Démocratique.* Kinshasa: Afrique éditions, 2008.

Ndongala, Maduku Ignace. "Autoritarisme étatiques et régulation religieuse du politique en République Démocratique du Congo: Analyse discursive de la parole de épiscopale catholique sur les élections (1990–2015)." Ph.D. Dissertation, Université de Montréal, 2015.

———. "Le ministère des prêtres en Afrique." In E. Babissangana and Nsapo Kalamba (eds.), *Qu'as-tu fais de ton frère? Mélanges en l'honneur de Mgr Jan Dumon.* Kinshasa: Publications Universitaires Africaines, 2012.

Neill, Stephen. *Colonialism and Christian Missions.* New York: McGraw-Hill, 1966.

Nelson, Jack Edward. "Christian Missionizing and Social Transformation: A History of Conflict and Change in Eastern Zaire." Ph.D., Temple University, 1989.

———. *Christian Missionizing and Social Transformation: A History of Conflict and Change in Eastern Zaïre*. New York: Praeger, 1992.

Newman, Edward. "Liberal Peacebuilding Debates." In Edward Newman, Roland Paris, and Oliver P. Richmond (eds.), *New Perspectives on Liberal Peacebuilding*. New York: United Nations University Press, 2009.

Ngabu, Faustin. "Courage, n'ayez pas peur (Is 13:4)." *Pastoral Letter*, May 18th, 1996.

Ngomo Okitembo, Louis. *L'engagement politique de l'Eglise catholique au Zaïre, 1960–1992*. Paris: L'Harmattan, 1998.

Nkingi, Mweze Chirhulwire Dominique. "Eglise de réveil: Génese et modes opératoires." In Kinyamba Sylvain Shomba (ed.), *Les spiritualité du temps présent*. Kinshasa: Éditions M.E.S., 2012.

Nkomo, Stella M., and Hellicy Ngambi. "African Women in Leadership: Current Knowledge and a Framework for Future Studies." *International Journal of African Renaissance Studies—Multi-, Inter- and Transdisciplinarity* 4, no. 1 (2009): 49–68.

Nkunzi, Baciyunjuze Justin. *La naissance de l'*Église au Bushi: l'ère des pionniers 1906–*1908*. Rome: Gregorian University Press, 2005.

Nordstrom, Carolyn. "Contested Identities/Essentially Contested Powers." In Kumar Rupesinghe (ed.), *Conflict Transformation*. Houndmills, Basingstoke, Hampshire: Macmillan, 1995.

———, and Antonius C. G. M. Robben. *Fieldwork Under Fire: Contemporary Studies of Violence and Survival*. Berkeley: University of California Press, 1995.

Nougayrède, Natalie. "La France prépare une initiative de paix pour l'est de la République démocratique du Congo." *Le Monde* (19 janvier 2009).

Ntumba, Museka Lambert. "Les Églises independantes et charismatiques en République Democratique du Congo (RDC) et leur engagement dans le developpement du pays." In Manfred Schulz (ed.), *Les porteurs du développement durable en R.D.Congo: Évolutions récentes de la vie politique, économique, religieuse, culturelle et de la societé civile*. Kinshasa; Berlin: Cepas; Spektrum, 2010.

Nzongola-Ntalaja, Georges. *The Congo from Leopold to Kabila: A People's History*. London; New York: Zed Books, 2002.

———. "Ethnicity and State Politics in Africa." *African Journal of International Affairs* 2, no. 1 (1999): 31–59.

———. *Faillite de la gouvernance et crise de la construction nationale au Congo-Kinshasa: une analyse des luttes pour la démocratie et la souveraineté*. Kinshasa; Montréal; Washington, D.C.: ICREDES, 2015.

Oldenburg, Silke. "Everyday Entrepreneurs and Big Men: Facets of Entrepreneurship in Goma, Democratic Republic of Congo." In Dorothea Elisabeth Schulz and Ute Röschenthaler (eds.), *Cultural Entrepreneurship in Africa*. New York, NY: Routledge, Taylor & Francis, 2016.

Omer, Atalia. "Religious Peacebuilding: The Exotic, the Good, and the Theatrical." In Atalia Omer, R. Scott Appleby, and David Little (eds.), *The Oxford Handbook of Religion, Conflict, and Peacebuilding*. New York, NY: Oxford University Press, 2015.

Oryang, John. "Can Peace Succeed in the Democratic Republic of Congo." *Peace News*. May 4, 2017 (https://www.peacenews.com/single-post/2017/05/04/Can-Peace-Succeed-in-the-Democratic-Republic-of-the-Congo).

Otite, Onigu. *Ethnic Pluralism and Ethnicity in Nigeria: With Comparative Materials*. Ibadan: Shaneson C. I., 1990.

Oyatambwe, Wamu. Église catholique et pouvoir politique au Congo-Zaire la quête démocratique. Paris: L'Harmattan, 1997.

Paffenholz, Thania. "Civil Society and Peacebuilding." In Thania Paffenholz (ed.), *Civil Society & Peacebuilding: A Critical Assessment*. Boulder: Lynne Rienner, 2010.

Pakenham, Thomas. *The Scramble for Africa: 1876–1912*. New York: Random House, 1991.

Palmer, Michael D., and Stanley M. Burgess. "Introduction." In Michael D. Palmer and Stanley M. Burgess (eds.), *The Wiley-Blackwell Companion to Religion and Social Justice*. Chichester, West Sussex; Malden, MA: Wiley-Blackwell, 2012.

Paluck, Levy Elizabeth. "Methods and Ethics with Research Teams and NGOs: Comparing Experiences across the Border of Rwanda and Democratic Republic of Congo." In Chandra Lekha Sriram, John C. King, Julie A. Mertus, Olga Martin-Ortega, and Johanna Herman (eds.), *Surviving Field Research: Working in Violent and Difficult Situations*. London; New York: Routledge, 2009.

Parent, Geneviève. "Peacebuilding, Healing, Reconciliation: An Analysis of Unseen Connections for Peace." *International Peacekeeping* 18, no. 4 (2011): 379–395.

Paris, Roland. "Saving Liberal Peacebuilding." *Review of International Studies* 36, no. 02 (2010): 337–365.

Paris, Roland, and Timothy D. Sisk. "Introduction: Understanding the Contradictions of Postwar Statebuilding." In Roland Paris and Timothy D. Sisk (eds.), *The Dilemmas of Statebuilding: Confronting the Contradictions of Postwar Peace Operations*. Abingdon, UK: Routledge, 2009.

Parrinder, Edward Geoffrey. *African Traditional Religion*. (3rd ed.). London: Sheldon Press, 1974.

Paul VI. "Eucharistic Celebration at the Conclusion of the Symposium Organized by the Bishops of Africa: Homily of Paul VI." Kampala, Uganda. July 31st, 1969. https://w2.vatican.va/content/paul-vi/en/homilies/1969/documents/hf_p-vi_hom_19690731.html.

———. "Evangelii Nuntiandi." *Vatican Website*. December 8th, 1975.

———. "Populorum Progressio." *Vatican Website*. March 26, 1967.

Pauwels, Nathalie. "L' économie de guerre en RDC: un défi pour la paix et la reconstruction." In Eric Remacle, Rosoux Valérie-Barbara, and Saur Léon (eds.), *L'Afrique des Grands Lacs: des conflits à la paix?* Bruxelles; New York: P.I.E. Peter Lang, 2007.

Peiffer, Caryn, and Pierre Englebert. "Extraversion, Vulnerability to Donors, and Political Liberalization in Africa." *African Affairs* 111, no. 444 (2012): 355–378.

Peters, Manfred. "Approche conscientisante et entrepreneuriat feminin." In Fatou Sarr and Georges Thill (eds.), *Femmes et développements durables et solidaires: savoirs, science, entrepreneuriat*. Namur: Presses universitaires de Namur, 2006.

Phan, C. Peter. "Peacebuilding and Reconciliation: Interreligious Dialogue and Catholic Spirituality." In Robert J. Schreiter, R. Scott Appleby, and Gerard F. Powers (eds.), *Peacebuilding: Catholic Theology, Ethics, and Praxis*. Maryknoll, NY: Orbis Books, 2010.

Philpott, Daniel. *Just and Unjust Peace: An Ethic of Political Reconciliation.* New York: Oxford University Press, 2012.

Pierson, Paul. "The Limits of Design: Explaining Institutional Origins and Change." *Governance* 13, no. 4 (2000): 475–499.

Pilar Aquino, María. "Religious Peacebuilding." In Andrew R. Murphy (ed.), *The Blackwell Companion to Religion and Violence.* Malden, MA: Wiley-Blackwell, 2011.

Posner, Daniel. "Civil Society and the Reconstruction of Failed States." In Robert I. Rotberg (ed.), *When States Fail: Causes and Consequences.* Princeton, NJ: Princeton University Press, 2004.

Pourtier, Roland. "Le Kivu dans la guerre: acteurs et enjeux." *EchoGéo [online]*, 2009.

Powers, Gerard F. "Religion and Peacebuilding." In Daniel Philpott and Gerard F. Powers (eds.), *Strategies of Peace: Transforming Conflict in a Violent World.* New York: Oxford University Press, 2010.

Prudhomme, Claude. "Le rôle des missions chrétiennes dans la formation des identités nationales: le point de vue catholique." In Claude Prudhomme and Jean-François Zorn (eds.), *Missions chrétiennes et formation des identités nationales hors d'Europe, XIX–XXe s.* Lyon: CREDIC, 1995.

———. *Stratégie missionnaire du Saint-Siège sous Léon XIII (1878–1903): centralisation romaine et défis culturels.* Roma: Ecole française de Rome, 1994.

Prunier, Gérard. "The Catholic Church and the Kivu Conflict." *Journal of Religion in Africa* 31, no. 2 (2001): 139–162.

Rabie, Moḥamed. *Conflict Resolution and Ethnicity.* Westport, CT: Praeger, 1994.

Ramsbotham, Oliver, Hugh Miall, and Tom Woodhouse. *Contemporary Conflict Resolution: The Prevention, Management and Transformation of Deadly Conflicts.* (3rd ed.). Cambridge, UK; Malden, MA: Polity Press, 2011.

Randles, W. G. L. *L'ancien royaume du Congo des origines à la fin du XIXe siècle.* Paris: Mouton, 1968.

Ravitch, Sharon M., and Matthew Riggan. *Reason & Rigor: How Conceptual Frameworks Guide Research.* Thousand Oaks, CA: Sage 2012.

Rawls, John. *A Theory of Justice.* (Rev. ed.). Cambridge, MA: Belknap Press of Harvard University Press, 1999.

Reich, Hannah. "'Local Ownership' in Conflict Transformation Projects: Partnership, Participation or Patronage?" *Berghof Occasional Paper* 27 (2006).

Reinharz, Shulamit. "Who Am I? The Need for a Variety of Selves in the Field." In Rosanna Hertz (ed.), *Reflexivity & Voice.* Thousand Oaks, CA: Sage Publications, 1997.

Renguet, Jacques, "Monseigneur Busimba et la paroisse du Chant d'oiseau." In Gonzalve Gisamonyo Ntawihaye Twose and Mararo Bucyalimwe Stanislas (eds.), *Mgr Joseph Busimba Mikararanga (1912–1974), premier prêtre et Èvêque noir du Kivu, fondateur et grand pasteur du Diocèse de Goma.* Goma, Congo (Democratic Republic): Association Les Amis de Goma, 2012.

Reybrouck, David van. *Congo: The Epic History of a People.* London: Fourth Estate, 2014.

Richards, Lyn. *Handling Qualitative Data: A Practical Guide.* (2nd ed.). Los Angeles, CA: Sage, 2009.

Richmond, Oliver P. "Patterns of Peace." *Global Society* 20, no. 4 (2006a): 367–394.

———. "The Problem of Peace: Understanding the 'liberal peace.'" *Conflict, Security & Development* 6, no. 3 (2006b): 291–314.

———. *The Transformation of Peace.* New York: Palgrave Macmillan, 2005.

Richmond, Oliver P., and Audra Mitchell. *Hybrid Forms of Peace: From Everyday Agency to Post-liberalism*. Houndmills, Basingstoke, Hampshire; New York, NY: Palgrave Macmillan, 2012a.

———. "Towards a Post-Liberal Peace: Exploring Hybridity via Everyday Forms of Resistance, Agency and Autonomy." In Oliver P. Richmond and Audra Mitchell (eds.), *Hybrid Forms of Peace: From Everyday Agency to Post-liberalism*. Houndmills, Basingstoke, Hampshire; New York, NY: Palgrave Macmillan, 2012b.

Roberts, Allen F. *A Dance of Assassins: Performing Early Colonial Hegemony in the Congo*. Bloomington; Indianapolis: Indiana University Press, 2013.

Roberts, Les. *Mortality in Eastern DRC: Results from Five Mortality Surveys*. International Rescue Committee, 2000.

Roeykens, Auguste. *Les débuts de l'*œuvre africaine de Léopold II. Bruxelles: Académie royale des sciences coloniales, 1955.

Ross, Marc Howard. *The Culture of Conflict: Interpretations and Interests in Comparative Perspective*. New Haven, CT: Yale University Press, 1993.

Roy, Simon N. "L'étude de cas." In Benoît Gauthier (ed.), *Recherche sociale: de la problématique à la collecte des données*. Sainte-Foy: Presses de l'Université du Québec, 2006.

Rubin, Herbert J., and Irene Rubin. *Qualitative Interviewing: The Art of Hearing Data*. (3rd ed.). Los Angeles, CA: Sage, 2012.

Ryan, Stephen. *The Transformation of Violent Intercommunal Conflict*. Aldershot, England: Ashgate, 2007.

Samba, Kaputo. *Phénomène d'ethnicité et conflits ethnopolitiques en Afrique noire post-coloniale*. Kinshasa: Presses universitaires du Zaïre, 1982.

Sampson, Cynthia. "Religion and Peacebuilding." In I. William Zartman (ed.), *Peacemaking in International Conflict: Methods & Techniques*. Washington, D.C.: United States Institute of Peace, 2007.

Sarr, Fatou, and Georges Thill. *Femmes et développements durables et solidaires: savoirs, science, entrepreneuriat*. Namur: Presses universitaires de Namur, 2006.

Sartori, Giovanni. "Bien comparer, mal comparer." *Revue internationale de politique comparée* 1, no. 1 (1994): 19–36.

Schatzberg, Michael G. *The Dialectics of Oppression in Zaire*. Bloomington: Indiana University Press, 1988.

Schreiter, Robert J. "The Catholic Social Imaginary and Peacebuilding." In Robert J. Schreiter, R. Scott Appleby, and Gerard F. Powers (eds.), *Peacebuilding: Catholic Theology, Ethics, and Praxis*. Maryknoll, NY: Orbis Books, 2010.

Schreiter, Robert J., R. Scott Appleby, and Gerard F. Powers, eds. *Peacebuilding: Catholic Theology, Ethics, and Praxis*. Maryknoll, NY: Orbis Books, 2010.

Seay, Laura Elizabeth. "Authority at Twilight: Civil Society, Social Services, and the State in the Eastern Democratic Republic of Congo." Ph.D. Dissertation, The University of Texas at Austin, 2009.

———. "Effective Responses: Protestants, Catholics and the Provision of Health Care in the Post-war Kivus." *Review of African Political Economy* 40, no. 135 (2013): 83–97.

Sekanga, Freddy Bomay. "Les rôles d'un prophete: regard sur les prophetisme des églises de reveil de Kinshasa." Mémoire (Licence), Université Protestante au Congo, 2009.

Shorter, Aylward. *African Christian Theology: Adaptation or Incarnation?* London: G. Chapman, 1975a.

———. *Prayer in the Religious Traditions of Africa*. Nairobi: Oxford University Press, 1975b.

Simons, Helen. *Case Study Research in Practice*. Los Angeles: Sage, 2009.

Slade, Ruth M. *English-speaking Missions in the Congo Independent State (1878–1908)*. Bruxelles: Academie Royale des Sciences Coloniales, 1959.

Smith, Donald Eugene. *Religion and Political Development, an Analytic Study*. Boston: Little, Brown, 1970.

Smythe, Carlyle. *The Story of Belgium*. London: Hutchinson, 1900.

Springs, Jason A. "Structural and Cultural Violence in Religion and Peacebuilding." In Atalia Omer, R. Scott Appleby, and David Little (eds.), *The Oxford Handbook of Religion, Conflict, and Peacebuilding*. New York, NY: Oxford University Press, 2015.

Stake, Robert E. *The Art of Case Study Research*. Thousand Oaks: Sage Publications, 1995.

Stauffacher, Gladys. *Faster Beats the Drum*. Pearl River, NY: Africa Inland Mission, 1977.

Steele, David. "An Introductory Overview to Faith-Based Peacebuilding." In Rogers Mark, Tom Bamat, and Ideh Julie (eds.), *Pursuing Just Peace: An Overview and Case Studies for Faith-Based Peacebuilders*. Baltimore, MD: Catholic Relief Services, 2008.

Stenger, Friedrich. *White Fathers in Colonial Central Africa: A Critical Examination of V. Y. Mudimbe's Theories on Missionary Discourse in Africa*. Münster: Lit, 2001.

Storme, Marcel Benedictus. "Engagement de la Propagande pour l'organisation territoriale des Missions au Congo." In Josef Metzler (ed.), *Sacrae Congregations de Propaganda Fide Memoria Rerum, Vol. III/1, 1815–1972*. Freiburg: Herder, 1975.

———. *Rapports du Père Planque, de Mgr. Lavigerie et de Mgr. Comboni sur l'Association internationale africaine*. Bruxelles: Académie Royale des Sciences d'Outre-Mer, 1957.

Sullivan, Thomas J. *Methods of Social Research*. Fort Worth, TX; London: Harcourt College, 2001.

Sundberg, Ralph, and Lotta Harbom. "Systematic Data Collection: Experiences from the Uppsala Conflict Data Program." In Kristine Höglund and Magnus Öberg (eds.), *Understanding Peace Research: Methods and Challenges*. London: Routledge, 2011.

Szayna, Thomas S., and Ashley J. Tellis "Introduction." In Thomas S. Szayna (ed.), *Identifying Potential Ethnic Conflict: Application of a Process Model*. Santa Monica: Rand, 2000.

Szayna, Thomas S., Ashley J. Tellis, and James A. Winnefeld. "The Process Model for Anticipating Ethnic Conflict." In Thomas S. Szayna (ed.), *Identifying Potential Ethnic Conflict: Application of a Process Model*. Santa Monica: Rand, 2000.

Tale, Steen-Johnsen. *State and Politics in Religious Peacebuilding*. London: Palgrave Macmillan, 2017.

Taylor, Mark C. *After God*. Chicago: University of Chicago Press, 2007.

Tesfai, Yacob. *Holy Warriors, Infidels, and Peacemakers in Africa*. New York; Basingstoke, England: Palgrave Macmillan, 2010.

Thelen, Kathleen. "How Institutions Evolve: Insights from Comparative Historical Analysis." In James Mahoney and Dietrich Rueschemeyer (eds.), *Comparative Historical Analysis in the Social Sciences*. New York: Cambridge University Press, 2003.

Thomas, Gary. *How to Do Your Case Study: A Guide for Students and Researchers*. Los Angeles, CA: Sage, 2011.

Thomas, R. Murray. *Blending Qualitative & Quantitative Research Methods in Theses and Dissertations*. Thousand Oaks, CA: Corwin Press, 2003.

Toft, Monica Duffy. *Securing the Peace: The Durable Settlement of Civil Wars. Princeton,* NJ: Princeton University Press, 2010.

———, Daniel Philpott, and Timothy Samuel Shah. *God's Century: Resurgent Religion and Global Politics*. New York: W.W. Norton, 2011.

Touze, Dominique Le, Derrick Silove, and Anthony Zwi. "Can there be Healing without Justice? Lessons from the Commission for Reception, Truth and Reconciliation in East Timor." *Intervention: International Journal of Mental Health, Psychosocial Work & Counselling in Areas of Armed Conflict* 3, no. 3 (2005): 192–202.

Trefon, Theodore. *Congo Masquerade: The Political Culture of Aid Inefficiency and Reform Failure*. New York: Zed Books, 2011.

Tsudi wa Kibuti, Mambu-Lo. "L'Église du Christ au Congo (ECC) et son attitude face à la politique (1970–1997)." Diplôme d'études supérieures (D.E.S) en Sciences Historiques, Université de Kinshasa, 2003.

Tull, Denis. *The Reconfiguration of Political Order in Africa: A Case Study of North Kivu (DR Congo)*. Hamburg: Institute of African Affairs, 2005.

Turner, Thomas. *Congo*. Cambridge; Malden, MA: Polity Press, 2013.

Twose, Gonzalve Gisamonyo Ntawihaye, and Stanislas Bucyalimwe Mararo. *Mgr Joseph Busimba Mikararanga (1912–1974), premier prêtre et Èvêque noir du Kivu, fondateur et grand pasteur du Diocèse de Goma*. Goma, Congo (Democratic Republic): Association Les Amis de Goma, 2012.

Ugeux, Bernard. "La pastorale des petites communautés chrétiennes dans quelques diocèses du Zaïre." Ph.D. Thesis, Institut Catholique de Paris, 1987.

———. *Les petites communautés chrétiennes, une alternative aux paroisses?: l'expérience du Zaïre*. Paris: Éditions du Cerf, 1988.

Ukiwo, Ukoha. "Hidden Agendas in Conflict Research: Informants' Interests and Research Objectivity in the Niger Delta." In Christopher Cramer, Laura Hammond, and Johan Pottier (eds.), *Researching Violence in Africa: Ethical and Methodological Challenges*. Leiden; Boston: Brill, 2011.

UN Department of Peacekeeping Operations. *United Nations Peacekeeping Operations: Principles and Guidelines*. New York: United Nations, 2008.

UN Human Rights High Commissioner. "DRC: Mapping Human Rights Violations 1993–2003." United Nations, 2010.

UN Security Council 6943rd Meeting. *Report S/RES/2098/ (2013)*. March 28, 2013.

UN Security Council. *Special Report of the Secretary-General on the DRC and the Great Lakes region (S/2013/119)*. February 27, 2013.

United States Conference of Catholic Bishops. "The Challenge of Peace: God's Promise and Our Response A Pastoral Letter on War and Peace," 1983.

Van Acker, Frank. "La 'Pembenisation' du Haut-Kivu: opportunisme et droits fonciers revisités." In Stefaan Marysse and Filip Reyntjens (eds.), *L'Afrique des grands lacs: annuaire 1998–1999*. Paris: L'Harmattan, 1999.

Vatican Council II. "Gaudium et Spes." December 7th, 1965. http://www.vatican.va/archive/hist_councils/ii_vatican_council/documents/vat-ii_const_19651207_gaudium-et-spes_en.html

Väyrynen, Raimo. *New Directions in Conflict Theory: Conflict Resolution and Conflict Transformation*. London: International Social Science Council; Sage Publications, 1991.

———. "To Settle or to Transform? Perspectives on the Resolution of National and International Conflicts." In Raimo Väyrynen (ed.), *New Directions in Conflict Theory: Conflict Resolution and Conflict Transformation*. London: International Social Science Council; Sage Publications, 1991.

Vlassenroot, Koen, and Karen Büscher. "The City as a Frontier: Urban Development and Identity Processes in Goma." *Crisis States Working Paper 61 (Series 2)*. London: London School of Economics, 2009.

———. "Humanitarian Presence and Urban Development: New Opportunities and Contrasts in Goma, DRC." *Disasters* 34, no. 2 (2010): 256–273.

Wallensteen, Peter. *Quality Peace: Strategic Peacebuilding and World Order*. New York: Oxford University Press, 2015.

———. *Understanding Conflict Resolution: War, Peace, and the Global System*. London; Thousand Oaks, CA: Sage Publications, 2002.

Weber, Max. *Economy and Society: An Outline of Interpretive Sociology*. New York: Bedminster Press, 1968.

Westerlund, David. *African Indigenous Religions and Disease Causation: from Spiritual Beings to Living Humans*. Leiden; Boston: Brill, 2006.

Wijsen, Frans Jozef Servaas. *Seeds of Conflict in a Haven of Peace: From Religious Studies to Interreligious Studies in Africa*. New York, NY: Rodopi, 2007.

Wilén, Nina. "Capacity-building or Capacity-taking? Legitimizing Concepts in Peace and Development Operations." *International Peacekeeping* 16, no. 3 (2009): 337–351.

Willaert, Maurice. *Kivu redécouvert*. Bruxelles: Max Arnold, 1973.

Willaime, Jean-Paul. *La précarité protestante: sociologie du protestantisme contemporain*. Genève: Labor et Fides, 1992.

———. "La religion: un lien social articulé au don." *Revue du MAUSS* no. 22 (2003/2): 248–269.

———. *Sociologie des religions*. Paris: Presses universitaires de France, 1995.

Willame, Jean-Claude. *Banyarwanda et Banyamulenge: violences éthniques et gestion de l'identitaire au Kivu*. Bruxelles: CERAF, 1997.

———. *La guerre du Kivu: Vues de la salle climatisée et de la véranda*. Bruxelles: Éditions GRIP, 2010.

———. *Les "Faiseurs de Paix" au Congo: gestion d'une crise internationale dans un état sous tutelle*. Bruxelles: GRIP; Éditions Complexe, 2007.

Willame, Jean-Claude, and Benoit Verhaegen. *Les provinces du Congo: Structure et fonctionnement (Lomami—Kivu Central)*. Léopoldville: Université Lovanium, 1964a.

———. *Les provinces du Congo: Structure et fonctionnement (Nord-Kivu—Lac Léopold II)*. Léopoldville: Université Lovanium, 1964b.

Williams, Malcolm. *Making Sense of Social Research.* Thousand Oaks, CA: Sage, 2003.

Witness, Global. *Faced With a Gun, What Can You Do?: War and the Militarisation of Mining in Eastern Congo.* London: Global Witness, 2009.

Wolcott, Harry F. *Transforming Qualitative Data: Description, Analysis, and Interpretation.* Thousand Oaks, CA: Sage Publications, 1994.

Yates, Simeon. *Doing Social Science Research.* London; Thousand Oaks, CA: Sage Publications in association with The Open University, 2004.

Yin, Robert K. *Case Study Research: Design and Methods.* (4th ed.). Los Angeles: Sage Publications, 2009a.

———. *Case Study Research: Design and Methods.* (5th ed.). Thousand Oaks, CA: Sage, 2014.

———. "How to Do Better Case Studies (with illustrations from 20 exemplary case studies)." In Leonard Bickman and Debra J. Rog (eds.), *The SAGE Handbook of Applied Social Research Method.* Los Angeles: Sage, 2009b.

Young, Crawford. *The African Colonial State in Comparative Perspective.* New Haven: Yale University Press, 1994.

———. "Ethnic Diversity and Public Policy: An Overview." In Crawford Young (ed.), *Ethnic Diversity and Public Policy: A Comparative inquiry.* New York: St. Martin's Press, 1998.

———. *Politics in the Congo: Decolonization and Independence.* Princeton: Princeton University Press, 1965.

Yumba, Gaston Nkasa. "L'apport de l'Eglise Protestante au développement économique et social du Congo." In Centre de recherchers interdisciplinaires et de Publications Université Protestante au Congo (ed.), *L'Eglise dans la societé Congolaise: Hier, Aujourd'hui et Demain (Actes des journées scientifiques interfacultaires du 25 au 28 avril 2001).* Kinshasa: Editions de l'Université Protestante au Congo (EDUPC), 2001.

Zahan, Dominique. *The Religion, Spirituality, and Thought of Traditional Africa.* Chicago: University of Chicago Press, 1979.

Zartman, I. William. "Introduction: Posing the Problem of State Collapse." In I. William Zartman (ed.), *Elusive Peace: Negotiating an End to Civil Wars.* Washington, D.C.: Brookings Institution, 1995.

———. "Conclusions: The Last Mile." In I. William Zartman (ed.), *Elusive Peace: Negotiating an End to Civil Wars.* Washington, D.C.: Brookings Institution, 1995.

5

A Comparative Analysis of the Catholic, *3eme* CBCA, and *Arche* Churches in Goma

Introduction

The aim of this chapter is to not only make an explicit comparison of elements of my findings within each of the three churches, but also to make a broader institutional comparison between the three churches themselves. Indeed, I was often asked by my colleague researchers and informants two kinds of questions that required a comparative framework for me to answer. Some questions I categorized as quantitative, which is not the focus of this study, and others as qualitative. Quantitative questions were articulated in the form of "How many?" and "How much?" Qualitative questions included "Which one is better, and which one is worse than the other church?" Qualitative questions were further formulated for descriptive and explanatory purposes.

Elsewhere, people wanted to know not only the reasons for undertaking such a study but also the reasons for including three different churches: "Why are you studying three churches if you are not comparing them?" An examination of three churches inevitably includes a certain degree of comparison. For many scholars, like political scientists Giovanni Sartori (1994), Mamoudou Gazibo and Jane Jenson (2004), a comparative investigation offers several benefits. First, it seeks to reveal both the similarities and the differences between the subjects being studied, according to given criteria. Precisely for this book, where do the differences between the Catholic, *3ème* CBCA and *Arche* Churches reside? The examination of these differences may take several perspectives: ecclesiological, sociological, and institutional. Taking a holistic approach, I privilege these perspectives not only in this chapter, but throughout the entire book.

Second, comparisons allow us to generalize findings (Sartori 1994, 20, 22). The cross-church qualitative study has two benefits: to further our understanding of the three churches and, ultimately, to generalize the findings. Making those comparisons, at times, raises methodological questions and challenges.

I have subdivided this chapter into five different sections, beginning with an examination of the main phases of the life cycle of the three selected religious organizations. Contrary to mainline churches—whose memberships have been decreasing since the 1990s, to the benefit of new churches—the socio-political and economic contexts in which religious organizations arise strongly influence their sustainability and eventual demise. Second, I address the roles fulfilled by the Catholic, *3ème* CBCA and *Arche* Churches, both as institutions and as social actors in religious peacebuilding in Goma. The third and fourth sections seek to comparatively understand the "religious economy" of the three churches regarding the mobilization of resources: in terms of socio-political mobilizations and as a global phenomenon. The fifth and final section addresses the issue of competition, which I argue to be one of the main expressions of the three religious institutions as well as other churches in other provinces in the DRC.

Emergence, Maintenance and "Decay": A Three-Phase Cycle of Religious Institutions

The development of institutions, in general, and that of social and religious institutions, in particular, is characterized by a three-phase life cycle. Their genesis is often influenced by or the result of socio-political factors such as war (Gazibo and Jenson 2004; Thelen 2003). In his book *Church and Organization: A Sociological and Theological Enquiry*, the sociologist Joseph F. McCann specifically notes that "religious institutions evolve from the religious experiences of particular founders and their circles of followers" (1993, 57). While socio-political indicators are not the sole factors that determine the emergence of institutions, they serve to justify their maintenance, longevity and reproduction. Many scholars, especially political scientists, include such arguments in their theories of path dependence and layering (Gazibo and Jenson 2004; Mahoney 2000; Pierson 2000; Thelen 2003).

On the one hand, path dependence supporters argue that certain sequential historical events are crucial in determining certain outcomes such as institutional emergence and maintenance. On the other hand, a layering perspective represents new layers of institutional structure as being deposited on top of pre-existing ones (Gazibo and Jenson 2004; Thelen 2003). That is, not only do institutions depend on exogenous and endogenous forces for their "innovation," other factors different from those that triggered their genesis will also be required, as the political scientist Kathleen Thelen (2003, 212) points out, to ensure their perpetuation. The third and last institutional phase marks the institution's demise. This phase does not necessarily mean a complete disappearance. Depending on the type of institution, and especially for non-mainline churches, their demise usually follows the death or fall of the main leader or prophet. In fact, Max Weber observes in his "routinization of charisma"—where he distinguishes three types of pure authority (legal, traditional and charismatic[1])—that the conflictual environment of succession poses a serious threat to a church's own survival, especially ones with charismatic leaders (1968, 215–253). The examination of the three religious institutions in this book illustrates the three-phase institutional evolution.

The Catholic, *3ème Communauté Baptiste au Centre de l'Afrique* (*3ème* CBCA) and *Arche de l'Alliance* Churches in Goma arose in difficult contexts. The first two stemmed from Belgian and American missionaries, respectively, in the late 1950s, and were predominately influenced by the events surrounding the independence of the Congo. With the independence of the Congo, new structural layers controlled by the Congolese were built upon existing structures led mainly by Western missionaries. While the *Arche* Church had already been established in Kinshasa, a new one emerged in Goma in the 1990s. Although it was established almost forty years after the Catholic and *3ème* CBCA Churches, the sociopolitical environment of the 1990s (preceding the rise of the three religious institutions) was plagued with instability, conflict, violence and rebellions. Moreover, the post-independence leadership of all three remained predominately local, accompanied by a certain degree of foreign assistance or partnership, often Western. As mentioned in Chapter Three, of the three institutions, the *3ème* CBCA (previously known as CBK) Church has encountered the most severe institutional turmoil. This resulted in its splitting, primarily because of internal ethnic conflicts.

Institutional and Personal Roles of the Catholic, 3ème CBCA, and *Arche* Churches in Religious Peacebuilding in Goma

Although individuals establish institutions that they then represent, both influence each other in different ways. According to Mamoudou and Jenson (2004, 209), institutions determine the power dynamics between actors, who adjust their roles to fit their interests, depending on the position they occupy within the institution. Religious actors in general, and those in Goma in particular, play several crucial and spatial-temporal roles at different levels that have socio-political and economic consequences. Regarding conflicts, for example, churches have demonstrated their capacity for not only preventing violence (by mediating between belligerents), but for making humanitarian efforts as well. In Eastern Congo, where the role of the Congolese state is extremely reduced and non-existent in some areas, the contributions of the Catholic and *3ème* CBCA Churches in North Kivu are particularly influential (e.g., in the health and education sectors) (Cusimano 2009; Kabamba 2013; Katherine Marshall 2013; Mpisi 2008; Seay 2013; Tull 2005).

Both leaders and members at the grassroots level in the three churches in Goma play a personal role as far as religious peacebuilding is concerned. Whether in a position of leadership or in the capacity of a member, and irrespective of their religious affiliations, these individuals share the same geographic space, which commands their attention in addressing matters that concern their daily lives. While the view of a local member may not have the same resonance as that of a church leader, their religious traditions and structures remain equally important in terms of the reliability and audience of their views. As an individual, for instance, the voice of the Catholic Bishop of Goma will arguably be more "trusted" and requested than that of the pastor of *Arche de l'Alliance* at the international level. The international audience that the Catholic Church possesses by far exceeds that of the *3ème* CBCA and *Arche* Churches as religious institutions, mainly because of its established networks and the impact of the Pope's visibility in the media (Willaime 1992, 175). At the same time, members of the *3ème* CBCA and *Arche* Churches are highly active on social media such as Facebook, Twitter, WhatsApp and Imo, which offer them platforms for the dissemination of their activities and beliefs to a larger global audience. The use of social media in churches in Goma would certainly be an interesting topic to study. Furthermore, the Catholic Church receives double recognition: on the one hand, it is universally considered to be a religious entity while functioning as a sovereign state; on the other hand, its local sovereign bodies (dioceses) are territorial jurisdictions generally recognized by states (Katherine Marshall 2013, 59–64).

As previously mentioned, the roles of religious institutions and the individuals who represent them overlap in their activities. While leaders of the three churches shape the overall orientation of their institutions, many interpret their actions according to their ethnic affiliations. Unlike the *3ème* CBCA and *Arche* Churches, the association between activities with ethnic ties seems to stand out in their Catholic counterpart for two main reasons. First, the Catholic Church's organizational structure is a dominant factor that clearly showcases that association. For example, its structures in the North Kivu province, and elsewhere, are not only diversified, centralized and widely represented in the far-reaching territories, but they have demonstrated relative stability in its leadership over time. Besides the Curia, several lay positions are available and generally under the jurisdiction of the diocese bishop. While other Christian organizational structures, such as the *3ème* CBCA, are prone to shifting, internal leadership contestations in the Catholic Church affect only its membership base. Second, the mode of appointment of church leaders is another argument put forward to explain the different forms of church ascriptions. Each one of the three churches have their own mode of leadership appointment. While choosing Catholic bishops is the exclusive role of the Pope, an internal election (General Assembly) determines the *3ème* CBCA Church's legal representative for a five-year renewable term. As for the head pastor of the *Arche,* he is self-appointed (though initially introduced by his former pastor, Reverend Israel N'sembe). The three churches display three very different modes of leadership appointment. In addition, in the case of the Catholic Church, there is the question of whether academic achievement should play a role in leadership appointments. One opponent of this influence is Cardinal Joseph-Albert Malula[2] who criticized the abuse of many clerics who still perceive academic achievements as both an internal and external legitimacy for advancement in leadership positions.[3] The British political scientist Jeffrey Haynes stresses in his book *Religion, Politics and International Relations* that "those who make it to the top of ecclesiastical structures are selectively recruited according to educational attainments and perhaps ethnic affinity…" (2011, 63) These leaders, according to Haynes, are "gradually socialized into the world of the political and social elites, and rewarded materially for their loyalty to the struggle to maintain the political status quo" (2011, 63).

In *La précarité protestante: sociologie du protestantisme contemporain,* the French sociologist Jean-Paul Willaime (1992) observes that the legitimation of the authority of the Catholic Church, which also includes the church in Goma, is shaped by three hierarchical elements. First, the function of the Pope, as head of the whole Roman Catholic Church, represented at the diocese level by the importance given to the function of the Bishops as his representative; second, the person of the Pope, as having reached this high level of function merits respect and thus carries legitimacy. Third, the actions of the person of the Pope can also carry legitimacy among the followers. All three levels of legitimacy can be found also in the other two churches. Even if officeholders and their actions may in some way and in certain circumstances be interpreted or perceived as stained, the "charisma [of their] office," to borrow Max Weber's term (1968, 1140), will still be unblemished. To distinguish this Catholic form of legitimation, called the "institutional-ritual model," Willaime defines Protestant and Evangelical churches' legitimations according to the "institutional-ideological model" (*modèle institutionnel idéologique*) and the "charismatic-associative model" (*modèle associative idéologique*) respectively (1992, 15–29).

Protestants, including *3ème* CBCA and to some degree *Arche* followers, generally distance themselves from the Catholic form of legitimation—which is exclusively based on the offices of pope and bishops—and embrace an institutional-ideological model. Contrary to the institutional-ritual model advocated by the Catholic Church, Protestants relativize human regularizations of the believer. An institutional-ideological model, as Jean-Paul Willaime defines it, stresses the importance of the biblical truth upon which believers need to rely (1992, 19–20). In other words, the ultimate place of the truth does not rest on institutions, leaders or their actions, it rather lies on the Bible itself. This understanding stems from the 16th century Protestant Reformation that instituted the Scriptures as the infallible Word of God—the famous *Sola Scriptura* (scriptures only). Willaime's third model of institutionalization is the charismatic-associative model that rests primarily on personal charisma. A person who has this ability (a prophet) is legitimized by his adherents. The latter see the charisma in their leader that confers on him or her the power to operate in that religious institution.

The capacity of institutions in general, and particularly of religious institutions, to mobilize resources both internally and externally, not only justifies their existence and the reasons for their perpetuation and expansion, but it also enhances their competitiveness. A cautionary note is important here: one cannot only define mobilization numerically; it also involves the capacity to mobilize both organizational and actors' networks for a given objective or purpose (e.g., political, social, economic, etc.). Except for a state's exclusive monopoly of violence, religious institutions share similar attributes as nation-states with respect to their mobilizing capacities which may be socio-political and operate both locally and globally.

Membership as Social and Political Mobilizations

Religions are recognized as institutions mainly because of their direct and indirect influence over populations in a territory (Sampson 2007). This influence shapes the adhesion of their followers and supporters, who then become members of those institutions. Adhesion furthermore takes at least two broad forms. The first form is by birth, as in the automatic acquisition of citizenship. The three churches use the same concept with some differences, principally on theological grounds. While children of members of the Catholic Church are immediately considered members, essentially through baptism, *3ème* CBCA and *Arche* Churches, as well as other Protestant traditions, argue that only a mature person can be saved and thus become a member of a local congregation. Secondly, and this applies to all religious organizations, new members originate from adherents of other religions. In other words, and as I have already indicated in the preceding chapter (Chapter Four), shifting churches also constitute another form of membership expansion, which stirs competition and rivalry among Christian traditions (chiefly Catholic, *3ème* CBCA and *Arche* Churches). Keeping and increasing one's membership has its importance not only in social mobilization, but also reveals its relevance in the political arena.

In the Congo, as well as in several colonial and post-colonial African countries, church-state relationships (interactions) are constantly changing. They range from being cordial, to hostile or neutral, mainly because of their mutual influences as institutions and their representatives in a socio-political environment undergoing regular transformations (Haynes 2011). By institutional relationships I mean that those who represent their respective institutions directly or indirectly engage them (institutions). The Catholic, *3ème* CBCA and *Arche* Churches in Goma illustrate the dynamics of such changes, which often take the form of negotiations and bargaining over political issues such as elections, public visibility with political leaders, and participation in conflict mediations (Fox 2012; Mpisi 2008). The ethnic factor also plays a role in church-state relationships. The Catholic and *3ème* CBCA Churches are two of the religious institutions in Goma and the Kivu provinces that are generally seen through an ethnic lens. In the Congolese political field, many in Goma perceived both their actions and inactions as ethnically motivated. During the 2006 presidential and legislative elections, as some religious and secular leaders indicated to me, political candidates not only lobbied churches, but the churches mobilized their communities to ensure that they voted for their preferences, who in many instances represented their own ethnic group. In return, churches expected to be somehow favoured in their social endeavors. For instance, one *3ème* CBCA pastor disliked the fact that a state official would reject their invitation and would rather choose to participate in a Catholic event.

While internal mobilizations are generally initiated by leaders of churches who do not refrain from expressing ethnic sentiments, their support base serves to carry out church objectives in their surroundings (Haynes 2011). The Catholic and *3ème* CBCA Churches enjoy the strength of their institutional organization and structures, which have been built and tested over time, to pass their social (even political) projects across their local members. However, the *Arche* Church and many other Revival churches that do not have the same experience would rather opt for a closer proximity between leaders and local members. These social and political mobilizations are not limited to the internal and local levels; they also seek to mobilize individuals globally. In the next section, I focus on the global perspective of the mobilization of Christian religious institutions.

Mobilization beyond the Local Sphere as a Global Phenomenon

The role of religion is not only recognized at the local level; its impact and influences have been observed at the international level in recent years. In other words, as recognized in the literature, religious institutions and churches are increasingly becoming transnational entities (Haynes 2011; Toft, Philpott, and Shah 2011). The migration of many Congolese citizens—estimated at more than 500,000 refugees, students and people seeking "salvation," a way out, or better opportunities in general—principally to Western countries such as Belgium, France, Canada and the United States, has also facilitated the migration of beliefs and culture (Demart 2010; Mossière 2013). Catholics and Protestants alike will prefer, in some cases, to attend congregations with priests or pastors of African origin, and Congolese descent in particular. In other cases, notably Pentecostals, believers will start meeting in their homes before a church emerges. This situation constitutes a recruitment method used by Pentecostals to appeal to Catholics, other Christian denominations, as well as other religious members. This latter instance is the one that retains my attention in this section. I will not focus on churches and their overseas members; rather, I will seek to examine the way in which they mobilize resources beyond their local space.

As a transnational and well-established religious organization, the Catholic Church does not face the same challenges as other churches, especially administratively and in terms of infrastructure. Once abroad, Pentecostals and Revival churches generally start their churches afresh and from the bottom-up. However, they will continue to demonstrate their faithfulness both to their original churches and their leaders in DRC as they lobby for them in their new places. For instance, one of the long-term objectives of Pastor Estone Kasereka of the *Arche* Church in Goma is to build churches in places as far away as Canada and the US. Strong churches, as he defines them, are not locally-limited; rather, they are global churches in the light of those who inspire him, like the Ghanaian Mensa Otabil and the Nigerian David Oyedepo (interview with Pastor Estone Kasereka; for further details on Mensa Otabil and David Oyedepo see, for instance, Gifford 2004, 56–61; 113–190). In fact, these two Anglophone Western African pastors, Oyedepo and Otabil, have given their churches an international dimension even in their names (International Central Gospel Church and Winners Church International or Faith Church World Wide, respectively). Monica Duffy Toft, Daniel Philpott and Timothy Samuel Shah summarize it well in their book *God's Century: Resurgent Religion and Global Politics*: "Not only do religious actors think globally but they also act globally" (Toft et al., 2011).

While ordinary people are responsible for international mobilization of Pentecostal or Revival Churches, including *Arche*, mainline churches (Catholic and *3ème* CBCA) exploit their institutional networks at the top-down level with religious and political partners. These relationships not only benefit their respective institutions insofar as mobilization is concerned, but as their representatives and intermediaries of their members they are personally beneficiaries, adopting what Jean-Francois Bayart (1989) and others call the *politique du ventre* (the politic of the belly; (Haynes 2011, 65, 70)). For example, during violent conflicts, as broadly experienced in Eastern Congo and particularly in Goma, humanitarian projects primarily financed by international non-governmental organizations (INGOs) are given to leaders of these mainline churches (Haynes 2011; Tull 2005). My research has also shown, as reported elsewhere (Cooley and Ron 2002, 16), that the situation equally benefited members of the same INGOs operating in the region, financially and even materially. My intention here is not to imply that this is a generalized *modus operandus*, or that these organizations do not alleviate the suffering of many. In fact, they do indeed rescue numerous individuals from hopeless situations and save the lives of many. They also gain various benefits from doing so.

Resource Mobilization and Competition: The Crux of Christian Religious Institution Relationships

The main characteristic of Christian religious institutions in Goma is their competition over diverse resources. While inter-church competition does not immediately trigger conflict and violence, their roles as peacebuilders are weakened in the eyes of their protagonists and members. That is, as moral authorities and potential mediators, people see them as being partial. As a neutral component, competition may connote two perspectives. On the one hand, a positive kind of competition strives to bring out or to attain a higher level of an anticipated positive objective while causing no negative consequences. In other words, this positive perspective of competition does not entail mutual competition; however, it fosters self-competition with the benefits of others in mind. On the other hand, the negative perspective of competition seeks the promotion of oneself at all costs and to the detriment of others. Instead of creating an atmosphere of mutual respect, the negative form of competition maintains an antagonistic relationship between actors and organizations.

Competition between Christian religious institutions and actors over resources, especially scarce ones, is like the continuation of colonial relationships between the Catholic and Protestant Churches in the Congo. In the late 1800s and early 1900s, as examined in Chapter Three, in several instances King Leopold II and Congo's Belgian authorities favored Belgian Catholic missionaries at the expense of other missionaries, including non-Belgian Catholics (Markowitz 1973; Moerschbacher 2010). As chief beneficiaries of advantageous considerations—such as state protection and education subsidies, among other things—Catholic missionaries ensured their preservation and their monopoly over them, whereas other missionary denominations increasingly sought to be included for similar advantages and privileges (Moerschbacher 2010; Prunier 2001). The inclusion of other Christian groups meant not only sharing state advantages and privileges, but also implied their renegotiation, which resulted in the use of negative forms of competition such as demonization and legitimacy questioning. Catholics and Protestants also competed in the mobilization of indigenous populations. Each religious group claimed to be working for the good of the local population by providing them with goods and services (e.g., basic education, health care, etc.).

In return, indigenous leaders disposed of their lands to one group over the other (Allen F. Roberts 2013). In eastern districts of the country, local peoples had to choose between the Muslim Arabs and the Christian missionaries (united as Western Christians against the Muslim Arabs). Alliances developed due to common goals (Slade 1959).

The context of post-independence Congo presented similar contentions and alliance games between the state and religious institutions on the one hand, and among religious institutions themselves on the other. First, in the face of a strong national religious institution such as the Catholic Church, which was inherited from the Belgians, the new state under Mobutu used all possible means to dismantle what appeared to be a religious monopoly. One way was to enhance competition among religious institutions by strategically weakening Catholics while increasingly promoting Protestants—coerced into uniting as one religious structure, the *Église du Christ au Zaïre/Congo* (ECZ/C)—and indigenous religious groups such as the Kimbanguists (Kabongo-Mbaya 1992; Nguindu Mushete 1972; 1974). The latter strongly supported the Mobutu regime, especially in the 1970s when the President introduced his politics of *authenticité*. This presidential measure likely targeted Catholics in that all foreign and so-called imported values (e.g. dress), including Christian names and geographical names, were abolished and replaced by local ones (Nguindu Mushete 1974; Prunier 2001). However, the relationship between the Mobutu regime and the Catholic Church was not solely hostile and its effects were only limited to the national level. It periodically improved and had subnational consequences as well (Prunier 2001).

In the early 1990s, Mobutu's regime, as well as many other African dictatorships, began to falter. Its relationship with the Catholic Church was still difficult, despite the policy of socio-political openness he called the "Third Republic," which included, among other things, the reinstatement of Christian names and religious and press freedoms (Prunier 2001). With this political turnaround, both in Zaïre and elsewhere, observe Stephen Ellis and Gerrie Ter Haar, emerged a wave of spiritual movements into the political space (2004, 100). Several events that transformed the socio-political context of the Great Lakes region occurred in that decade. First, in the same period, 1994, a genocide accompanied the death of the Rwandan President Juvenal Habyarimana, who was Mobutu's friend. Second, three years later, Mobutu's regime speedily crumbled with the rise of the RCD rebellion which overthrew him in late 1997. Third, Laurent-Desiré Kabila, chairman of the rebellion and self-proclaimed head of the Congo (ex-Zaïre), took over the country for four years before his assassination in January 2001. While these changes occurred, a rapid mushrooming of new churches, particularly Revival

Churches, was also taking place (Ellis and Haar 2004, 100). Consequently, the official arrival of these new actors increased the competition between mainline churches and Revival churches.

Conclusion

The risk of a comparative analysis was worth taking, despite its limitations in terms of religious diversity and their periods of existence. Nevertheless, it helped increase our understanding of Goma's churches. This tentative assignment has highlighted at least three main differences in the three phases of their life-cycles. First, mainline (Catholic and Protestant) churches do not have existential challenges as Revival churches do. While Catholic and Protestant churches share their concerns about losing adherents to their counterpart Revival churches, the latter (Revival churches) suffer from their contested legitimacies in the face of the former (Catholic and Protestant churches). In addition, the relationship of the leaders of these three Christian institutions with the state reveals the games of alliances they entertain, and the competitive nature of their relationships, especially during conflicts and elections.

Although the socio-political environment has had a certain influence in the trajectory of each church, the personality of their leaders equally shaped, directly or indirectly, their churches' reputations. First, many interpreted the action or inaction of the leaders of these churches from an ethnic perspective, overriding their religious identity. For instance, amidst conflict, the position of a Catholic bishop, seen as an ally of the Rwandans, likely carried much more ethnic connotation and resonance than a pastor of the *Arche* Church, whose views were perceived as being more theological. Equally, the posture of the leader of the *3ème* CBCA Church, from the Nande ethnic group, carried ethnic and community weight. Consequently, the relationship of these churches, including their adherents, often had a mobilization perspective (membership and socio-political).

Endnotes

1. While legal authority rests on the legality of the office held by an individual one owes due respect, traditional authority consists of a set of values and beliefs which regulate a society on the grounds of their traditional status. In other words, a person in the position of authority, traditionally speaking, is followed and respected because of the given tradition. Max Weber, *Economy and Society: An Outline of Interpretive Sociology*, New York: Bedminster Press, 1968, p. 226.

2. Cardinal Joseph-Albert Malula expressed his regrets over the futile pursuits of several young priests, who have abandoned their clerical tasks for earthly concerns such as titles and positions. He writes: Today, we observe that new generation priests strongly crave titles. Thus, the race for university degrees. They hastily strive for positions: faculty professors, bishopric secretary, dean, priest, bishop, etc. (author's translation). See, Joseph-Albert Malula, "Essai de profil des prêtres de l'an 2000 au Zaïre: Message du Cardinal Malula," *in Documentation Catholique*, (1er mai 1988).
3. The current diocesan bishop of the Goma Catholic Church, Theophile Ruboneka Kaboy, completed his doctoral studies at the Pontifical Gregorian University of Rome (Italy) entitled "Implantation missionaire au Kivu (Zaïre). Une étude historique des établissement des Pères Blancs: 1880–1945, 1980." Several unsuccessful attempts were made to access the full copy of this dissertation. First, while in Goma I received a written authorization from a church officer, but I was still unable to access the church libraries. However, during a very brief meeting with Bishop Kaboy in one of his offices, he handed me his small book *Le diocèse de Goma: Un aperçu historique de ses origines et de son développement (1911–1985)*. Second, three years ago (2014) the library of the University of Montreal was neither able to borrow the dissertation from the Gregorian University, which replied the following in Italian: *"In questi casi non ci è possibile fare copie o estratti da inviare ad altre Università/Biblioteche. È solamente possibile consultarne il contenuto qui sul posto per una sola ora e una sola volta. Mi dispiace non poter fare di più ma questo è il regolamento."* [...You cannot make copies or extracts to be sent to other Universities/Libraries. It is only possible to browse the content here on the spot for an hour and only once. I regret not being able to do more but that's the rules].

    In 1988, the *3ème* CBCA church's legal representative, Kakule Molo Pheresie, defended his PhD dissertation at the Christ Seminary in St. Louis Missouri (US), "Quest for Ecclesiological self-understanding of the Church of Christ in Zaïre: Toward the retrieval of Contextual models of Church in an African Setting." In 2006, Reverend Molo was elected a member of the Congolese national parliament to represent the territory of Beni (North Kivu) under the Démocratie chrétienne féderaliste—convention des fédéralistes pour la démocratie chrétienne (DCF-COFEDEC) party, headed by Pierre Pay Pay. Pastor Estone Kasereka of the Goma *Arche de l'Alliance* church did his theological studies in the early 1990s in West Africa.

Bibliography

Bayart, Jean-Francois. "Les Églises chrétiennes et la politique du ventre: le partage du gâteau ecclesial." *Politique Africaine* 39 (1989): 3–26.

Cooley, Alexander, and James Ron. "The NGO Scramble: Organizational Insecurity and the Political Economy of Transnational Action." *International Security* 27, no. 1 (2002): 5–39.

Cusimano, Maryann K. "God and Global Governance: Resurgent Religion in World Politics." In Maryann K. Cusimano (ed.), *Beyond Sovereignty: Issues for a Global Agenda*. Boston, NY: Wadsworth, 2009.

Demart, Sarah. "Les territoires de la délivrance: mises en perspectives historique et plurilocalisée du Réveil congolais (Bruxelles, Kinshasa, Paris, Toulouse)." Doctorat, Université Toulouse-Le-Mirail and Université catholique de Louvain-La-Neuve, 2010.

Ellis, Stephen, and Gerrie ter Haar. *Worlds of Power: Religious Thought and Political Practice in Africa*. Oxford, NY: Oxford University Press, 2004.

Fox, Jonathan. "Introduction." In Jonathan Fox (ed), *Religion, Politics, Society, and the State*. New York: Oxford University Press, 2012.

Gazibo, Mamoudou, and Jane Jenson. *La politique comparée: fondements, enjeux et approches théoriques*. Montréal: Presses de l'Université de Montréal, 2004.

Gifford, Paul. *Ghana's New Christianity: Pentecostalism in a Globalising African Economy*. London: Hurst, 2004.

Haynes, Jeffrey. *Religion, Politics and International Relations: Selected Essays*. New York: Routledge, 2011.

Kabamba, Patience. *Business of Civil War: New Forms of Life in the Debris of the Democratic Republic of Congo*. Dakar: Codesria, 2013.

Kabongo-Mbaya, Philippe B. *L'Eglise du Christ au Zaïre: formation et adaptation d'un protestantisme en situation de dictature*. Paris: Karthala, 1992.

Kaboy, Theophile Ruboneka. *Le diocèse de Goma: Un aperçu historique de ses origines et de son développement (1911–1985)*. Goma: Construire ensemble, 1986.

Mahoney, James. "Path Dependence in Historical Sociology." *Theory and Society* 29, no. 4 (2000): 507–548.

Malula, Joseph-Albert. "Essai de profil des prêtres de l'an 2000 au Zaïre: Message du Cardinal Malula." *in Documentation Catholique*, no. 1961 (1er mai 1988): 463–469.

Markowitz, Marvin D. *Cross and Sword: The Political Role of Christian Missions in the Belgian Congo, 1908–1960*. Stanford, CA: Hoover Institution Press, 1973.

Marshall, Katherine. *Global Institutions of Religion: Ancient Movers, Modern Shakers*. Abingdon, Oxon; New York: Routledge, 2013.

McCann, Joseph F. *Church and Organization: A Sociological and Theological Enquiry*. Scranton: University of Scranton Press, 1993.

Moerschbacher, Marco. "La mission catholique en RDC et sa contribution au développement." In Manfred Schulz (ed.), *Les porteurs du développement durable en R.D.Congo: Évolutions récentes de la vie politique, économique, religieuse, culturelle et de la societé civile*. Kinshasa; Berlin: Cepas; Spektrum, 2010.

Mossière, Géraldine. "Églises de réveil, ONG confessionnelles et transnationalisme congolais: une théologie du développement." *Canadian Journal of Development Studies/Revue canadienne d'*études du développement 34, no. 2 (2013): 257–274.

Mpisi, Jean. *Kivu, RDC: La paix à tout prix!: La Conférence de Goma (6–23 janvier 2008)*. Paris: L'Harmattan, 2008.

Mushete, Ngindu. "Simon Kimbangu et le Kimbanguisme: une lecture historique à propos d'un colloque recent." *Cahiers des religions Africaines* 6 (1972): 91–103.

———. "Le propos du recours à l'authenticité et le christianisme au Zaïre." *Cahiers des religions Africaines* 8, no. 16 (1974): 209–230.

Philpott, Daniel. *Just and Unjust Peace: An Ethic of Political Reconciliation.* New York: Oxford University Press, 2012.

Pierson, Paul. "The Limits of Design: Explaining Institutional Origins and Change." *Governance* 13, no. 4 (2000): 475–499.

Prunier, Gérard. "The Catholic Church and the Kivu Conflict." *Journal of Religion in Africa* 31, no. 2 (2001): 139–162.

Roberts, Allen F. *A Dance of Assassins: Performing Early Colonial Hegemony in the Congo.* Bloomington; Indianapolis: Indiana University Press, 2013.

Sampson, Cynthia. "Religion and Peacebuilding." In I. William Zartman (ed.), *Peacemaking in International Conflict: Methods & Techniques.* Washington, D.C.: United States Institute of Peace, 2007.

Sartori, Giovanni. "Bien comparer, mal comparer." *Revue internationale de politique comparée* 1, no. 1 (1994): 19–36.

Seay, Laura Elizabeth. "Effective Responses: Protestants, Catholics and the Provision of Health Care in the Post-war Kivus." *Review of African Political Economy* 40, no. 135 (2013): 83–97.

Slade, Ruth M. *English-speaking Missions in the Congo Independent State (1878–1908).* Bruxelles: Academie Royale des Sciences Coloniales, 1959.

Thelen, Kathleen. "How Institutions Evolve: Insights from Comparative Historical Analysis." In James Mahoney and Dietrich Rueschemeyer (eds.), *Comparative Historical Analysis in the Social Sciences.* New York: Cambridge University Press, 2003.

Toft, Monica Duffy; Philpott, Daniel, and Shah, Timothy Samuel. *God's Century: Resurgent Religion and Global Politics.* New York: W.W. Norton, 2011.

Tull, Denis. *The Reconfiguration of Political Order in Africa: A Case Study of North Kivu (DR Congo).* Hamburg: Institute of African Affairs, 2005.

Weber, Max. *Economy and Society: An Outline of Interpretive Sociology.* New York: Bedminster Press, 1968.

Willaime, Jean-Paul. *La précarité protestante: sociologie du protestantisme contemporain.* Genève: Labor et Fides, 1992.

6 General Conclusions

Overview

The main purpose of undertaking this qualitative research, as noted in both the General Introduction, was to understand the role played by the Catholic, *3ème Communauté Baptiste au centre d'Afrique* (CBCA) and *Arche de l'Alliance*/Goma (*Arche*) Churches in religious peacebuilding in the city of Goma. My main argument was that religious actors, in general, and Christians, in particular, have the potential to contribute to peacebuilding in the DRC and notably in Goma. Capturing their perceptions and definitions of peace and conflict, as examined, particularly in Chapter Four, was crucial since studies about religious actors in the North Kivu province have rarely focused on church leaders, and never on grassroots members. In addition, the nature of the relationship between religious actors both within and between churches revealed the existence of a knowledge gap (especially an empirical one).

This book not only covered the Catholic Church in Goma in its peacebuilding role at the leadership level, as others have previously done (Mararo 2005a, 2005b; Mujynya and Sebisogo 2012; Seay 2009; Twose and Mararo 2012), but it also included leaders of the *3ème* CBCA and *Arche* Churches in the same city, as well as ordinary lay members of these three churches. In the literature on religious peacebuilding and conflict transformation (as introduced in the General Introduction and elaborated in Chapter One) relationships, change, transformation and historical understanding of conflicts are pivotal. In respect to Goma, it is critical to understand the historical and dynamic social relationships between those who identify themselves as indigenous *versus* immigrants. Churches are not exempt from these kinds of discourses. Thus, the aim of this book was to understand the role of three particular churches in religious peacebuilding and conflict transformation. In other words, how do these religious actors transform negative forces that entice conflicts and violence into healthy and peaceful relationships?

The main question I answered in this book was "How do members of the Catholic, *3ème* CBCA and *Arche* Churches perceive and describe their roles in religious peacebuilding in Goma?" In addition, answering the four sub-questions that emerged from the main one has helped provide a deeper understanding of the roles of churches in Goma in relation to religious peacebuilding.

In this final concluding chapter, I summarize my findings in three sections. I begin with a brief recapitulation of key findings of my research, which was largely laid out in preceding chapters. The significance of these findings is discussed in the second section in terms of their theoretical and practical implications. These two implications offer lenses through which the role of both religious institutions and their actors can be better understood, especially in conflict-ridden societies such as Goma and its surrounding areas. These theoretical and practical implications are important for researchers who wish to conduct fieldwork in war zones. Third, I propose an agenda (not exhaustive) for future research, such as the inclusion of other churches and the expansion of similar research in other parts of the DRC.

Catholic, *3ème* CBCA, and *Arche*: A Religious Peacebuilding Project

This exploratory qualitative research sought, as much as possible, to reflect the views and perspectives of participants concerning their role in religious peacebuilding. While the participants' views and perspectives illustrated in this book included those of leaders of the three churches (Catholic, *3ème* CBCA and *Arche*), one should not directly and necessarily impute them to the rest of their religious institutions (churches). One should also refrain from making hasty generalizations regarding the information collected.

Members of the Catholic, *3ème* CBCA and *Arche* Churches did not limit their broad understanding of peace and conflict to the traditional dichotomy of presence or absence of war, thus leading to another common dichotomous way of describing peace, namely as either negative or positive peace. While many of my interviewees perceived such dichotomies through spiritual and religious lenses that made them critical of such binary explanations, they also distinguished, in their own ways, what they called either a "*semblant* and a *soi-disant* peace" or a "*véritable* peace." These two kinds of peace sharply contrast with each other. Paradoxically, the respondents did not see how the proposed alternative wording also rests on a binary conceptualization.

Contrary to a *semblant* and *soi-disant* kind of peace that participants related to both the absence of war and to harmony, a *véritable* kind of peace reflects harmony not only at the individual level, but also at a collective level. In regard to both *semblant* and *soi-disant* kind of peace, for example, they required relatively less energy and time to attain. A *véritable* kind of peace, on the other hand, was considered much more difficult (if not impossible) to reach, because of two requirements it demands: (1) diligence (e.g., requiring the inclusion of divine, personal and community objectives), and (2) time (i.e., occurring over the long-term). If one risks quantifying or qualifying peace without necessarily demeaning the importance of the first kind (*semblant* and *soi-disant*), the second kind of peace (*véritable*) would be far better rated in general. In conflict areas, they both carry weight and have their pros and cons. From these definitions and different understandings of the concepts of peace and conflict, which were addressed in the first research sub-question, stemmed the second sub-question pertaining to the causes of conflicts.

Five main interrelated root causes of conflicts emerged from the participants. None of the causes stood out as the predominant cause as they were always combined with at least one other cause. The first cause of conflict in Goma, as well as elsewhere in the North Kivu province, regarded the spatial and geographical importance of the city, with it being an object of attraction. Since Goma attracts not only what were perceived as good people and things, and for good purposes; yet it also attracts unpleasant and even dreadful ones. As a result, many have portrayed Goma either as a *blessed* or a *cursed* city.

Interconnected land and natural resources' issues in the North and South Kivu provinces as well as in Goma have been perceived as the second factor influencing conflicts. While Goma does not necessarily have many natural resources compared to the interior areas of the province of North Kivu, the city acts as a node that connects those places where resources are extracted to their selling destinations. In addition, land-related conflicts are common in the region, mainly because of the high population density.

The third cause of conflict related to identity issues such as ethnicity that take centre stage in determining the nature of relationships in social organizations (including churches). While religious belonging characterized in itself one's identity, it was still perceived through the lenses of ethnic identity categorization. In other words, churches carried the ethnic label of the group a leader or the majority of congregants belong to. For instance, churched were identified as *Kanisa ya Banyarwanda* (Church of the people from Rwanda or those who speak Kinyarwanda) or *Kanisa ya Banande* (church of those who speak Kinande). Some informants went even so far as to call certain religious institutions, organizations, and subgroups as belonging to such ethic groups as Tutsi, Hutu or Hunde (e.g., association *ya ba Tutsi/Hutu/Hunde* [association of people of the Tutsi/Hutu/Hunde]).

The fourth cause of conflicts participants identified is leadership failure at both the state and ecclesial levels. For many, not only did the Congolese State fail in its responsibility to its citizens/population, but church leaders have equally failed in their respective mission.[1] Instead of denouncing injustices and the like that have been perpetrated by Congolese State's officials, participants argued that both religious and secular leaders have chosen to remain silent. The Catholic Church of Bukavu, notably the episcopacies of Bishops Christophe Munzihirwa and Emmanuel Kataliko, has stood out as an example of resistance against injustice, which many grassroots members have compared to churches in Goma that, according to them, side directly or indirectly with peace spoilers—particularly rebels who dissociate from peace agreements or individuals and groups who are supported by foreigners or whose interests they (spoilers) incarnate and defend. My informants, who identified themselves with one of the three churches, bridged the concepts of peace and conflict with their own theological meanings.

The third sub-question this book attempted to answer regarded the place of a theology of peace from the perspective of the three churches in Goma, i.e., Catholic, *3ème* CBCA and *Arche*). On the one hand, peace and conflict carried different theological meanings and areas of emphasis depending on the religious institution with which one was aligned, along with his or her personal experience. On the other hand, these churches still demonstrated some convergences in theologically explaining root causes or sources of conflicts and their possible solutions. Conflict and war were observed as the result of the "evil condition of people's heart," which was described as "sinful" and required salvation through Jesus Christ, who was often referred to as the Prince of Peace.

The fourth and last sub-question this book explored dealt with the nature of relationships in and between churches. Although the fourth sub-question specifically examined the issues of relationships within and between the Catholic,

3ème CBCA and *Arche* Churches, these issues transpired throughout the first three sub-questions as power dynamics. First, my findings showed that the nature of relationships at the internal level of the three churches in Goma was dominated by the race for positions especially among clergies, identity-based conflicts and grassroot issues like their participation in decision-making processes. Second, inter-church relationships, as shown in Chapter Four, occurred not only at the leadership level, but also at the grassroot level. This research revealed three kinds of inter-church relationships, which I categorized as (1) "opaque," (2) "competitive" or "rivals," and (3) "cooperative" or "complicit."

Theoretical and Practical Implications of Religious Peacebuilding in Goma

This book raises theoretical implications for peace, conflict, and religious studies (including peacebuilding, conflict transformation, and local ownership), but also contains practical implications to serve as lessons to other researchers interested in conducting studies in conflict zones and addressing issues related to non-state actors, including both mainline/mainstream and non-mainline/mainstream church members. While mainline churches have been included in recent studies of religious peacebuilding and conflict transformation efforts, none of them, as I see it, have included Revival churches in their investigation, especially in the case of Eastern Congo. Therefore, one of the main contributions of this research resides in this inclusion.

Theoretical Implications

I will discuss the question I previously categorized as "qualitative" and "quantitative": "Which one [church] is better and which one is worse than the other?" The qualification of religious institutions or organizations was not the purpose of this book, nor do I have the tools for such an endeavour. My purpose was to examine the role of religious institutions/organizations in religious peacebuilding and to recommend ways for improvement in such fields of study as religious peacebuilding and conflict transformation.

This book builds on the conceptual frameworks for religious peacebuilding and conflict transformation. Change, relationships, and proper selection of key participants in the transformation processes are three vital elements in both religious peacebuilding and conflict transformation. These elements facilitate both an adequate and effective examination of conflict and prospect of a lasting peace.

One of the first and undeniable implications of this study is the importance, omnipresence and ubiquity of religion and religious actors, especially Christianity and Christian churches, in the Congolese socio-political landscape. While this omnipresence may have been culturally facilitated, particularly in the postcolonial Congo, the fragility of the Congolese state has contributed to its (religious ubiquity) reproduction over time. This presence bears sociopolitical implications. The role of such non-state actors as churches in religious peacebuilding is therefore paramount. Therein lies the rationale of having chosen the Catholic, *3ème* CBCA, and *Arche* Churches.

While many continue to portray religion and its actors negatively, chiefly as sources of conflict, their roles need to be nuanced and further explored regarding their contributions to peace. In the case of Goma, my findings supported that churches play "ethnic games," and they also revealed that churches mitigate the suffering of many, especially in contexts where the state's role is relatively absent. Besides some doctrinal differences, the spiritual dimension that religion, in general, and churches, in particular, offer can be an asset in peacebuilding (Johnston and Sampson 1994; Schreiter, Appleby, Powers 2010). For example, while the organizational structure and resources of both the Catholic and *3ème* CBCA Churches in Goma (and the entire province of North Kivu) cannot be underestimated, the influence of the *Arche* Church and other Revival churches at the grassroots level and their rapid growth cannot be undermined either. One determining factor in religious peacebuilding and conflict transformation successes may lie in the transformation of inter-church relationships at the social and structural level with *justice* (especially social and economic justices) being the core value (Abu-Nimer 2012; Lederach 1999; Rawls 1999).

As previously noted, the nature of the relationships that the Catholic, *3ème* CBCA and *Arche* Churches have with each other, at both the institutional and congregational levels (top-down and grassroots) is crucial, in that it can either foster or harm the religious peacebuilding processes. Therefore, a transformation of at least two kinds of relationships should be encouraged. First, there is the indifferent or "opaque" kind, especially at the top-down level, which in some way facilitates negative perceptions of one another and should be discouraged and denounced. It is also important to note that the first steps would not be necessary easy. They may happen quickly or may automatically eliminate existing doctrinal differences. However, with time and the building of trust, some potential positive outcomes (of breaking inter-church opacities include the mitigation of tensions and conflicts between leaders and grassroots members) may take place.

The second kind of relationship that needs transformation is negative competition. As elaborated in Chapter Four and Chapter Five, the competition between religious leaders including those from the Catholic, *3ème* CBCA, and *Arche* Churches is notably over resources and visibility in the Congolese socio-political arena. These factors, in combination with others, fuel institutional competition while maintaining a distrustful and suspicious environment. Rather than being a positive incentive, competition has actually sustained a negative relationship between the three religious institutions. Moreover, the competitive nature of the leaders' relationships transpires also to grassroots members sustaining the kind of questions indicated in the introduction of this section. That is, "Which one [church] is better and which one is worse than the other church?" In addition, the other theoretical implication of this study regards the nature of relationships in terms of local *versus* external.

From Chapter Four emerged my findings that support the existence of a state of dependency of the three religious institutions and their related organizations to external assistance and solutions. *External* not only refer to Western sources as opposed to African or Congolese sources, it also includes the relations of grassroots members and their Congolese local leaders, provincial *versus* national, and so on.[2] In other words, these relationship dependencies are framed or designed in spatial and geographical layers. I illustrate these layers of dependency through two examples.

First, I was invited by one bishop to attend a meeting between a foreign donor's representative and a group of civil society members which included two women from Eastern Congo. While the purpose of the meeting was to strategize about the political situation surrounding the choice of a civil society member to head the *Commission Électorale Nationale Indépendante* (Independent National Electoral Commission, CENI), it became altered and discussions were geared toward the donor's representative for financial assistance. At the same time, the two ladies wanted to express their objections, which included being discriminated against because, according to them, they were from the interior (provinces). In fact, I observed that not only were they rarely given the opportunity to speak by their Kinshasa's colleagues, they were also spoken over and prevented (cut off) from speaking.

The second illustration regards projects funded by foreign donors and implemented by Congolese churches. Although I use an example from the Catholic Church, similar issues have been reported elsewhere. The Catholic Church in

Goma, which possesses well-established structures such as the commission *Justice et Paix* (Justice and Peace commission) at local and national levels, contains leaders that still expect officials from Kinshasa to constantly support their activities (financially and through training). Two church officials mentioned to me that the viability of their peace-related projects was dependent on *partenaires étrangers* (foreign partners). As a result, my findings demonstrate that many *partenaires* impose their own conditions, views, and approaches, which do not necessarily respond to local needs and, in some cases, impede freedom of choice and local ownership. Séverine Autesserre reports in *Peaceland* a "beggars can't be choosers'" problem (2014, 101). Elsewhere, and still within the religious context, I was told that funding from *partenaires* was, in some instances, conditional on the presence of one of their agents (usually a foreigner) and foreign funding was interrupted when this condition was challenged.

Practical Implications

This book has revealed several practical implications not only for practitioners in the field of religious peacebuilding, but also for those conducting fieldwork with religious actors amidst conflict and war. Being influenced by their environment and numerous interests, religious institutions need to be studied like any other social or political organization. As discussed in As discussed earlier on in this book, when conducting research in a risky and volatile environment such as Goma (at least during 2013), researchers must constantly pay attention to local advice and rely on local guidance. In addition, I strongly encourage the use of a triangulation approach when choosing data collection methods. As I have already noted in the General Introduction and particularly in the section of the methodology of this research, a triangulation approach helped me to cross-check what I was told in interviews.

By triangulation, I encourage researchers to actually be present—while at the same time being discrete—in their environment of study. This, which I call "proxy research," does not offer the same insight as "proximity research." Discretion is, however, important. Physical and linguistic discretion might be difficult, for example, for someone who is not the same skin colour as the majority of participants or who is accompanied by an interpreter (especially if the interpreter is well known to participants). Furthermore, interviews have the potential of being easily biased, as do other data collection methods. While participants were reticent to share their stories, they also chose which parts to share and where to place emphasis, factors that I had no control over. As a result, a researcher can easily be influenced during his or her study, especially when hearing stories of violence that are emotionally loaded.

Beyond a Christian Religious Peacebuilding in Goma

In addition to covering what other researchers (e.g., Büscher 2011; Tull 2005) have identified as future research agendas, my research has also suggested far broader future areas of research, as already indicated in my limitations section in the General Introduction of this book.

While this research focused primarily on Christian churches in Goma, the role of other religious actors both from the top-down and bottom-up levels remain a subject of study. In Chapter Three, it was seen that Islam played an important role in shaping the sociopolitical and cultural landscapes of the eastern Congolese areas; however, their role in religious peacebuilding in the postcolonial period is barely, if at all, mentioned in the literature. Moreover, in Goma, several local non-state actors, including mainline churches, largely rely on their partners (mostly Western) for the financing of their peace-related projects.

In fact, as indicated in Chapter Four, international non-profit organizations (INGOs) prefer, at the expense of the Congolese state, to partner with non-state actors. Even though the aim of my research was not to study the role of INGOs operating within churches in financing peacebuilding activities, many research participants were concerned about the use of these funds by their religious leaders. To what extent, one can then ask, does the funding of INGOs operating within churches influence conflict in Goma, as well as elsewhere?

In response to one of the sub-questions pertaining to the causes of conflicts in the DRC and in Goma in particular, many participants stated that people from neighbouring Rwanda, especially the Tutsi, were the instigators. While some nuanced their argument, asserting that the current regime in Rwanda was to blame, others maintained that such an alibi only demonstrated the incapacity of the Congolese state to protect its own population and borders. Even though these issues have their place and several United Nations reports from experts have addressed the issue, my own interest would have been the role of religious actors, from a comparative perspective, in religious peacebuilding. The Catholic, *3ème* CBCA and *Arche* Churches have each, to a certain degree, been involved in peacebuilding activities with their denominational partners in Rwanda. For instance, the Catholic Churches of both countries already work, at the macro-level (state and national), through its *Association des Conférences Épiscopales de l'Afrique*

Centrale (Association of Episcopal Conferences of Central Africa).[3] The *3ème* CBCA Church organizes meetings with their Rwandan partners and, in many instances, choir exchanges. One *3ème* CBCA pastor observed that "they [Rwandans] are more secure in Birere, because of their proximity to the border. If something goes wrong, they can easily escape and go back to their country." An official at the *Arche* Church astutely noted that several members of their church cross the border every Sunday for worship services. These three illustrations show how insightful an international study of religious peacebuilding could be, especially at the grassroots level.

Endnotes

1. A warning must be given here, again concerning the inferences between the views of informants and those of religious institutions. The views of informants, although they may have included those of leaders, do not necessarily impute those of the communal representation of the churches.
2. For further details on the "attitude" of foreign peacebuilders (including researchers) towards the Congolese, and local perceptions of such attitudes, see Séverine Autesserre's book, notably Chapter 3, "Local Reaction": Séverine Autesserre, *Peaceland: Conflict Resolution and the Everyday Politics of International Intervention*, 2014.
3. Although the two Catholic Churches (in the DRC and Rwanda) work already together at the national level in peace endeavors, many observers still question whether mutual trust exists between the two populations (especially between the clergies). For instance, during the 2013 Plenary Assembly of the Symposium of Episcopal Conferences of Africa and Madagascar, one clergyman interpreted an incident that involved two bishops from the Association of Episcopal Conferences of Central Africa, observing: "Trust has still not been established between the populations of Rwanda and DRC, especially in the East—Goma, Bukavu and so on. For instance, they [the bishops] usually take a specific route here to their meeting place. But, due to traffic, when their Congolese driver attempted to change his regular route, he was immediately and strongly discouraged to do so. I just think that they were scared of being kidnapped. This is the kind of atmosphere that dominates between us."

Bibliography

Abu-Nimer, Mohammed. "Building Peace in the Pursuit of Social Justice." In Michael D. Palmer and Stanley M. Burgess (eds.). *The Wiley-Blackwell Companion to Religion and Social Justice.* Chichester, West Sussex; Malden, MA: Wiley-Blackwell, 2012.

Autesserre, Séverine. *Peaceland: Conflict Resolution and the Everyday Politics of International Intervention*. New York, NY: Cambridge University Press 2014.

Büscher, Karen. "Conflict, State Failure and Urban Transformation in Eastern Congolese Periphery: The Case of Goma " Ph.D., University of Ghent, 2011.

Johnston, Douglas, and Cynthia Sampson. *Religion, the Missing Dimension of Statecraft*. New York, NY: Oxford University Press, 1994.

Lederach, John Paul. "Justpeace: The Challenge of the 21st Century." In Paul van Tongeren (ed.), *People Building Peace: 35 Inspiring Stories from Around the World.* Utrecht, The Netherlands: European Centre for Conflict Prevention, 1999.

Mararo, Stanislas Bucyalimwe, "Kinshasa et le Kivu depuis 1987: Une histoire ambigue." In S. Marysse and Filip Reyntjens (eds.), *L'Afrique des grands lacs : annuaire 2004–2005.* Paris: L' Harmattan, 2005a.

———."Kivu and Ituri in the Congo War: The Roots and Nature of a Linkage." In S. Marysse and Filip Reyntjens (eds.), *The Political Economy of the Great Lakes Region in Africa: The Pitfalls of Enforced Democracy and Globalization.* New York, NY: Palgrave Macmillan, 2005b.

Mujynya, Edmond, and Laurent Sebisogo. "Monseigneur Joseph Busimba: Pionnier, pasteur et homme de Dieu. " In Ntawihaye Gisamonyo Gonzalve Twose and Bucyalimwe Stanislas Mararo (eds), *Mgr Joseph Busimba Mikararanga (1912–1974), premier prêtre et Èvêque noir du Kivu, fondateur et grand pasteur du Diocèse de Goma.* Goma, Congo (Democratic Republic): Association Les Amis de Goma, 2012.

Rawls, John. *A Theory of Justice*. (Rev. ed.). Cambridge, MA: Belknap Press of Harvard University Press, 1999.

Schreiter, Robert J., R. Scott Appleby, and Gerard F. Powers. *Peacebuilding: Catholic Theology, Ethics, and Praxis.* Maryknoll, NY: Orbis Books, 2010.

Seay, Laura Elizabeth. "Authority at Twilight: Civil Society, Social Services, and the State in the Eastern Democratic Republic of Congo." Ph.D. Dissertation, The University of Texas at Austin, 2009.

Tull, Denis. *The Reconfiguration of Political Order in Africa: A Case Study of North Kivu (DR Congo).* Hamburg: Institute of African Affairs, 2005.

Twose, Ntawihaye Gisamonyo Gonzalve, and Stanislas Bucyalimwe Mararo. *Mgr Joseph Busimba Mikararanga (1912–1974), premier prêtre et Èvêque noir du Kivu, fondateur et grand pasteur du Diocèse de Goma.* Goma, Congo (Democratic Republic): Association Les Amis de Goma, 2012.

[illegible], Peace [illegible]. [illegible] Man[illegible] [illegible] Harvard [illegible].

Index

A

B

C

J

K

L

M

N

O

P

Q

R

S

T

U

V

Knut Holter, *General Editor*

Both the social sciences and the humanities are currently witnessing an increasing research interest for the interface between religion and society in Africa and in the African diaspora. Religion and Society in Africa is an interdisciplinary and multidisciplinary series aiming to participate in these discourses by publishing studies that are analytically outstanding and provide new insights in the field. The series welcomes manuscripts that address religion and society in Africa and in the African diaspora from historical as well as contemporary perspectives.

Inquiries and manuscripts should be directed to:

Professor Knut Holter
Center for Mission and Global Studies
VID Specialized University
Misjonsmarka 12
N-4024 Stavanger, Norway
knut.holter@vid.no

To order other books in this series, please contact our Customer Service Department:

(800) 770-LANG (within the U.S.)
(212) 647-7706 (outside the U.S.)
(212) 647-7707 FAX

Or browse online by series:

www.peterlang.com